The
Written Wars

The
Written Wars:

*American War Prose Through
the Civil War*

Joseph T. Cox

Archon Books
1996

Library of Congress Cataloging-in-Publication Data

The written wars : American war prose through the Civil War /
   [compiled by] Joseph T. Cox.
      p.   cm.
   Includes bibliographical references (p.   ) and index.
   ISBN 0-208-02344-5 (alk. paper)
   1. United States—History, Military—To 1900—Sources.
2. American prose literature.   I. Cox, Joseph T., 1946–   .
E181.W963   1995
973—dc20   95-32374
                                                  CIP

Text design by Dutton & Sherman Design
Printed in the United States of America

for Brig. Gen. Herbert M. Wassom
(20 December 1938—17 August 1988)

Contents

III. The War of 1812

IV. The War with Mexico

V. The Civil War

Acknowledgments

I am indebted to many people for help in writing this book. First, Peter Stromberg gave me the chance to study and to teach, and I thank him for his encouragement throughout my military and academic careers. Generous and wonderful people at the University of North Carolina at Chapel Hill provided the necessary assistance, advice, and facilities to pursue this goal. As he has for so many students, Louis Rubin pointed me in the right direction. Townsend Ludington provided wise and timely advice throughout this project and encouraged me to think for myself. Bob Bain added his friendship, his sense of humor, and his wide historical, literary, and human perspective. Richard Rust provided an example of scholarly thoroughness, integrity, and genuine decency that continues to inspire me to do better. Despite the tremendous demands on her time, Erica Lindemann gave generous attention to my work, and her enthusiasm and rhetorical wisdom kept me on track. Fellow pilgrims Marilyn Elkins and Michele Ware provided invaluable and timely peer support.

Lunches at the Northwest table offered a weekly measure of healthy skepticism, intellectual stimulation, and needed friendship throughout the early stages. My colleagues at West Point provided similar encouragement and advice, especially Elliott Gruner, who pointed out my many critical limitations and tried to help me overcome them. Without Steve Luebke's help, the computer would have won.

I owe much to Diantha Thorpe, who, during a very difficult period, found the time and the energy to bring this project to fruition. She and my editor and friend, James Thorpe III, had much more patience with me than I deserved. As did the people I need to thank most of all, my wife Joanne, my son Matthew, and my daughter Ansley, who gave their love and support as I wrestled with the details of what is in more ways than one a never-ending tale.

xi

Introduction

*Myth may clothe history as fiction, but it persuades in proportion to
its capacity to help people act in history.*

—Sacvan Bercovitch   *The American Jeremiad*

This book is a chronicle of the transformation of war experience into language
and image and story, and the impact of that translation on American consciousness and culture. It began as an examination of personal assumptions
about the use of force and evolved into a broad review of American soldier
accounts of combat from colonial times to the end of the Civil War. The questions to which I continually return are these: How do Americans construct
coherent written representations out of the often incomprehensible realities
of war? What are the rhetorical techniques they employ? What are the consequences of the social myths that result from the construction of American
justifications of war and warmaking?

I divide this book into five major parts, each covering a specific war or
period of conflict, from colonial times to the Civil War. Each part has a general
introduction and a chronology that provides the reader with a broad historical
framework within which to place the selected texts and, in order to further
explain the circumstances and significance of the narratives that follow, individual prose selections have their own introductory remarks that comment on
the developing national war discourse.

The collection ends with the Civil War because that conflict marks both
the extremity of an historical dynamic that ordered earlier events and—despite
Henry Adams's arguments for 1812—the conclusion of a period of evolution
that saw the united states become The United States. Except for parts of the
chapter, "The War with Mexico," the selections in this anthology describe conflicts fought on native soil and reflect critical periods of national uncertainty
and circumspection. The collected authors contribute to a national consciousness and mythology that subsequent writers draw upon to justify and explicate
America's post-Civil War global military involvement.

In this study I do not try to give a complete or comprehensive account of each period of American conflict, nor do I comment in depth on the cultural, ideological, or literary presuppositions that support each prose fragment. Rather, I offer an anthology of war writing that invites further analysis of the history, mythology, and rhetoric of American warmaking.

I have selected both first-person and third-person accounts. Because they offer a perspective on the private world of battle sometimes overlooked by those who study war, individual soldier accounts predominate. Although first-person narratives do not always provide the most reliable record of the details of historical events, they do chronicle human psychological and physical limits, and that process of recording extreme physical and mental dissociations reveals much about the language of and imagination in American war prose.

Juxtaposed to these are more public interpretations of the nation's wars that further manipulate these accounts into acceptable public myth. Together, these written accounts reveal recurring themes, offer sketches of developing American character types, and inscribe emerging, shared cultural ideals. They document the way Americans organize and explain incoherent, inchoate sets of experiences into familiar, and thus comforting, comprehensible, and ideologically acceptable patterns.

The transformation of war to word and combat to collective myth is a varied, often paradoxical, and sometimes self-canceling process. Yet, some themes appear repeatedly and follow predictable rhetorical courses. For example, two of the earliest ways of looking at war continue to influence this nation's justifications for the use of arms. Captain John Smith's self-promotional prose of the early 1600s sets in motion an American frontier hubris that still shapes the self-fashioning narratives of individual American warriors; and our Puritan forefathers provide rhetorical exemplars for commentators and political figures who still interpret the events of war as validation of national morality and mission. In the American imagination, individual soldiers continue to pursue knighthood, and warmaking still seeks the moral status of crusade. This is a powerful synergism reinforced in many of the following selections. Read critically, these accounts could help policymakers and future participants in this nation's conflicts decipher the rhetoric of combat and the long-standing cultural assumptions Americans rely on to talk themselves into war.

The warrior may at first tell stories because unusual experience compels it. However, more often than not, the desire of the soldier to regain admission into and to attain stature in the community ultimately shapes combat accounts into the acceptable and psychologically expected hero quest motif: The veteran returns from war or enemy captivity to impart the grace and wisdom gained through the ordeal. At the same time, the community rewrites individual narratives in ways that reinforce values and sentiments the public most wants to believe about itself, and the details of combat experience are often subordinated to cultural truisms.

This continual reworking and reshaping of national war prose sets the stage for future drama. When confronted with the task of remembering a past war or justifying the next one, subsequent generations begin with a repository of shared myths that generally disregard the details of human suffering. In addition, even though the ideological scaffolding of some of these narratives may not be relevant to contemporary experience, familiar prose patterns continue to justify American involvement in conflict, to imaginatively shape the anticipated combat experience, and to influence the subsequent histories of those events. American war prose is itself a larger tale of the power of myth and the many ways Americans revise reality to serve the present.

This anthology collects some of these multiple interpretations of combat in order to reveal a master narrative that continues to shape today's rhetoric of war, and, in Bercovitch's words, helps the American people "act in history." Early American war prose leads us back to unique cultural headwaters of intellectual, ideological, and emotional currents that continue to carry us into the future. Because we may pay for our storytelling with the blood of our young men and women, it is a stream of consciousness that deserves our most critical examination.

Editor's Note

The accounts collected in this volume appear essentially in their original form. Some of the prose, especially in the colonial section, contains spellings, punctuation, and vocabulary that may be unfamiliar to a modern audience. A minimal amount of editing has been done in order to improve readability while preserving the individual voices of the authors.

The following selections are reprinted here with permission:

For **Rice C. Bull:** *Soldiering: The Civil War Diary of Rice C. Bull* by Rice C. Bull, edited by K. Jack Bauer. Reprinted with permission from *Soldiering* by Rice C. Bull © 1977. Published by Presidio Press, Novato, CA.

For **John Haley:** From *The Rebel Yell and the Yankees Hurrah: The Civil War Journal of a Maine Volunteer,* edited by Ruth L. Silliker. Published by DownEast Books, Camden, Maine, 1985. Reprinted by permission of DownEast Books.

For **Charles Woodward Hutson:** Selected material from the Charles Woodward Hutson Papers, #362. Reprinted with permission from the Southern Historical Collection, Library of the University of North Carolina at Chapel Hill.

For **Joseph Plumb Martin:** From *Private Yankee Doodle: Being a Narrative of Some of the Adventures, Dangers, and Sufferings of a Revolutionary War Soldier* by Joseph Plumb Martin, edited by George F. Scheer. Copyright © 1962 by George F. Scheer. By permission of Little, Brown, and Company.

For **James Miller,** "Letters"; for **Napoleon J. T. Dana,** "Letters to His Wife"; for **Ulysses S. Grant,** "Letters to John W. Lowe"; for **Edmund B. Alexander,** "Letters"; for **Robert E. Lee,** "Letter to His Family": All approved for publication by Alan C. Aimone, Head of Special Collections, USMA, West Point, NY.

For **Nathan Newsom:** From *Diary of Nathan Newsom, 1812–1813.* Reprinted by permission of The Ohio Historical Society.

For **James K. Newton:** "Letter to His Family, 12 April 1862." In *A Wisconsin Boy in Dixie: Civil War Letters of James K. Newton,* edited by Stephen E. Ambrose, © 1961 (Madison: University of Wisconsin Press). Reprinted by permission of The University of Wisconsin Press.

For **Private Carr White:** "Letter to His Sister." Reprinted by permission of The Ohio Historical Society.

Part I

The Colonial Period

Brave spirits that advanced themselves from poor soldiers to great captains, their posterity to great lords.

—Captain John Smith   *True Travels*

The noble Acts Jehovah wrought his Israel to redeem, Surely this second work of his shall far more glorious seem.

—Benjamin Tompson   *New England's Crisis*

Introduction

America's written wars begin with the narrative of a professional English soldier of fortune, Captain John Smith, who transported chivalric legend to the American wilderness and cast himself in the role of leading knight errant. In doing so, he gave birth to the most persistent and forceful of American myths: the belief that in the New World one becomes a new man: the American myth of becoming. According to Smith, frontier deeds, especially those opportunities afforded by combat with native Americans, produced a uniquely self-reliant kind of leader.

Further north, Puritan forefathers preached that wilderness hardships forged a new and improved social order. Their war prose interpreted Indian conflicts as paradoxical tokens of God's approval of Puritan theocracy and His unique way of canonizing new English saints: War was a test of the body politic and a sure sign that God took an interest in the new "chosen people." Because bloodshed in America was part of God's plan, combat provided the proving ground for New England moral exceptionalism.

While Captain John Smith exploited the trappings of single-combat heraldry to define his version of New World heroism, the Puritans compared their hardships to Old Testament accounts of the Israelites in order to cast themselves in the role of a "chosen people." War was terrible but necessary proof of their unique social and spiritual mission in history. By finding in the fear and horror of frontier combat worthy personal and social ends, both early justifications of war convinced colonial Americans to accept violence as preordained confirmation of positive physical and spiritual values, rather than as an unfortunate, bitter, dangerous, or possibly avoidable patterns of behavior.

These earliest colonial justifications of hostilities have continued to influence the way Americans look at war, at themselves individually, and at their society. Supernatural divine purpose and great righteousness (at times, self-righteousness) are certainly not unique to public American myth, but they are its predominant elements.

Throughout American history, storytellers have simultaneously embellished John Smith's abstract myth of romantic frontier heroism and incorpo-

3

rated Puritan religious typology to help shape subsequent accounts of combat. Other colonial soldiers and commentators embroidered this fundamental early American war prose and, in doing so, helped accommodate the New World consciousness to a violent frontier.

A good example of the manipulation of combat experience is Puritan leader Increase Mather's treatment of militia captain Thomas Wheeler's account. Wheeler, a plain and simple soldier and an embodiment of the Puritan culture's heroic Christian ideal, reflects little chivalric or millennial myth-making in his first-person narrative. Instead, he focuses on the physical hardships of his ordeal and celebrates the importance of comradeship within a military unit. In contrast, the details he faithfully reports are transformed into millennial symbols by Increase Mather. When Mather retells Wheeler's story, war's reality has little to do with the suffering of soldiers, but everything to do with the idea of a people chosen by God to set an example for the rest of the world.

Mather focuses on the ends and not the means of combat. He presents King Philip's War as a conflict between the forces of good and evil, where victory must wait until God uses violence to cleanse his chosen but backsliding people. It suggests a pattern of interpretation common to most of America's wars. Popular faith in war's ability to purge society's weaknesses and instill discipline remains strong, and cultural myths continue to describe each war as the last violent prelude to a millennium of peace. In our own time, the war to end all wars, the war to make the world safe for democracy, the Cold War to cleanse the evil scourge of godless communism, and the Gulf War were all supposed to usher in a period of prosperity and to confirm America's superiority and moral obligation to lead the new world order.

This optimism extends to individual as well as national prospects. As in these 300-year-old accounts, America continues to expect its champions to be larger-than-life masters of solitary combat, always fighting outnumbered and always winning. Taking their cue from Captain John Smith's prose, early war stories stress individual rather than corporate effort.

One early soldier whose prose helped perpetuate the image of this solitary, New World champion was Benjamin Church. Although Puritan faith in the predestination of their transcendental mission seems to leave little room for his kind of self-celebration, Colonel Church's account neatly supplements the rugged-individual and ring-tailed-roarer myth begun by Captain John Smith. As the hero who fights outnumbered and finally conquers his enemy by becoming like him, Church offers an early version of the American prototype we later associate with real-life personages Daniel Boone and Davy Crockett, and the fictional Natty Bumppo—not to mention Sylvester "Rambo" Stallone, Clint Eastwood, or another mythic parody and inversion—Dr. Strangelove himself.

Another sub-genre of war prose, prisoner-of-war narratives, provides extended insight into the formation of American regeneration-through-violence myths. Like Indian captives Captain John Smith and Mary Rowlandson before him, John Williams in *The Redeemed Captive* reads captivity as symbolic social drama. Pitting the forces of Protestantism against the Anti-Christ Roman Catholic Church, Williams's account demonstrates the power of the early American myth of Puritan exceptionalism and New World interpretations of millennialism to shape a prisoner's tortured realities.

The narrative expectations created by war prose can even shape perceptions of history. Major Robert Rogers so successfully wrote himself into the frontier hero tradition that he is generally accepted as a prototype of the essential, patriotic American warrior despite having shady ethical dealings and fighting on the side of the British during the Revolution. His journal account suggests that if one repeats the story popular culture expects its heroes to tell, people will forgive many sins.

In a similar incorporation of tried and tested mythology, Colonel Benjamin Franklin gives a temporal twist to the Puritan myth of moral exceptionalism. His account begins a secular interpretation of the unique American mission that would emerge more fully in Revolutionary War narratives. By criticizing British General Braddock's defeat as a failure of European character, Franklin endorses a popular faith in the unique colonial predisposition for combat, and by substituting rational for religious moral exceptionalism, he helps secularize American faith in its preordained mission.

The following narratives offer insight into how early Americans used prose accounts of combat to formulate national notions of singular and social moral uniqueness. For the most part in these selections, the rhetoric of violence confirms both individual and collective values, but in doing so it fosters a uniquely American schizophrenia. On the one hand, these early war narratives celebrate the individual warrior, and on the other hand they describe war as God's angry scourge of disapproval and approval. These early American views of war expect killers to be God's angels or at least God's agents; yet, the exact proportion of saint to sniper is never quite right. This imbalance of psychic harmony inspires further and more complex individual and collective justifications of war in the American experience.

Nevertheless, these colonial American war narratives help us understand how three centuries later, General Dwight Eisenhower could entitle his history of World War II *Crusade in Europe*, apparently without a sense of irony. His choice of the word *miracles* to describe America's arms build-up and the success of the Allied coalition illustrates how, in the American consciousness, the fusion of secular and sacred history forged by early American war experiences continued to inform a faith in American moral exceptionalism and destiny hundreds of years and dozens of wars later.

Chronology

1492	Columbus discovers America.
1497	Cabot establishes foundation for English claims in New World.
1539	De Soto lands in Florida.
1578	Gilbert and Raleigh granted charter for colonization of North America.

1585		Raleigh lands with 107 men on Roanoke Island.
1587		The "Lost Colony" on Roanoke Island vanishes.
1607		Jamestown, first permanent English settlement in North America, established.
1620		Pilgrims land on shore of Massachusetts Bay.
1627		Charter granted to Massachusetts Bay Company.
1630		"Great Migration" of Puritans to Massachusetts Bay.
1637		Pilgrims destroy the Pequots.
1642		Civil War in England.
1649		Charles I executed.
1660		Restoration of Charles II.
1662		Wamsutta (Alexander), chief of Wampanoags and Metacom's (Philip's) brother, called to answer if he is plotting war; dies of fever.
1668–71		Philip involved in land disputes, fined by Plymouth.

King Philip's War, 1675–76

1675		
29	Jan	Philip's secretary, John Sassamon, murdered.
1–8	Jun	Sassamon's murderers tried and executed.
20	Jun	Wampanoags under Philip attack Swansea.
30	Jun	Colonial army sweeps Mount Hope Neck; Philip escapes.
8	Jul	Church's "pease" fight.
28	Jul	Captains Hutchinson and Wheeler march to meet Nipmuck chiefs near Brookfield.
2–4	Aug	Hutchinson and Wheeler besieged at Brookfield.
4–5	Aug	Springfield attacked and partially burned.
19	Dec	Great Swamp fight: 80 English, 600 Narragansetts (half women and children) killed.
1676		
10	Feb	Lancaster attacked. Mary Rowlandson captured.
14	Mar	Praying Indians removed to Deer Island.
	April	Epidemic kills many colonists, including Governor Winthrop.
21	Apr	Indians attack Sudbury, their high-water mark.
2–3	May	Mary Rowlandson ransomed.

18–19 May		Battle of Turners Falls.
1	Aug	Benjamin Church, leading an army of white and Indian soldiers, captures Philip's wife and son; Philip escapes.
10–12 Aug		Church ambushes Philip; Philip shot and killed by Indian named Alderman.
1688		"Glorious Revolution" in England.

King William's War, 1689–97

1690		
9	May	Battle of Port Royal. Under Sir William Phips, colonial militia loots Port Royal.
21	Aug	Phips begins Quebec expedition.
17	Oct	Unsuccessful attack on Quebec.
1692		Salem witchcraft hysteria.
1696		Chubb surrenders Fort William Henry.

Queen Anne's War 1702–14

1702	Governor James Moore of South Carolina attacks St. Augustine.
1704	Deerfield Massacre.
1710	Successful attack on Port Royal.
1711	Unsuccessful attack on Quebec.
1713	Treaty of Utrecht gives England all French claims to Arcadia, Newfoundland, and the Hudson Bay.
1718	New Orleans founded.

King George's War, 1740–48

1742	Spanish invasion of Georgia and Carolinas defeated by James Oglethorpe.
1745	Successful attack on Louisbourg; first foreign military expedition planned, supplied, and conducted by New England.
1748	Treaty of Aix-la-Chapelle ends war.
1753	French seize Ohio country.

French and Indian War, 1754–60

1754	Washington defeated at Great Meadow.

1755	British defeated in effort to take Fort Duquesne; Braddock killed.
1756	Montcalm captures Fort Oswego.
1757	French capture Fort William Henry; British attack on Fort Ticonderoga fails.
1758	British take Louisbourg.
1759	British and Americans take Fort Ticonderoga, Niagara, and Quebec, where Montcalm and Wolfe die of wounds.
1760	War concludes in America but not in Europe; Franklin pleads for annexation of Canada.
1763	Treaty of Paris; England claims all of Canada from France; rumors that England plans to tax colonies for cost of the war.
1765	Stamp Act, pamphlet war in colonies; Stamp Act repealed.
1767	Townshend Acts.
1770	Boston Massacre; Townshend Acts repealed.
1773	Boston Tea Party.
1774	"Intolerable Acts."
1775	Skirmishes at Lexington and Concord.

John Smith

(1580–1631)

The first extended written imaginative response to experience in the land that would become America belonged to a career soldier prosaically named John Smith. A yeoman-born, Renaissance Achilles who championed a Christian army against the Turks in three single combats, a prisoner of war who killed his slave master and made his way back to Western Europe, the English Captain Smith was also the first American frontier hero. He was the paradigmatic rugged individual who single-handedly subdued the American wilderness; he was the feared Indian killer "Nantaquond."

John Smith's history reads like fiction and presents a truth that transcends fact. Yet, whether you accept his words as fact or fiction, his narrative—written in the third person—delineates the fundamental representation of individual heroism still powerfully at work in the collective American consciousness today. By creating himself as a mythic figure, Smith begins a uniquely American celebration of violent individual regeneration through martial self-reliance. The following account of his self-promoting heroic exploits, and ironically naive description of ritual acceptance into an indigenous culture, demonstrate and delineate New World standards of the individual hero-myth lurking in most American written wars.

from John Smith's *True Travels*

[Smith describes his adventures with the Turks in Transylvania in 1602, in which he kills three men in single combat. Note how he transports the narrative framework of this experience to the New World in the second selection.]

That to delight the Ladies, who did long to see some court-like pastime, the Lord Turbashaw did defie any Captaine, that had the command of a Company, who durst combate with him for his head: The matter being discussed, it was accepted, but so many questions grew for the undertaking, it was decided by lots, which fell upon Captaine Smith, before spoken of.

Truce being made for that time, the Rampiers all beset with faire Dames, and men in Armes, the Christians in Battalio; Turbashaw with a noise of Howboyes [haughtboys] entered the field well mounted and armed; on his shoulders were fixed a paire of great wings, compacted of Eagles feathers within a ridge of silver, richly garnished with gold and precious stones, a Janizary before him, bearing his Lance, on each side another leading his horse; were long he stayed not, ere Smith with a noise of Trumpets, only a Page bearing his Lance, passing by him with a courteous salute, tooke his ground with such good successe, that at the sound of the charge, he passed the Turke thorow the sight of his Beaver, face, head and all, that he fell dead to the ground, where alighting and unbracing his Helmet, cut off his head, and the Turkes tooke his body; and so returned without any hurt at all. The head he presented to the Lord Moses, the General, who kindly accepted it, and with joy to the whole armie he was generally welcomed.

The death of this Captaine so swelled in the heart of one Grualgo, his vowed friend, as rather inraged with madnesse than choller, he directed a particular challenge to the Conquerour, to regaine his friends head, or lose his owne, with his horse and Armour for advantage, which according to his desire, was the next day undertaken: as before upon the sound of the Trumpets, their Lances flew in peeces upon a cleare passage, but the Turke was neere unhorsed. Their Pistolls was the next, which marked Smith upon the placard; but the next shot the Turke was so wounded in the left arme, that being not able to rule his horse, and defend himselfe, he was throwne to the ground, and so bruised with the fall, that he lost his head, as his friend before him; with his horse and Armour; but his body and his rich apparell was sent backe to the Towne.

Every day the Turks made some sallies, but few skirmishes would they endure to any purpose. Our workes and approaches being not yet advanced to that height and effect which was of necessitie to be performed; to delude time, Smith with so many incontradictable perswading reasons, obtained leave that the Ladies might know he was not so much enamoured of their servants heads, but if any Turke of their ranke would come to the place of combate to redeeme them, should have his also upon the like conditions, if he could win it.

The challenge presently was accepted by Bonny Mulgro. The next day both the Champions entering the field as before, each discharging their Pistoll, having no Lances, but such martial weapons as the defendant appointed, no hurt was done; their Battle-axes was the next, whose piercing bills made sometime the one, sometime the other to have scarce sense to keep their saddles, specially the Christian received such a blow that he lost his Battle-axe, and failed not much to have fallen after it, wharat the supposing conquering Turk, had a great shout from the Rampiers. The Turk prosecuted his advantage to the uttermost of his power; yet the other, what by the readinesse of his horse, and his judgement and dexterity in such a businesse, beyond all mens expectation, by God's assistance, not only avoided the Turks violence, but having drawne his Faulchion, pierced the Turke so under the Culets thorow back and body, that although he alighted from his horse, he stood not long ere he lost his head, as the rest had done.

This good success gave such great encouragement to the whole Armie, that with a guard of six thousand, three spare horses, before each a Turkes head upon a Lance, he as conducted to the Generalls Pavillion with his Presents. Moyses received both him and them with as much respect as the occasion deserved, embracing him in his armes; gave him a faire Horse richly furnished, a Scimitar and belt worth three hundred ducats; and Meldritch made him Sergeant major of his Regiment. But now to the siege.

[Following these 1602 acts of heroism in Transylvania, John Smith was wounded in battle, rescued by pillagers, but sold into slavery. In 1603 he killed his Turkish master and made his way alone back to Christian Europe. By December 1606 Smith was in Jamestown, the first permanent English colony in America, complaining about his lack of status.

After two-and-a-half years, he had to return to England to recover from serious burns to his legs and groin, but in 1614 he explored the New England coast. He published his best known of nine works, The General Historie of Virginia, New England, and the Summer Isles, *in 1624, in which he offers the following description of his transformation from Old World knight into a frontier hero able to survive tremendous odds thanks to his personal bravery, his culture's technological superiority, and, perhaps, the good nature of his Indian captors.*

Smith's account of his rescue by Pocahontas is most likely a description of a ceremony marking his ritualistic rebirth as a member of the Powhatan tribe, but, with characteristic self-absorption, Smith explains that it is just one more fortunate escape.

Smith sees his redemption from captivity as a sign of his personal greatness and a key to special knowledge and social privilege. He returns to Jamestown, foils his enemies' plans to arrest him, and convinces his fellow colonists not to abandon the settlement. His story begins what becomes a unique American confidence in the potential of the individual to build a New World, and thus redeem the Old World, with the rhetoric of ego.]

from Smith's *General Historie of Virginia*

But our Comedies never endured long with out a Tragedie; some idle exceptions being muttered against Captaine Smith, for not discovering the head of Chickahamania river, and taxed by the Councell, to be too slow in so worthy an attempt. The next voyage hee proceeded so farre that with much labour by cutting of trees in sunder he made his passage, but when his Barge could passe no farther, he left her in a broad bay out of danger of shot, commanding none should goe a shore till his returne: himself with two English and two Salvages [savages] went up higher in a Canoowe, but hee was not long absent, but his men went a shore, whose want of government, gave both occasion and opportunity to the Salvages to surprise one George Cassen, whom they slew, and much failed not to have cut off the boat all the rest.

Smith little dreaming of that accident, being got to the marshes at the rivers head, twentie myles in the desert, had his two men slaine (as is supposed) sleeping by the Canowe, whilste himself by fowling sought them victual, who finding he was beset with 200 Salvages, two of them he slew, still defending himself with the ayd of a Salvage his guid, whom he bound to his arme with his garters, and used him as a buckler [shield], yet hee was shot in his thigh a litle, and had many arrowes that stucke in his cloathes but no great hurt, till at last they took him prisoner. When this newes came to James towne, much was their sorrow for his losse, fewe expecting what ensued. Six or seven weekes those Barbarians kept him prisoner, many strange triumphes and conjurations they made of him, yet hee so demeaned [comported] himselfe amongst them as he not only diverted them from surprising the Fort, but procured his owne libertie, and got himselfe and his company such estimation amongst them, that those Salvages admired him more then their owne Quiyouckosucks [petty gods]. The manner how they used and delivered him, is as followeth.

The Salvages having drawne from George Cassen whether Captaine Smith was gone, prosecuting that opportunity they followed him with 300 bowmen, conducted by the King of Pamaunkee, who in divisions searching the turnings of the river, found Robinson and Emry by the fire side, those they shot full of arrowes and slew. Then finding the Captaine, as is said, that used the Salvage that was his guide as his sheld (three of them being slaine and divers other so gauld) all the rest would not come neere him. Thinking thus to have returned to his boat, regarding them, as he marched, more then his way slipped up to the middle in an oasie creeke and his Salvage with him, yet durst they not come to him till being neere dead with cold, he threw away his armes. Then according to their composition they drew him forth and led him to the fire, where his men were slaine. Diligently they chafed his benummed limbs. He demanding for their Captaine, they shewed him Opechankanough, King of the Pamaunkee, to whom he gave a round of Ivory double compass Dyall [dial]. Much they marvailed at the playing of the Fly and Needle, which they could see so plainely, and yet not touch it, because of the glasse that covered them. But when he demonstrated by that Globe-like Jewell, the roundnesse of the earth, and the skies, the spheare of the Sunne, Moon, and starres, and how the Sunne did chase the night round about the world continually; the greatnesse of the Land and Sea, the diversitie of Nations, varietie of complexions, and how we were to them Antipodes, they all stood as amazed with admiration. Notwithstanding, within an houre after they tyed him to a tree, and as many as could stand about him prepared to shoot him, but the King holding up the Compass in his hand, they all laid downe their Bowes and Arrowes, and in a triumphant manner led him to Orapaks, where he was after their manner kindly feasted, and well used.

Their order in conducting him was thus; Drawing themselves all in fyle, the King in the middest had all their Peeces and Swords borne before him. Captaine Smith was led after him by three great Salvages, holding him fast by each arme: and on each side six went in fyle with their Arrowes nocked. But arriving at the Towne (which was but onely thirtie or fortie hunting houses made of Mats, which they remove as they please, as we our tents) all the women and children staring to behold him, the souldiers first all in fyle performed the forme of a Bissone so well as could be; and on each flanke, officers as Serjeants to see them keepe their order. A good time they continued this exercise, and then cast themselves in a ring, dauncing in such severall Postures, and singing and yelling out such hellish notes and screeches; being strangely painted, every one his quiver of Arrowes, and at his backe a club; on his arme a Fox or an Otters skinne, or some such matter for his vambrace [forearm protector]; their heads and shoulders painted red, with Oyle and Pocones mingled together, which Scarlet-like colour made an exceeding handsome shew; his Bow in his hand, and the skinne of a Bird with her wings abroad dryed, tyed on his head, a peece of copper, a white shell, a long feather, with a small rattle growing at the tayles of their snakes tyed to it, or some such like toy. All this while Smith and the King stood in the middest guarded, as before is said, and after three dances they all departed. Smith they conducted to a long house, where they all departed, where thirtie or fortie tall fellowes did guard him, and ere long more bread and venison was brought him then would have served twentie men, I thinke his stomacke at the time was not very good; what he left they put in baskets and tyed over his head. About midnight they set the meate againe before him, till the next morning they brought him as much more, and then did they eate all the old, and reserved the new as they had done the other, which made him think they would fat him to eat him. Yet in this desperate estate to defend him from the cold, one Maocassater brought him his gowne, in requitall of some beads and toyes Smith had given him at his first arrivall in Virginia.

Two days after a man would have slaine him (but that the guard prevented it) for the death of his sonne, to whom they conducted him to recover the poore man then breathing his last. Smith told them that at James towne he had a water would doe it, if they would let him fetch it, but they would not permit that; but made all the preparations they could to assault James towne, craving his advice, and for recompence he should have life, libertie, land, and women. In part of a Table booke he writ his minde to them at the Fort, what was intended, how they should follow that direction to affright the messengers, and without fayle send him such things as he writ for. And an Inventory with them.

The difficultie and danger, he told the Salvages, of the Mines, great gunnes, and other Engins exceedingly affrighted them, yet according to his request they went to James towne, in as bitter weather as could be of frost and snow, and within three dayes returned with an answer.

But when they came to James towne, seeing men sally out as he had told them they would, they fled; yet in the night they came againe to the same place where he had told them they should receive an answer, and such things as he had promised them, which they found accordingly, and with which they returned with no small expedition, to the wonder of them all that heard it, that he could either divine, or the paper could speake: then they led him to the Youghtanunds, the Mattapanients, the Payankatanks, the Nantaughtacunds, and Onawmanients upon the rivers of Rapahanock, and Patawomck, . . . to the Kings habitation at Pamaunkee, where they entertained him with most strange and fearefull Conjurations;

> *As if neare led to hell*
> *Amongst the Devils to dwell.*

Not long after, early in a morning a great fire was made in a long house, and a mat spread on the one side, as on the other, on the one they caused him to sit, and all the guard went out of the house, and presently came skipping in a great grim fellow, all painted over with coale, mingled with oyle; and many Snakes and Wesels skins stuffed with mosse, and all their tayles tyed together, so as they met on the crowne of his head in a tassell was as a Coronet of feathers, the skins hanging round about his head, backe, and shoulders, and in a manner covered his face; with a hellish voyce and a rattle in his hand. With most strange gestures and passions he began his invocation, and environed the fire with a circle of meale; which done, three more such like devils came rushing in with the like antique tricks, painted white, and some red stroakes like Mutchato's along their cheekes: round about him those fiends daunced a pretty while, and then came in three more as ugly as the rest; with red eyes, and white stroakes over their blacke faces, at last they all sat downe right against him; three of them on the one hand of the chiefe Priest, and three on the other. Then all with their rattles began a song, which ended, the chiefe Priest layd downe five wheat cornes: then strayning his armes and hands with such violence that he sweat, and his veynes swelled, he began a short Oration:

at the conclusion they all gave a short groane; and then layd down three graines more. After that, began their song againe, and then another Oration, ever laying downe so many cornes as before, till they had twice incirculed the fire; that done, they tooke a bunch of little stickes prepared for that purpose, continuing still their devotion, and at the end of every song and Oration, they layd downe a sticke betwixt the divisions of Corne. Till night, neither he nor they did either eate or drinke, and then they feasted merrily, with the best provisions they could make. Three dayes they used this Ceremony; the meaning whereof they told him, was to know if he intended them well or no. The circle of meale signified his Country. They imagined the world to be flat and round, like a trencher, and they in the middest. After this they brought him a bagge of gunpowder which they carefully preserved till the next spring, to plant as they did their corne; because they would be acquainted with the nature of that seede. Opitchapam the Kings brother invited him to his house, where, with as many platters of bread, foule, and wild beasts, as did environ him, he bid him wellcome; but not any of them would eate a bit with him, but put up all the remainder in Baskets. At his returne to Opechancanoughs, all the Kings women, and their children, flocked about him for their parts, as a due by Custome, to be merry with such fragments.

> *But his waking mind in hydeous dreames did oft*
> *see wondrous shapes,*
> *Of bodies strange, and huge in growth, and of*
> *stupendious makes.*

At last they brought him to Meronocomoco where was Powhatan their Emperor. Here more than two hundred of those grim Courtiers stood wondering at him, as he had beene a monster; till Powhatan and his trayne had put themselves in their greatest braveries. Before a fire upon a seat like a bedsted, he sat covered with a great robe, made of Rarowcun [raccoon] skinnes, and all the tayles hanging by. On either hand did sit a young wench of 16 or 18 yeares, and along on each side the house, two rowes of men, and behind them as many women, with all their heads and shoulders painted red; many of their heads bedecked with the white downe of Birds; but every one with something: and a great chayne of white beads about their necks. At his [Smith's] entrance before the King, all the people gave a great shout. The

Queene of Appamatuck was appointed to bring him water to wash his hands, and another brought him a bunch of feathers, in stead of a Towell to dry them: having feasted him after their best barbarous manner they could, a long consultation was held, but the conclusion was, two great stones were brought before Powhatan: then as many as could layd hands on him [Smith], dragged him to them, and thereon laid his head, and being ready with their clubs, to beat out his braines, Pocahontas the Kings dearest daughter, when no intreaty could prevaile, got his head in her armes, and laid her owne upon his to save him from death: whereat the Emperour was contented he should live to make him hatchets, and her bells, beads, and copper; for they thought him as well of all occupations as themselves. For the King himselfe will make his owne robes, shooes, bowes, arrowes, pots; plant, hunt, or doe any thing so well as the rest.

> *They say he bore a pleasant shew,*
> *But sure his heart was sad.*
> *For who can pleasant be, and rest,*
> *That lives in feare and dread:*
> *And having life suspected, doth*
> *It still suspected lead.*

Two dayes after, Powhatan having disguised himselfe in the most fearefullest manner he could, caused Captaine Smith to be brought forth to a great house in the woods, and there upon a mat by the fire to be left alone. Not long after from behinde a mat that divided the house, was made the most dolefullest noyse he ever heard; then Powhatan more like a devill then a man with some two hundred more as blacke as himselfe, came unto him and told him now they were friends, and presently he should goe to James towne, to send him [Powhatan] two great gunnes, and a gryndstone, for which he would give him the Country of Capahowosick.

William Bradford

(1590–1657)

Elected governor of Plymouth Plantation in 1621, pious, wise, courageous yet humble, William Bradford governed Plymouth for over thirty years. His *History of Plymouth Plantation* is an epic record of the discrepancy between the activities of the settlement's very human inhabitants and the Puritan ideal. To Bradford's credit, he does not blink but reports the worst of his community's sins to include a case of bestiality and the grisly details of the earliest colonial wars.

In the following account of the burning of the Pequot village, he attributes his fellow Pilgrims' brutality to God's will. It is a passage that reveals both an enduring human fascination with cataclysmic destruction—what philosopher J. Glenn Gray calls the "lust of the eye"—and the penchant for total war in the name of self-justifying idealism. Bradford's faith that war is a trial by fire to test Puritan mettle for future challenges contributes to the enduring rhetorical association between combat and American exceptionalism and mission. Out of their need to explain and justify, William Bradford and other Puritan narrators begin to develop a collective sense of war as a divinely sanctioned, inevitable part of national destiny.

from Bradford's *History of Plymouth Plantation*

Boston, the 20. of the 3. month, 1637.

In the mean time, the Pequents, espetially in the winter before, sought to make peace with the Narigansets, and used very pernicious arguments to move them therunto: as that the English were strangers and begane to overspred their countrie, and would deprive them therof in time, if they were suffered to grow and increase; and if the Narigansets did assist the English to subdue them, they did but make way for their owne overthrow, for if they were rooted out, the English would soone take occasion to subjugate them; and if they would harken to them, they should not neede to fear the strength of the English; for they would not come to open battle with them, but fire their houses, kill their katle, and lye in ambush for them as they went abroad upon their occasions; and all this they might easily doe without any or litle danger to themselves. The which course being held, they well saw the English could not long subsiste, but they would either be starved with hunger, or be forced to forsake the countrie; with many the like things; insomuch that the Narigansets were once wavering, and were halfe minded to have made peace with them, and joyned against the English. But againe when they considered, how much wrong they had received from the Pequents, and what an oppertunitie they now had by the help of the English to right them selves, revenge was so sweete unto them, as it prevailed above all the rest; so as they resolved to joyne with the English against them, & did. The Court here agreed forwith to send 50. men at their owne charg; & with as much speed as posible they could, gott them armed, & had made them ready under sufficiente leaders, & provided a barke to carrie them provisions & tend upon them for all occasions; but when they were ready to march (with a supply from the Bay) they had word to stay, for the enimie was as good as vanquished, and their would be no neede.

I shall not take upon me exactly to describe their proceedings in these things, because I expect it will be fully done by them selves, who best know the carrage & circumstances of things; I shall therfore but touch them in generall. From Conightecute [Connecticut] (who were most sencible of the hurt sustained, & the present danger), they sett out a partie of men, and an other partie mett them from the Bay, at the Narigansets, who were to joyne with them. The Narigansets were ernest to be gone before the English were well rested and refreshte, espetially some of them which came last. It should seeme their desire was to come upon the enimie sudenly & undiscovered. Ther was a barke of this place, newly put in ther, which was come from Conightecute, who did incourage them to lay hold of the Indeans forwardnes, and to shew as great forwardnes as they, for it would incorage them, and expedition might prove to their great advantage. So they went on, and so ordered their march, as the Indeans brought them to a forte of the enimies (in which most of their cheefe men were) before day. They approached the same with great silence, and surrounded it both with English & Indeans, that they might not breake out; and so assualted them with great courage, shooting amongst them, and entered the forte with all speed; and those that first entered found sharp resistance from the enimy, who both shott at & grapled with them; others rane to their howses, & brought out fire, and sett them on fire, which soone tooke in their matts, &, standing close togeather, with the wind, all was quickly on a flame, and therby more were burnte to death then was otherwise slain; it burnte their bowstrings, and made them unservisable. Those that scaped the fire were slaine with the sword; some hewed to peeces, others rune throw with their rapiers, so as they were quickly dispatchte, and very few escaped. It was conceived they [the English] thus destroyed about 400. at this time. It was a fearfull sight to see them thus frying in the fryer, and the streams of blood quenching the same, and horrible was the stinke & sente ther of; but the victory seemed a sweet sacrifice, and they [the English] gave the prays therof to God, who had wrought so wonderfuly for them, thus to inclose their enimies in their hands, and give them so speedy a victory over so proud & insulting an enimie. The Nariganset Indeans, all this while, stood round aboute, but aloofe from all danger, and left the whole execution to the English, except it were the stoping of any [Pequots] that broke away, insulting over their enimies in this their ruine & miserie, when they saw them dancing in the flames, calling them by a word in their owne language, signifing, O brave Pequents!

Captain Thomas Wheeler

(1620?–1686)

Thomas Wheeler came to America a freeman in 1642. Having seen service as a sergeant of infantry in the Concord, Massachusetts, Bay Colony militia in 1662, he was appointed captain of a horse company when it was formed in 1669. In July, 1675, his company joined the fight against the Indians led by King Philip. In the following account of the confusion, fear, and fatigue of combat, Wheeler attributes his deliverance to God's providence, but he does not ignore the worldly details of war: the terrain, the logistics, and especially the human cost of combat.

In marked contrast to Increase Mather's account of the incident, which follows here, Wheeler's comrades are not simply personifications of Biblical allegory. Instead, Wheeler provides a prototypical frame for future frontier war stories with all the details of the most popular westerns: flaming arrows, a demoniac enemy, a beleaguered outpost, and its last-minute rescue. His account also reflects the New World emphasis on the ability of the colonial soldier to defeat numerically superior forces; in doing so, it contributes to the rhetorical strategy of national self-idealization.

from Wheeler's *A Thankful Remembrance of Gods Mercy to Several Persons at Quabaug or Brookfield*

The said Captain Hutchinson, and my self with about twenty men or more from Cambridge to Sudbury, July 28. 75. and from thence into the Nipmuck Country, and finding that the Indians had deserted their Towns, and we having gone until we came within twenty miles of New Norwitch, on July 31. (only we saw two Indians having an Horse with them, whom we would have spoke with, but they fled from us and left their Horse, which we took) We then thought it not expedient to march any further that way, but set our march for Brookfield, whither we came on the Lords day about noon.

From thence the same day (being August 1) we understanding that the Indians were about Ten Miles Northwest from us, we sent out four men to acquaint the Indians that we were not come to harm them, but our business was only to deliver a Message from our Honored Governour and Council to them, and to receive their Answer, we desiring to come to a Treaty of Peace with them, they having before professed Friendship, and promised Fidelity to the English. When the Messengers came to them; they made an Alarm, and gathered together about an hundred and Fifty fighting men as near as they could judge; The young men amongst them were stout in their Speeches, and surly in their Carriage; But at length three of the chief Sachems promised to meet us on the next morning about eight of the Clock upon a plain within three miles of Brookfield.

Whereupon though their speech and carriage did much discourage diverse of our company, yet we conceived that we had a clear Call to go to meet them at the place whither they had promised to come. Accordingly we with our men accompanied with three of the Principle Inhabitants of the Town marched to the plain appointed; but the Treacherous Heathen intending mischief (if they could have the opportunity) came not to the said place, and so failed our hopes of speaking with them there. Whereupon the said Captain Hutchinson and my self with the rest of our Company Considered what was best to be done, whether we should go any further towards them, or Return, divers of us apprehending much danger in Case we did proceed, but because the Indians kept not promise there with us: But the three men who belonged to Brookfield were so strongly perswaded of their Freedom from any ill intentions towards us, (as upon other grounds, so especially because the greatest part of those Indians belonged to David one of the Chief Sachems, who was taken to be great Friend to the English) That the said Captain Hutchinson (who was principally intrusted with the Matter of Treaty with them) was thereby encouraged to proceed and march forward towards a Swampe where the Indians then were. When we came near the said Swampe, the way was so very bad that we could march only in a single File, there being a very Rocky Hill on the right hand, and a thick Swampe on the left. In which there were many of those cruel blood-thirsty Heathen, who there way-laid us, waiting an opportunity to cut us off; there being also much brush on the side of said Hill, where they lay in Ambush to surprize us.

When we had marched there about sixty or seventy Rods, the said perfidious Indians sent out their shot upon us as a showre of haile, they being (as we supposed) two hundred men or more. We seeing ourselves so beset, not having room to fight, Endeavoured to fly for the safety of our lives. In which Flight we were no small danger to be all Cut off, there being a very miry Swamp before us into which we could not enter with our horse to go forwards, and there being no safety in retreating the way we came, because many of our Enemies, who lay behind the Bushes, and had let us pass by them quietly; when others had shot, they came out, and stopt our way back: so that we were forced as we could to get up the steep and Rocky Hill: but the greater our danger was, the greater was Gods mercy in the preservation of so many of us from sudden destruction.

My self being gone up part of the Hill without any hurt, and perceiving some of my men to be fallen by the Enemies shot: I wheeled about upon the Indians, not calling on my men who were left to Accompany me, which they in all probability would have done had they known of my Return upon the Enemy. They firing violently out of the Swamp, and from behind the bushes on the Hillside wounded me sorely, and shot my Horse under me, so that he Faultering and Falling, I was forced to leave him, divers of the Indians being then but a few Rods distant from me, My Son Thomas Wheeler flying with the rest of Company missed me amongst them, and fearing that I was either slain, or much endangered returned towards the Swampe again, though he had from them received a dangerous wound in the Reins [kidneys]; where he saw me in the danger aforesaid: Whereupon he endeavored to Rescue me, shewing himself therein a loving and dutiful Son, he adventuring himself into great peril of his Life to help me in that distress, there being many of the Enemies about him. My son set me on his own horse, and so escaped a while on Foot himself until he Caught an Horse whose Rider was slain, on which he mounted, and so through Gods great mercy we both escaped: But in this attempt for my deliverance he received another dangerous wound by their shot in his left arm.

[Captain Wheeler lists the men killed and wounded in what he calls this "sudden and unexpected blow given us wherein we desire to look higher than man the instrument." He goes on to describe the survivors' hasty retreat to Quabaug where they garrison in "one of the largest and strongest houses therein."]

Within two hours after our coming to the said house, or less, the said Captain Hutchinson and my self posted away Ephraim Curtis of Sudbury, and Henry Young of Concord to go to the Honoured Council at Boston to give them an Account of the Lords dealings with us, and our present Condition. When they came to the further end of the Town they saw the enemy Rifling of houses which the Inhabitants had forsaken. The Post fired upon them, and immediately returned to us again, they discerning no safety in going forward, and being desirous to inform us of the Enemies Actings, that we might the more prepare for a sudden Assault by them. Which indeed presently followed, for as soon as the said Post was come back to us, the Barbarous Heathen pressed upon us in the house with great violence, sending in their Shot amongst us like haile through the walls, and shouting as if they would have swallowed us up alive; but our good God wrought wonderfully for us, so that there was but one man wounded within the house, viz the said Henry Young who looking out a garret window that Evening was mortally wounded by a Shot, of which wound he died within two dayes after.

There was the same day another man slain, but not in the house, a son of Sergeant Prichards adventuring out of the house wherein we were, to his Father's house not far from it, to fetch more goods out of it was Caught [by] those Cruel Enemies as they were coming towards us, who cut off his head, kicked it about like a Football, and then putting it upon a Pole, they set it up, before the door of his Fathers house in our sight. The night following the said blow, they did roar against us like so many wild Bulls, sending in their Shot amongst us till towards the Moon rising, which was about three of the Clock; at which time they Attempted to fire our house by Hay and other Combustible matter which they brought to one Corner of the house, and set it on fire. Whereupon some of our company were necessitated to expose themselves to very great danger to put it out; Simon Davis one of the three appointed by my self as Captain, to supply my place by Reason of my wounds as aforesaid, he being of lively Spirit encouraged the Souldiers within the house to fire upon the Indians; and also those that Adventured out to put out the Fire (which began to rage and kindle upon the house side) with these and the like words, That God is with us, and fights for us, and will deliver us out of the hands of these Heathen; which Expressions of his the Indians hearing, they shouted and scoffed saying: now see how your God delivers you, or will deliver you, sending in many shots whilst our men were putting out the Fire. But the Lord of Hosts wrought very graciously for us, in preserving our Bodies within and without the house from their shot, and our house from being consumed by Fire, we had but two men wounded in that Attempt of theirs, but we apprehended that we killed divers of our Enemies.

[Wheeler sends out another messenger to Boston. On his third try Ephraim Curtis evades the Indians and gets word to Major Williams in Marlborough.]

The next day being August 3d, they continued shooting & Shouting, & proceeded in their former wickedness blaspheming the Name of the Lord, and reproaching us his Afflicted Servants, scoffing at our prayers as they were sending in their shot upon all quarters of the house[.] And many of them went to the Towns meeting house (which was within twenty Rods of the house in which we were) who mocked saying, Come and pray, & sing Psalms, & in Contempt made an hideous noise somewhat resembling singing. But we to our power did endeavor our own defence, sending our shot amongst them the Lord giving us Courage to resist them, & preserving us from the destruction they sought to bring upon us.

[Wheeler reports the Indians carrying off their dead and wounded and their reinforcement. The enemy once again tries to set fire to the house with flaming arrows, "cotton and linen rags with Brimstone in them."]

So we were preserved by the keeper of Israel, both our Bodies from their shot, which they sent thick against us, and the house from being consumed to Ashes, although we were but weak to defend our selves, we being not above twenty and six men with those of that small Town, who were able for any Service, and our Enemies as I Judged them about (if not above) three hundred, I speak of the least, for many there present did guess them to be four or five hundred.

[The next day, Wednesday, August 4, rain thwarted further Indian at-
tempts to burn them out. Major Willard with Captain Parker of Groton and
a company of forty-six white men and five Indians, relieved the Hutchinson
and Wheeler party. Wheeler continues to describe the tactical details of their
relief and goes on to discuss the further suffering of the wounded during their
fortnight travel to Marlborough. Captain Hutchinson died of his wounds on
August 19. Captain Wheeler returned to Concord on August 21, "though
not thoroughly recovered of my wound." His son Thomas fully recovered.]

Increase Mather

(1639–1723)

A spokesman for the second generation of Puritan saints, Increase Mather interpreted King Philip's War as God's promised punishment, a test of spiritual resolve, and a confirmation of election. Because his generation of Puritans failed to live up to the spiritual standards of their fathers, Mather believed God punished them with war. Paradoxically, because God chose to test them, Mather infers that the war also confirmed their special place in His divine plan. He ignores the details of the Indian conflict and urges his followers to accept war as one of God's many trials.

In the following account, Mather argues that King Philip's War is a conflict between the forces of good and evil, but the triumph of good over evil must wait until God cleanses his backsliding chosen people. For Mather, war's reality had little to do with the suffering of soldiers but everything to do with God's plan and the confirmation of Puritan cultural identity. Thus, he contributes to a discourse that describes war as simply God's violent prelude to a millennium of peace. Mather's thesis is a wellspring of faith in war's ability to purge social wickedness and instill discipline, a theme repeated during America's many subsequent wars.

from Mather's *A Brief History of the Warr with the Indians in New England.*

July 19. Our Army pursued Philip who fled unto a dismal Swamp for refuge: the English Souldiers followed him, and killed many of his Men, also about fifteen of the English were then slain. The Swamp was so Boggy and thick of Bushes, as that it was judged to proceed further therein would be but to throw away Mens lives. It could not there be discerned who were English and who the Indians. Our Men when in that hideous place if they did but see a Bush stir would fire presently, whereby 'tis verily feared, that they did sometimes unhappily shoot English men instead of Indians. Wherefore a Retreat was Sounded, and night coming on, the Army withdrew from that place. This was because the desperate Distress which the Enemy was in was unknown to us: for the Indians have since said, that if the English had continued at the Swamp all night, nay, if they had but followed them but one half hour longer, Philip had come and yielded up himself. But God saw that we were not yet fit for Deliverance, nor could Health be restored unto us except a great deal more Blood be first taken from us: and other places as well as Plimouth stood in need of such a course to be taken with them.

It might rationally be conjectured that the unsuccessfulness of this Expedition against Philip would embolden the Heathen in other parts to do as he had done, and so it came to pass. For July 14, the Nipnep (or Nipmuck) Indians began their mischief at a Town called Mendam (had we amended our ways as we should have done, this Misery might have been prevented) where they committed Barbarous Murders. This Day deserves to have a Remark set upon it, considering that Blood was never shed in Massachusetts Colony in a way of Hostility before this day. Moreover the Providence of God herein is the more awful and tremendous, in that this very day the Church in Dorchester was before the Lord, humbling themselves by Fasting and Prayer, on account of the Day of trouble now begun amongst us.

The news of this Bloodshed came to us at Boston the next day in Lecture time, in the midst of the Sermon, the Scripture then improved being that, Isai.42.24. Who gave Jacob to the spoil, and Israel to the robbers? did not the Lord, He against whom we have sinned?

As yet Philip kept in the Swamp at Pocasset, but August 1. (being the Lords day) he fled. The English hearing that Philip was upon flight, pursued him, with a party of Monhegins, i. e. Unkas (who approved himself faithful to the English almost forty years ago in the time of the Pequod Wars, and now also in this present War) his Indians. They overtook Philips Party and killed about thirty of his men, none of ours being at that time cut off. Had the English pursued the Enemy they might easily have overtaken the Women and Children that were with Philip, yea and himself also, and so have put an end to these tumults: but though Deliverance was according to all Humane probability near, God saw it no good for us as yet. Wherefore Philip escaped and went to the Nipmuck Indians who had newly (as hath been intimated) done Acts of Hostility against the English. But mean while endeavours were used to keep those Indians from engaging in this War, and that those persons who had committed the Murder at Mendam might be delivered up to Justice. Captain Hutchinson with a small party was sent to Quabaog where there was a great Rendezvouze of Nipnep [Nipmuck] Indians. They appointed time and place of Treaty to be attended, August 2. accordingly Captain Hutchinson rode to the Place fixed on to Treat in. But the Indians came not thither according to their Agreement, whereupon Captain Hutchinson resolved to go further to seek after them elsewhere, and as he was riding along, the Perfidious Indians lying in Ambuscado in a Swamp, shot at him and wounded him, of which Wounds he after dyed, and eight men that were with him were struck down dead upon the place. Captain Wheeler who was in that Company was shot through the Arm, his dutiful Son alighting to relieve his Father, was himself shot and sorely wounded, willingly hazarding his own life to save the life of his Father. The English were not in a capacity to look after their dead, but those dead bodies were left as meat for the Fowls of Heaven, and their Flesh unto the Beasts of the Earth, and there was none to bury them.

Captain Hutchinson and the rest that escaped with their lives, hastened to Quabaog, and the Indians speedily followed, violently set upon the Town, killed divers, burning all the Houses therein down to the ground, except only one unto which the Inhabitants fled for succour, and now also (as since we have understood) did Philip with his broken Party come to Quabaog. Hundreds of Indians beset the House, and took possession of a Barn belonging thereunto, from whence they often shot into the House, and also attempted to fire lit six times, but could not prevail, at last they took a Cart full of Flax and other combustible matter, and brought it near the House, intending to set it on fire; and then there was no appearing possibility, but all the English there, Men and Women, and Children must have perished, either by unmerciful flames, or more unmerciful hands of wicked Men whose tender Mercies are cruelties, so that all hope that they should be saved was then taken away: but behold in this Mount of Difficulty and Extremity. The Lord is seen.

For in the very nick of opportunity God sent that worthy Major

Willard, who with forty and eight men set upon the Indians and caused them to turn their backs, so that poor People who were given up for dead, had their lives given then for a prey. Surely this was a token for good, that however we may be diminished and brought low through Oppression, Affliction, and Sorrow, yet our God will have compassion on us, and this his People shall not utterly perish. And this Salvation is the more remarkable, for that albeit the Indians had ordered Scouts to lye in the way, and to give notice by firing three Guns, if any English came to the relief of the Distressed; yet although the Scouts fired when Major Willard and his Souldiers were past them, the Indians were so busie and made such a noise about the House, that they heard not the report of those Guns; which if they had heard, in all probability not only the People then living at Quabaog, but those also that came to succour them had been cut off.

Colonel Benjamin Church
(1639–1718)

Another Puritan participant in the conflict with King Philip was Benjamin Church who, like Captain John Smith, discusses his exploits in the third person and extols the virtues of frontier self-reliance. A refreshingly candid narrator, Church describes mistakes made during the beginning of King Philip's War and attributes them to a lack of discipline and proper military training, to citizen soldiers' fear when under fire for the first time, and to the enemy's tenacity and familiarity with the terrain. One of the first colonists to adopt Indian tactics, Church's account is an excellent light infantry field manual.

The following prose is also a reconciliation of rugged individualism and religious myth. For Church, as it was for Smith, war is the best opportunity for upward social mobility and, even in his theocratic society, the best proving ground for civic leadership. That Church could reconcile the romantic fascination with the ability of colonial soldiers to win when outnumbered with the religious interpretation that such victories confirm national purpose, serves as a rhetorical model for generations of Americans who would interpret the details of their wars according to these early romantic and religious narrative frameworks.

from Church's *The Entertaining History of King Philip's War*

The Enemy who began their Hostilities with plundering and destroying Cattel, did not long content themselves with that game; they thirsted for English blood, and they soon broached it; killing two Men in the way not far from Mr. Miles's Garison, and soon after, eight more at Mattapoiset: Upon whose bodies they exercised more than brutish barbarities; beheading, dismembering and mangling them, and exposing them in the most inhumane manner, which gashed and ghostly objects struck a damp on all beholders.

The Enemy flushed with these exploits, grew yet bolder and skulking every where in the bushes, shot at all passengers, and killed many that ventured abroad. They came so near as to shoot down two Sentinels at Miles's Garrison, under the very noses of most of our Forces. These provocations drew out some of Capt. Prentices Troops, who desired they might have liberty to go out and seek the enemy in their own quarters. Quartermasters Gill & Belcher commanded the parties drawn out, who earnestly desired Mr. Churche's company. They provided him a Horse and Furniture (his own being out of the way). He readily comply'd with their desires, and was soon mounted.

This party was no sooner over Miles' Bridge, but were fired on by an Ambuscade of about a dozen Indians, as they were afterwards discovered to be. When they drew off, the pilot was mortally wounded, Mr. Belcher received a shot in his knee, and his Horse was killed under him. Mr. Gill was struck with a musket-ball on the side of his body; but being clad with a buff Coat and some thickness of Paper under it, it never broke his skin. The troopers were surprised to see both their commanders wounded and wheeled off; but Mr. Church persuaded, at length stormed and stamped, and told them was a shame to run, and leave a wounded Man there to become a prey to the barbarous Enemy; for the pilot yet sat his Horse, though amazed with the shot as not to have sense to guide him. Mr. Gill seconded him, and offered, though much disabled, to assist in bringing him off. Mr. Church asked a stranger, who gave him his company in that action, if he would go with him and fetch off the wounded man. He readily consented, and they with Mr. Gill went; but the wounded man fainted and fell off his horse before they came to him. But Mr. Church and the Stranger dismounted, took up the man, dead, and laid him before Mr. Gill on his Horse. Mr. Church told the other two, if they would take care of the dead man, he would go and fetch his horse back, which was going off the Causeway toward the enemy; but before he got over the Causeway he saw the enemy run to the right into the neck. He brought back the horse, and called earnestly and repeatedly to the Army to come over and fight the Enemy; and while he stood calling & persuading, the skulking Enemy returned to their old stand, and all discharged their guns at him at one clap; [and] though every shot missed him, yet, one of the army on the other side of the river received one of the balls in his foot. Mr. Church now began (no succour coming to him) to think it time to retreat: Saying, "The Lord have Mercy on us, if such a handful of Indians shall thus dare such an Army!"

Upon this 'twas immediately resolved, and orders were given to March down into the neck, and having passed the bridge, and Causeway, the direction was to extend both wings, which being not well headed, by those that remained in the center, some of them mistook their friends for their enemies, and made a fire upon them in the right wing, and wounded that noble heroick Youth, Ensign Savage, in the thigh, but it happily proved but a flesh wound. They marched until they came to the narrow of the neck, at a Place called Keekamuit, where they took down the heads of Eight Englishmen that were killed at the head of Matapoiset Neck, and set upon polls, after the barbarous manner of those Salvages. There Philip had staved all his Drums, and conveyed all his Canoe's to the East-side of Metapoiset River. Hence it was concluded by those that were aquainted with the motions of those people, that they had quitted the neck. Mr. Church told them that Philip was doubtless gone over to Pocasset side to engage those Indians in a rebellion with him, which they soon found to be true. The Enemy were not really beaten out of Mounthope neck, though it was true that they fled from thence; yet it was before any pursued them. It was but to strengthen themselves, and to gain a more advantageous Post. However, some, and not a few, pleased themselves with the fancy of a mighty conquest.

A grand council was held, and a resolve past, to build a Fort there, to maintain the first ground they had gained, by the Indians leaving it to them. And to speak the truth, it must be said, that as they gained not that field by their sword, nor their bow; so it was rather their fear than their courage that obliged them to set up the marks of their Conquest.

Mr. Church looked upon it, and talked of it with contempt, and urged hard the pursuing [of] the Enemy on Pocasset side; and with the greater earnestness, because the promise made to Awashonks, before mentioned.

The Council adjourned themselves from Mounthope to Rehoboth, where Mr. Treasurer Southworth being weary of his charge of Commissary General, (provision being scarce and difficult to be obtained, for the Army, that now lay still to cover the people from no-body, while they were building a fort for nothing) retired, and the power and trouble of that post was left with Mr. Church, who still urged the commanding officers to move over to Pocasset side, to pursue the Enemy and kill Philip, which would in his opinion be more probable to keep possession of the neck, than to tarry to build a Fort.

He was still restless on that side of the river, and the rather, be-cause of his promise to [Awashonks] the Squaw Sachem of Sogkonate. And Captain Fuller also urged the same, until at length there came further orders concerning the fort, and withal an order for Captain Fuller with six files to cross the river to the side so much insisted on, and to try if he could get speech with any of the Pocasset or Sogkonate Indians, and that Mr. Church should go [as] his second.

Upon the Captains receiving his orders, he asked Mr. Church whither he was willing to engage in this enterprise; to whom it was indeed too agreeable to be declined; though he thought the enterprise was hazardous enough for them to have [had] more men assigned them. Captain Fuller told him, that for his own part, he was grown ancient and heavy, [and] he feared the travel and fatigue would be too much for him. But Mr. Church urged him, and told him that he would cheerfully excuse him his hardship and travel, and take that part to himself, if he might but go; for he had rather do any thing in the world than stay there to build the fort.

Then they drew out the number assigned them and marched the same night to the ferry, and were transported to Rhode island, from whence the next night they got a passage over to Pocasset side in Rhode island boats, and concluded there to dispose themselves in two Ambuscadoes before day, hoping to surprise some of the enemy by their falling into one or other of their Ambushments. But Captain Full-er's party being troubled with the epidemical plague of lust after to-bacco, must needs strike fire to smoke it. And thereby discovered themselves to a party of the enemy coming up to them, who immedi-ately fled with great precipitation.

This Ambuscade drew off about break of day, perceiving [that] they were discovered, the other continued in their post until the time assigned them, and the light and heat of the sun rendered their station both insignificant and troublesome, and then returned, unto the place of Rendezvous; where they were acquainted with the other party's disappointment, and the occasion of it.

[After a "slender breakfast," Mr. Church consolidated his command. He and his company of thirty-six men moved off toward Sogkonat where they discovered fresh Indian tracks.]

"Now," says Mr. Church to his men, "if we follow this track no doubt but we shall soon see Indians enough." They express'd their willingness to follow the track, and moved [on] in it, but [they] had not gone far, before one of them narrowly escaped being bit with a rattlesnake; and the woods that the track lead them through was haunted much with those snakes, which the little company seemed more to be afraid of then the black serpents they were in quest of; and therefore bent their course another way to a place where they thought it probable to find some of the Enemy. Had they kept the track to the pine swamp, they had been certain of meeting Indians enough, but not so certain that any of them should have returned to give [an] account how many.

Now they pass'd down into Punkatees Neck; and in their march discovered a large wigwam full of Indian truck, which the soldiers were for loading themselves with, until Mr. Church forbid it; telling them they might expect soon to have their hands full and business without caring for plunder. Then crossing the head of the creek into the neck, they again discovered fresh Indian tracks; [which had] very lately passed before them into the neck. They then got privately and undiscovered unto the fence of Captain Almy's Peas field, and divided into two parties, Mr. Church keeping the one party with himself sent the other with Lake who was acquainted with the ground on the other side. Two Indians were soon discovered coming out of the peas field towards them, when Mr. Church and those that were with him concealed themselves from them by falling flat on the ground, but the other division, not using the same caution, was seen by the Enemy, which occasioned them to run, which, when Mr. Church perceived, he shewed himself to them, and call'd; telling them he desired but to speak with them, and would not hurt them. But they ran, and Church pursued.

The Indians climbed over a fence, and one of them facing about, discharged his piece, but without effect, on the English. One of the

English soldiers ran up to the fence and fired upon him that had discharged his piece, and they concluded by the yelling they heard, that the Indian was wounded. But the Indians soon got into the thickets, whence they [the English] saw them no more for the present.

Mr. Church then marching over a plane piece of ground where the woods were very thick on one side, ordered his little company to march at double distance, to make as big a show, (if they should be discovered,) as might be. But before they saw any body, they were saluted with a volley of fifty or sixty guns. Some bullets came very surprizingly near Mr. Church, who starting looked behind him to see what was become of his men, expecting to have seen half of them dead; but seeing them all upon their legs and briskly firing at the smokes of the Enemies Guns, (for that was all that was then to be seen). He blesses God, and called to his Men not to discharge all their guns at once, lest the enemy should take the advantage of such an opportunity to run upon them with their hatchets.

Their next motion was immediately into the peas field. When they came to the fence, Mr. Church bid as many as had not discharged their Guns to clap under the Fence and lie close, while the other at some distance in the field stood to charge; hoping, that if the enemy should creep to the fence, (to gain a shot at those that were charging their guns,) they might be surprised by those that lie under the fence. But casting his eyes to the side of the hill above them, the hill seemed to move, being covered with Indians, with their bright guns glittering in the sun, and running in a circumference with a design to surround them.

Seeing such multitudes surrounding him and his little company, it put him [Church] upon thinking what was become of the boats that were ordered to attend him, and looking up, he spyed them ashore at Sandypoint on the island side of the river, with a number of horse and foot by them, and wondered what should be the occasion; until he was afterwards informed that the boats had been over that morning from the Island, and had landed a party of men at Fogland, that were designed in Punkatees neck to fetch off some cattle and horses, but were ambuscadoed, and many of them wounded by the enemy.

Now our gentleman's courage and conduct were both put to the test. He encouraged his men, and orders some to run and take a wall for shelter before the enemy gained it. It was time for them now to think of escaping if they knew which way. Mr. Church orders his men to strip to their white Shirts, that the islanders might discover them to be Englishmen, and then orders three guns to be fired distinctly, hoping [that] it might be observed by their friends on the opposite shore. The men that were ordered to take the wall being very hungry, stopped a while among the peas to gather a few, being about four rod from the wall. The Enemy from behind, hailed them with a shower of bullets. But soon all but one came tumbling over an old hedge, down the bank, where Mr. Church and the rest were, and told him, that his Brother B. Southworth, who was the man that was missing, was killed; that they saw him fall. And so they did indeed see him fall, but it was without a shot, and lay no longer than till he had opportunity to clap a bullet into one of the enemies forehead, and then came running to his Company.

The meanness of the English's powder was now their greatest misfortune. When they were immediately upon this beset with multitudes of Indians, who possessed themselves of every rock, stump, tree, or fence that was in sight, firing upon them without ceasing; while they had no other shelter but a small bank and bit of a water Fence. And yet, to add to the disadvantage of this little handful of distressed men, the Indians also possessed themselves of the ruins of a stone house that overlooked them. So that now they had no way to prevent lying quite open to some or other of the enemy, but to heap up stones before them, as they did; and still bravely and wonderfully defended themselves against all the members of the Enemy.

At length came over one of the boats from the island shore, but the enemy plied their shot so warmly to her as made her keep at some distance. Mr. Church desired them to send their canoe ashore, to fetch them on board; but no persuasions nor arguments could prevail with them to bring their canoe to shore; which some of Mr. Church's men perceiving, began to cry out, for God's sake to take them off, for their ammunition was spent! Mr. Church being sensible of the danger of the enemys hearing their Complaints, and being made acquainted with the weakness and scantiness of their ammunition, fiercely called to the Boat's master, and bid either send his Canoe ashore, or else begone presently, or he would fire upon him.

Away goes the boat, and leaves them still to shift for themselves. But then another difficulty arose; the enemy seeing the boat leave them, were reanimated and fired thicker and faster than ever, upon which, some of the men, that were lightest of foot, began to talk of attempting an escape by flight, until Mr. Church solidly convinced them of the impracticableness of it, and encouraged them yet. [He] told them, that he had observed so much of the remarkable and wonderful providence of God [in] hitherto preserving them, that encouraged him to believe with much confidence that God would yet preserve them; that not a hair of their heads should fall to the ground; bid them be patient, courageous and prudently sparing of their Ammunition, and he made no doubt but they should come well off yet. [Thus] until his little army again resolve, one and all, to stay with and stick by him. One of them by Mr. Church's order was pitching a flat stone up on end before him in the sand, when a bullet from the enemy with a full force struck the stone while he was pitching it on end, which put the poor fellow to a miserable start, till Mr. Church called upon him to observe how God directed the Bullets, that the Enemy could not hit him when in the same place, [and] yet could hit the stone as it was erected.

While they were thus making the best defense they could against their numerous Enemies, that made the woods ring with their constant yelling and shouting. And night coming on, somebody told Mr. Church, [that] they spied a sloop up the river as far as Gold island, that seemed to be coming down towards them. He looked up and told them, that, succor was now coming, for he believed it was Captain Golding, whom he knew to be a man for business, and would certainly fetch them off if he came. The wind being fair, the Vessel was soon with them, and Captain Golding it was. Mr. Church (as soon as they came to Speak one with another) desired him to come to anchor at such a distance from the shore that he might veer out his cable, and ride afloat; and let slip his canoe that it might drive a shore; which directions Captain Golding observed. But the Enemy gave him such a warm salute, that his sails, colours, and stern were full of bullet holes.

The Canoe came ashore, but was so small that she would not bear above two men at a time; and when two were got aboard, they turned her loose to drive ashore for two more. And the sloop's company kept the Indians in play the while. But when at last it came to Mr. Church's turn to go aboard, he had left his hat and cutlash at the well where he went to drink when he first came down; he told his company, [that] he would never go off and leave his hat and cutlash for the Indians, [that] they should never have that to reflect upon him. Though he was much dissuaded from it, yet he would go fetch them. He put all the powder he had left into his gun, (and a poor charge it was) and went presenting his gun at the enemy, until he took up what he went for. At his return he discharged his gun at the enemy to bid them farewell for that time; but had not Powder enough to carry the bullet half way to them.

Two bullets from the enemy struck the canoe as he went on board, one grazed the hair of his head a little before, another struck in a small stake that stood right against the middle of his breast.

Now this Gentleman with his army, making in all twenty men, himself, and his Pilot being numbered with them, got all safe on board after six hours engagement with three hundred Indians; [of] whose numbers we were told afterwards by some of themselves. A deliverance which that good gentleman often mentions to the Glory of God, and His Protecting Providence.

John Williams
(1664–1729)

Although not a soldier, Congregational minister John Williams became an active participant in Queen Anne's War when he was taken prisoner by a French-Canadian and Indian force in February 1704. Two of his children were killed in the attack on Deerfield, Massachusetts, and his family captured. His wife, Eunice Mather, the niece of Increase Mather and stepdaughter of Solomon Stoddard, could not keep up on the long forced march and was killed by their captors before they reached Canada. Williams spent over two years in captivity and was exchanged for the French pirate Baptiste. Although his son Samuel briefly converted to Catholicism, Williams ransomed him and three other children. Daughter Eunice decided to remain with her Indian captors.

Like Indian captive Mary Rowlandson before him, Williams interprets his personal suffering as a fortunate affliction that promises God's special favor for American colonists. He sees his successful resistance to French Jesuit conversion as confirmation of God's grace and the righteousness of the Puritan experience. The following passages demonstrate the power of the American Puritan myth to shape one man's tortured reality and reinforce the persistent image of the prisoner of war as living verification of American cultural exceptionalism.

from Williams's *The Redeemed Captive Returning to Zion*

The history I am going to write proves that days of fasting and prayer, without reformation, will not avail to turn away the anger of God from a professing people. And yet witnesseth how very advantageous gracious supplications are to prepare particular Christians patiently to suffer the will of God in very trying public calamities! For some of us, moved with fear, set apart a day of prayer to ask of God, either to spare and save us from the hands of our enemies, or to prepare us to sanctify and honor Him in what way soever He should come forth towards us. The places of Scripture from whence we were entertained were Gen. 32:10–11: "I am not worthy of least of all the mercies and of all the truth which thou hast showed unto thy servant. Deliver me, I pray thee, from the hand of my brother, from the hand of Esau, for I fear him, lest he will come and smite me and the Mother with the children" (in the forenoon). And Gen. 32:36: "And he said, 'Let me go, for the day breaketh'; and he said, 'I will not let thee go, except thou bless me' " (in the afternoon). From which we were called upon to spread the causes of fear relating to our own selves or families before God; as also how it becomes us with an undeniable importunity to be following God with earnest prayers for His blessing in every condition. And it is very observable how God ordered our prayers in a peculiar manner to be going up to Him to prepare us with a right Christian spirit to undergo and endure suffering trials.

Not long after, the holy and righteous God brought us under great trial as to our persons and families which put us under a necessity of spreading before Him in a wilderness the distressing dangers and calamities of our relations; yea, that called on us notwithstanding seeming present frowns, to resolve by His grace not to be sent away with a blessing. Jacob in wrestling has the hollow of his thigh put out of joint, and it is said to him, "Let me go": yet he is rather animated to an heroical Christian resolution to continue earnest for the blessing than discouraged from asking.

[The Attack]

On the twenty-ninth of February 1704, not long before break of day, the enemy came in like a flood upon us, our watch being unfaithful: an evil, whose awful effects in a surprisal of our fort, should bespeak all watchmen to avoid, as they would not bring the charge of blood upon themselves. They came to my house in the beginning of the onset and, by their violent endeavors to break open doors and windows with axes and hatchets, awakened me out of sleep; on which I leaped out of bed, and running toward the door, perceived the enemy making their entrance into the house. I called to awaken two soldiers in the chamber and returned towards my bedside for my arms. The enemy immediately broke into the room I judge to the number of twenty, with painted faces and hideous acclamations. I reached up my hands to the bedtester for my pistol, uttering a short petition to God for everlasting mercies for me and mine on the account of the merits of our glorified redeemer, expecting a present passage through the Valley of the Shadow of Death, saying in myself as Isaiah 38:10–11: "I said in the cutting off my days, 'I shall go to the gates of the grave. I am deprived of the residue of my years.' I said, 'I shall not see the Lord, even the Lord in the land of the living. I shall behold man no more with the inhabitants of the world.' " Taking down my pistol, I cocked it and put it to the breast of the first Indian who came up, but my pistol missing fire, I was seized by three Indians who disarmed me and bound me naked, as I was in my shirt, and so I stood for near the space of an hour. Binding me, they told me they would carry me to Quebec. My pistol missing fire was an occasion of my life's being preserved, since which I have also found it profitable to be crossed in my own will. The judgment of God did not long slumber against one of the three which took me, who was a captain, for by sunrising he received a mortal shot from my neighbor's house, who opposed so great a number of French and Indians as three hundred and yet were not more than seven men in an ungarrisoned house.

I cannot relate the distressing care I had for my dear wife, who had lain-in [given birth] but a few weeks before, and for my poor children, family, and Christian neighbors. The enemy fell to rifling the house and entered in great numbers into the house. I begged of God to remember mercy in the midst of judgment, that He would so far restrain their wrath as to prevent their murdering of us, that we might have grace to glorify His name, whether in life or death, and, as I was able, committed our state to God. The enemies who entered the house were all of them Indians and Mohawks, insulted over me awhile, holding hatchets over my head threatening to burn all I had. But yet God beyond expectation made us in a great measure to be pitied, for though some were so cruel and barbarous as to take and carry to the door two of my children and murder them, as also a Negro woman, yet they gave me liberty to put on my clothes, keeping me bound with a cord on one arm till I put on my clothes to the other, and then changing my cord, they let me dress myself and then pinioned me again. [They] gave liberty to my dear wife to dress herself and our children.

About sun an hour high we were all carried out of the house for a march and saw many of the houses of my neighbors in flames, perceiving the whole fort, one excepted, to be taken. Who can tell what sorrows pierced our souls when we saw ourselves carried away from God's sanctuary to go into a strange land exposed to so many trials, the journey being at least three hundred miles we were to travel, the snow up to the knees, and we never inured to such hardships and fatigues, the place we were to be carried to a popish country?

Upon my parting from the town, they fired my house and barn. We were carried over the river to the foot of the mountain, about a mile from my house, where we found a great number of our Christian neighbors, men, women, and children, to the number of a hundred, nineteen of which were afterward murdered by the way and two starved to death near Cowass in a time of great scarcity or famine the savages underwent there. When we came to the foot of our mountain, they took away our shoes and gave us Indian shoes to prepare us for our travel. While we were there, the English beat out a company that remained in the town and pursued them to the river, killing and wounding many of them, but the body of the army, being alarmed, they repulsed those few English that pursued them.

I am not able to give you an account of the number of the enemy slain, but I observed after this fight no great insulting mirth as I expected and saw many wounded persons, and for several days together they buried [several] of their party and one of chief note among the Mohawks. The governor of Canada told me his army had that success with the loss but of eleven men, three Frenchmen, one of which was the lieutenant of the army, five Mohawks, and three Indians; but after my arrival at Quebec I spoke with an Englishman, who was taken the last war and married there and of their religion, who told me they lost above forty and that many were wounded. I replied the governor of Canada said they lost but eleven men. He answered, " 'Tis true that there were but eleven killed outright at the taking of the fort, but that many others were wounded, among who was the ensign of the French." But, said he, "They had a fight in the meadow, and that in both engagements they lost more than forty. Some of the soldiers, both French and Indians then present, told me so," said he, adding that, "The French always endeavor to conceal the number of their slain."

[The Journey Northward]

After this we went up the mountain and saw the smoke of the fires in the town and beheld the awful desolations of our town, and, before we marched any farther, they killed a sucking child of the English. There were slain by the enemy of the inhabitants of our town to the number of thirty-eight besides nine of the neighboring towns. We traveled not far the first day; God made the heathen so to pity our children that, though they had several wounded persons of their own to carry upon their shoulders for thirty miles before they came to the river, yet they carried our children, incapable of traveling, upon their shoulders and in their arms.

When we came to our lodging-place the first night, they dug away the snow and made some wigwams, cut down some of the small branches of spruce trees to lie down on, and gave the prisoners somewhat to eat, but we had but little appetite. I was pinioned and bound down that night, and so I was every night while I was with the army. Some of the enemy who brought drink with them from the town fell to drinking, and in their drunken fit they killed my Negro man, the only dead person I either saw at the town or on the way. In the night an Englishman made his escape; in the morning I was called for and ordered by the general to tell the English that, if any more made their escape, they would burn the rest of the prisoners.

He that took me was unwilling to let me speak with any of the prisoners as we marched; but on the morning of the second day, he being appointed to guard the rear, I was put into the hands of my other master who permitted me to speak to my wife when I overtook her and to walk with her to help her in her journey. On the way we discoursed of the happiness of them who had a right to a house not made with hands, eternal in the heavens and God for a father and a friend; as also that it was our reasonable duty quietly to submit to the will of God and to say the will of the Lord be done. My wife told me her strength of body began to fail and that I must expect to part with her, saying she hoped God would preserve my life and the lives of some, if not all of our children with us, and commended to me, under God, the care of them. She never spoke any discontented word as to what had befallen us, but with suitable expressions justified God in what had befallen us.

We soon made a halt in which time my chief surviving master came up, upon which I was put upon marching with the foremost, and so made to take my last farewell of my dear wife, the desire of my eyes, and companion in many mercies and afflictions. Upon our separation from each other we asked, for each other, grace sufficient for what God should call us to. After our being parted from one another, she spent the few remaining minutes of her stay in reading the holy Scriptures, which she was wont personally every day to delight her soul in reading, praying, meditating of and over, by herself in her closet, over and above what she heard out of them in our family worship.

I was made to wade over a small river and so were all the English, the water above knee-deep, the stream very swift; and after that to travel up a small mountain; my strength was almost spent before I came to the top of it. No sooner had I overcome the difficulty of the ascent, but I was permitted to sit down and be unburdened of my pack; I sat pitying those who were behind and entreated my master to let me go down and help up my wife, but he refused and would not let me stir from him. I asked each of the prisoners as they passed by me after her, and heard that in passing through the above said river, she fell down and was plunged over head and ears in the water; after which she traveled not far, for at the foot of this mountain the cruel and bloodthirsty savage who took her, slew her with his hatchet at one stroke, the tidings of which were very awful; and yet such was the hard-heartedness of the adversary that my tears were reckoned to me as a reproach.

My loss and the loss of my children was great; our hearts were so filled with sorrow that nothing but the comfortable hopes of her being taken away in mercy, to herself, from the evils we were to see, feel, and suffer under (and joined to the assembly of the spirits of just men made perfect, to rest in peace and joy unspeakable, and full of glory, and the good pleasure of God thus to exercise us) could have kept us from sinking under at that time. That Scripture, Job 1:21, "Naked came I out of my Mother's womb, and naked shall I return thither. The Lord gave and the Lord hath taken away, blessed be the name of the Lord," was brought to my mind and from it that an afflicting God was to be glorified, with some other places of Scripture to persuade to a patient bearing my afflictions.

Robert Rogers

(1731–1795)

Born on a farm in Methuen, Massachusetts, Rogers grew up near what is now Concord, New Hampshire. He hunted and traded with the Indians on the frontier and helped raise a company of men for William Shirley's expedition to Nova Scotia. To escape prosecution for counterfeiting, he enlisted in the New Hampshire regiment, where he rose to the rank of captain. In 1758 his ability as a scout led to his promotion to major and the command of nine ranger companies charged with scouting responsibilities for the entire British army.

His military success during the French and Indian War did not follow him into civilian life, where he amassed enormous debts that forced him to flee to England. There he published his journals and wrote *Ponteach: or the Savages of America,* one of the first dramas written by a native New Englander. He returned to America in 1775, but in 1776 General Washington arrested him as a spy. He escaped and led a company of Queen's American rangers to defeat at White Plains. In 1780, he fled to England, where he died. Today, Rogers's positive reputation has more to do with the endurance of the frontier warrior myth than with the facts of his life. Like John Smith and Benjamin Church before him, he wrote himself favorably into history.

from *Journals of Major Robert Rogers*

It would be offering an affront to the public should I pretend to have no private views in publishing the following Journals; but they will excuse me if I leave them to conjecture what my particular views are and claim the merit of impartially relating matters of fact without disguise or equivocation. Most of those which relate to myself can at present be attested by living witnesses.

And should the troubles in America be renewed and the savages repeat those scenes of barbarity they so often have acted on the British subjects, which there is great reason to believe will happen, I flatter myself that such as are immediately concerned may reap some advantage from these pages.

Should any one take offense at what they may here meet with, before they venture upon exhibiting a charge, they are desired in favour to themselves to consider that I am in a situation where they cannot attack me to their own advantage; that it is the soldier not the scholar that writes; and that many things here were written not with silence and leisure but in forests, on rocks and mountains, amidst the hurries, disorders, and noise of war, and under that depression of spirits which is the natural consequence of exhausting fatigue. This was my situation when the following journals or accounts were transmitted to the generals and commanders I acted under, which I am now at liberty to correct except in some very gross and palpable errors.

[In the following letter of January, 1758, Lord Louden ordered Rogers to raise additional companies of rangers. They were composed of Indians and New Englanders like himself: early Natty Bumppos, self-reliant frontiersmen using Indian tactics and techniques. His instructions follow, along with an account of the rangers' first enemy engagement.]

Robert Rogers:

Your men to find their own arms which must be such as upon examination shall be found fit and be approved of. They are likewise to provide themselves with good warm clothing which must be uniform in every company, and likewise with good warm blankets. And the company of Indians to be dressed in all respects in the true Indian fashion, and they are all to be subject to the rules and articles of war. You will forthwith acquaint the officers appointed to these companies, that they are immediately to set out on the recruiting service, and you will not fail to instruct them that they are not to enlist any man for a less term than one year, nor any but what are able-bodied, well acquainted with the woods, used to hunting, and every way qualified for the ranging service. You are also to observe that the number of men requisite to complete the said five companies are all to be at Fort Edward on or before the 15th day of

March next ensuing, and those that shall come by the way of Albany are to be mustered there by the officer commanding, as shall those who go straight to Fort Edward by the office commanding there. Given under my hand, at New York, the 11th day of January 1758.

By his Excellency's command,
Louden

In pursuance of the above instructions, I immediately sent officers into the New England provinces, where, by the assistance of my friend, the requested augmentation of Rangers was quickly completed, the whole five companies being ready for service by the 4th day of March.

Four of these companies were sent to Louisbourg to join General Amherst, and one joined the corps under my command; and tho' I was at the whole expense of raising the five companies, I never got the least allowance for it, and one of the Captains dying, to whom I had delivered a thousand dollars as advance pay for his company, which, agreeable to the instructions I received, I had a right to do, yet was obliged to account with the government for this money, and entirely lost every penny of it.

It has already been mentioned that the garrison at Fort Edward was this winter under the command of Lieut. Col. Haviland. This gentleman, about the 28th of February, ordered out a scout under the direction of one Putnam, Captain of a company of one of the Connecticut provincial regiments, with some of my men, giving out publicly at the same time that, upon Putnam's return, I should be sent to the French forts with a strong party of 400 Rangers. This was known not only to all the officers but soldiers also at Fort Edward before Putnam's departure.

While this party was out, a servant of Mr. Best, a sutler to the Rangers, was captured by a flying party [scouting party] of the enemy from Ticonderoga; unfortunately too one of Putnam's men had left him at Lake George and deserted to the enemy. Upon Captain Putnam's return, we were informed he had ventured within eight miles of the French fort at Ticonderoga, and that a party he had sent to make discoveries had reported to him that there were near 600 Indians not far from the enemy's quarters.

March 10, 1758. Soon after the said Captain Putnam's return, in consequence of positive orders from Col. Haviland, I this day began a march from Fort Edward for the neighbourhood of Carillon, not with a party of 400 men as at first given out but of 180 men only, officers included, one Captain, one Lieutenant, and one Ensign, and three volunteers, viz. Messrs. Creed, Kent and Wrightson, one sergeant, and one private, all volunteers of the 27th Regiment; and a detachment from the four companies of Rangers quartered on the island near Fort Edward, viz. Capt. Bulkley, Lieutenants Philips, Moore, Crafton, Campbell, and Pottinger; Ensigns Ross, Wait, M'Donald, and White, and 162 private men. I acknowledge I entered upon this service and viewed this small detachment of brave men march out with no little concern and uneasiness of mind; for as there was the greatest reason to suspect that the French were, by the prisoner and deserter above mentioned, fully informed of the design of sending me out upon Putnam's return: what could I think! to see my party, instead of being strengthened and augmented, reduced to less than one half of the number at first proposed. I must confess it appeared too incomprehensible (ignorant and unskilled as I then was in politics and the arts of war); but my commander doubtless has his reasons and is able to vindicate his own conduct. We marched to the halfway brook in the road leading to Lake George and there encamped the first night.

The 11th we proceeded as far as the first Narrows on Lake George and encamped that evening on the east side of the lake; and after dark I sent a party three miles further down to see if the enemy might be coming towards our forts, but they returned without discovering any. We were however on our guard, and kept parties walking on the lake all night, besides sentries at all necessary places on the land.

The 12th we marched from our encampment at sunrise, and having distanced it about three miles. I saw a dog running across the lake whereupon I sent a detachment to reconnoitre the island, thinking the Indians might have laid in ambush there for us; but no such could be discovered; upon which I thought it expedient to put to shore, and lay by till night to prevent any party from descrying us on the lake, from hills or otherwise. We halted at a place called Sabbath Day Point on the west side on the lake, and sent out parties to look down the lake with perspective glasses which we had for that purpose. As soon as it was dark we proceeded down the lake. I sent Lieutenant Phillips with fifteen men as an advanced guard some of whom went before him on skates while Ensign Ross flanked us on the left under the west shore, near which we kept the main body marching as close as possible to prevent separation, it being a very dark night. In this manner we continued our march till within eight miles of the French advanced guards, when Lieutenant Philips sent a man on skates back to me to desire me to halt; upon which I ordered my men to squat down upon the ice. Mr. Philips soon came to me himself, leaving his party to look out, and said, he imagined he had discovered a fire on the east shore but was not certain; upon which I sent with him Ensign White, to make further discovery. In about an hour they returned, fully persuaded that a party of the enemy was encamped there. I then called in the advanced guard and flanking party, and marched on to the west shore where in a thicket we hid our sleds and packs, leaving a small guard with them, and with the remainder I marched to attack the enemy's encampment, if there was any; but when we came near the place, no fires were to be seen, where made us conclude that we had mistaken some bleach patches of snow, or pieces of rotten wood, for fire (which in the night, at distance, resembles it) whereupon we returned to our packs, and there lay the remainder of the night without fire.

The 13th, in the morning I deliberated with the officers how to proceed, who were unanimously of opinion that it was best to go by land in snowshoes lest the enemy should discover us on the lake; we accordingly continued our march on the west side, keeping on the back of the mountain that overlooked the French advance guards. At twelve of the clock we halted two miles west of those guards, and there refreshed ourselves till three, that the dayscout from the fort might be returned home before we advanced; intending at night to ambuscade some of their roads in order to entrap them in the morning. We then marched in two divisions, the one headed by Captain Bulky, the other by myself: Ensigns White and Wait had the rear guard; the other officers were posted properly in each division, having a rivulet at a small distance on our left and a steep mountain on our right. We kept close to the mountain that the advance guard might better observe the rivulet, on the ice of which I imagined they would travel if out, as the snow was four feet deep and very bad travelling on snowshoes. In this manner we marched a mile and a half, when our advanced guard informed me of the enemy being in their view; and soon after, that they had ascertained their number to be ninety-six, chiefly Indians. We immediately laid down our packs, and prepared for battle, supposing there to be the whole number or main body of the enemy, who were marching on our left up the rivulet upon the ice. I ordered Ensign M'Donald to the command of the advanced guard which, as we faced to the left, made a flanking party to our right. We marched to within a few yards of the bank which was higher than the ground we occupied; and observing the ground gradually to descend from the bank of the rivulet to the foot of the mountain, we extended our party along the bank far enough to command the whole of the enemy's at once; we waited till their front was nearly opposite to our left wing when I fired a gun as a signal for a general discharge upon them; whereupon we gave them the first fire which killed above forty Indians; the rest retreated and were pursued by about one half of our people. I now imagined the enemy totally defeated, and ordered Ensign M'Donald to head the flying remains of them that none might escape; but we soon found our mistake, and that the party we had attacked were only their advance guard, their main body coming up, consisting of 600 more, Canadians and Indians; upon which I ordered our people to their own ground, which we gained at the expense of fifty men killed; the remainder I rallied, and drew up in pretty good order, where they fought with such intrepidity and bravery as obliged the enemy (tho' seven to one in number) to retreat a second time; but we not being in a condition to pursue them, they rallied again, and recovered their groun[1], and warmly pushed us in front and both wings, while the mountain defended our rear; but they were so warmly received that their flanking parties soon retreated to their main body with considerable loss. This threw the whole again into disorder, and they retreated a third time; but our number being now too far reduced to take advantage of their disorder, they rallied again, and made a fresh attack upon us. About this time we discovered 200 Indians going up the mountain on our right, as we supposed, to get possession of the rising ground and attack our rear; to prevent which I sent Lieutenant Philips with eighteen men to gain the first possession and beat them back; which he did: and being suspicious that the enemy would go round on our left and take possession of the other part of the hill, I sent Lieutenant Crafton with fifteen men to prevent them there; and soon after desired two Gentlemen who were volunteer[2] in the party, with a few men to go and support him, which they did with great bravery.

The enemy pushed us so close in front that the parties were not more than twenty yards asunder in general and sometimes intermixed with each other. The fire continued almost constant for an hour and a half from the beginning of the attack, in which time we lost eight officers and more than 100 private men killed on the spot. We were at last obliged to break, and I with about twenty men ran up the hill to Philips and Crafton, where we flopped and fired on the Indians who were eagerly pushing us with numbers that we could not withstand. Lieutenant Philips being surrounded by 300 Indians, was at this time capitulating for himself and party on the other part of the hill. He spoke to me and said if the enemy would give them good quarters, he thought it best to surrender, otherwise that he would fight while he had one man left to fire a gun.

I now thought it most prudent to retreat and bring off with me as many of my party as I possibly could, which I immediately did; the Indians closely pursuing us at the same time took several prisoners. We came to Lake George in the evening, where we found several wounded men whom we took with us to the place were we had left our sleds, from whence I sent an express to Fort Edward, desiring Mr. Haviland to send a party to meet us and assist in bringing in the wounded; with the remainder I tarried there the whole night, without fire or blankets, and in the morning we proceeded up the lake, and met with Captain Stark at Hoop Island, six miles north from Fort William Henry, and encamped there that night; the next day being the 15th, in the evening, we arrived at Fort Edward.

The number of the enemy was about 700, 600 of which were Indians. By the best accounts we could get, we killed 150 of them and wounded as many more. I will not pretend to determine what we should have done had we been 400 or more strong; but this I am obliged to say of those brave men who attended me (most of whom are now no more) both officers and soldiers in their respective stations behaved with uncommon resolution and courage; nor do I know an instance during the whole action in which I can justly impeach the prudence or good conduct of any one of them.

Colonel Benjamin Franklin

(1706–1790)

Benjamin Franklin fused Puritan morality to the secular culture of the Age of Reason, and with wit and charm he created a persona of the practical American everyman. It should not surprise us that a man of many occupations, devoted to public service, also found time to be a part-time soldier. The following account of his brief command during the French and Indian War reveals a developing pragmatic American attitude toward national defense.

Franklin believed in an intuitive American predisposition for combat. He points out that the British government sent General Braddock and two regiments to defend the western settlements not out of a paternal motive, but out of fear that colonials who had banded together for the common defense would "grow too military." According to Franklin, Braddock's defeat "gave us Americans the first suspicion that our exalted ideas of the prowess of British regulars had not been well founded."

Like the Puritans of his birthplace, Boston, Franklin argued that there are moral imperatives for training for the common defense, but he does not turn to scripture for justification. Instead, he invokes the new god of reason and begins to secularize American war rhetoric.

from *The Autobiography of Benjamin Franklin*

This, being notified to the House, was accepted in lieu of their share of a general tax, and a new bill was form'd, with an exempting clause, which passed accordingly. By this act I was appointed one of the commissioners for disposing of the money, sixty thousand pounds. I had been active in modeling the bill and procuring its passage, and had, at the same time, drawn a bill for establishing and disciplining a voluntary militia, which I carried thro' the House without much difficulty, as care was taken in it to leave the Quakers at their liberty. To promote the association necessary to form the militia, I wrote a dialogue, stating and answering all the objections I could think of to such a militia, which was printed, and had, as I thought, great effect.

While the several companies in the city and country were forming, and learning their exercise, the governor prevail'd with me to take charge of our North-western frontier, which was infested by the enemy, and provide for the defense of the inhabitants by raising troops and building a line of forts. I undertook this military business, tho' I did not conceive myself well qualified for it. He gave me a commission with full powers, and a parcel of blank commissions for officers, to be given to whom I thought fit. I had but little difficulty in raising men, having soon five hundred and sixty under my command. My son, who had in the preceding war been an officer in the army rais'd against Canada, was my aid-de-camp, and of great use to me. The Indians had burned Gnadenhut, a village settled by the Moravians, and massacred the inhabitants; but the place was thought a good situation for one of the forts.

In order to march thither, I assembled the companies at Bethlehem, the chief establishment of those people. I was surprised to find it in so good a posture of defense; the destruction of Gnadenhut had made them apprehend danger. The principal buildings were defended by a stockade; they had purchased a quantity of arms and ammunition from New York, and had even plac'd quantities of small paving stones between the windows of their high stone houses, for their women to throw down upon the heads of any Indians that should attempt to force into them. The armed brethren, too, kept watch, and reliev'd as methodically as in any garrison town. In conversation with the bishop, Spangenberg, I mention'd this my surprise; for, knowing they had obtained an act of Parliament exempting them from military duties in the colonies, I had suppos'd they were conscientiously scrupulous of bearing arms. He answer'd me that it was not one of their established principles, but that, at the time of their obtaining that act, it was thought to be a principle with many of their people. On this occasion, however, they, to their surprise, found it adopted by but a few. It seems they were either deceiv'd in themselves, or deceiv'd the Parliament; but common sense, aided by present danger, will sometimes be too strong for whimsical opinions.

It was the beginning of January when we set out upon this business of building forts. I sent one detachment toward the Minisink, with instructions to erect one for the security of that upper part of the country, and another to the lower part, with similar instructions; and I concluded to go myself with the rest of my force to Gnadenhut, where a fort was tho't more immediately necessary. The Moravians procur'd me five wagons for our tools, stores, baggage, etc.

Just before we left Bethlehem, eleven farmers, who had been driven from their plantations by the Indians, came to me requesting a supply of firearms, that they might go back and fetch off their cattle. I gave them each a gun with suitable ammunition. We had not march'd many miles before it began to rain, and it continued raining all day; there were no habitations on the road to shelter us, till we arriv'd near night at the house of a German where, in his barn, we were all huddled together, as wet as water could make us. It was well we were not attacked in our march, for our arms were of the most ordinary sort, and our men could not keep their gun locks dry. The Indians are dexterous in contrivances for that purpose, which we had not. They met that day the poor farmers above mentioned, and killed ten of them. The one who escap'd inform'd that his and his companions' guns would not go off, the priming being wet with the rain.

The next day being fair, we continu'd our march, and arriv'd at the desolated Gnadenhut. There was a saw-mill near, round which were left several piles of boards, with which we soon hutted ourselves; an operation the more necessary at that inclement season, as we had no tents. Our first work was to bury more effectually the dead we found there, who had been half interr'd by the country people.

The next morning our fort was plann'd and mark'd out, the circumference measuring four hundred and fifty-five feet, which would require as many palisades to be made of trees, one with another, of a foot diameter each. Our axes, of which we had seventy, were immediately set to work to cut down trees, and, our men being dexterous in the use of them, great dispatch was made. Seeing the trees fall so fast, I had the curiosity to look at my watch when two men began to cut at a pine; in six minutes they had it upon the ground, and I found it fourteen inches diameter. Each pine made three palisades of eighteen feet long, pointed at one end. While these were preparing, our other men dug a trench all round, of three feet deep, in which the palisades were to be planted; and, our wagons, the bodys being taken off, and the fore and hind wheels separated by taking out the pin which united the two parts of the perch, we had ten carriages, with two horses each, to bring the palisades from the woods to the spot. When they were set up, our carpenters built a stage of boards all round within, about six feet high, for the men to stand on when to fire thro' the loopholes. We had one swivel gun, which we mounted on one of the angles, and fir'd it as soon as fix'd, to let the Indians know, if any were within hearing, that we had such pieces; and thus our fort, if such a magnificent name may be given to so miserable a stockade, was finish'd in a week, though it rain'd so hard every other day that the men could not work.

This gave me occasion to observe, that, when men are employ'd, they are best content'd; for on the days they worked they were good-natur'd and cheerful, and, with the consciousness of having done a good day's work, they spent the evening jollily; but on our idle days they were mutinous and quarrelsome, finding fault with their pork, the bread, etc., and in continual ill-humor, which put me in mind of a sea-captain, whose rule it was to keep his men constantly at work; and, when his mate once told him that they had done every thing, and there was nothing further to employ them about, "Oh," says he, "make them scour the anchor."

This kind of fort, however contemptible, is a sufficient defense against Indians, who have no cannon. Finding ourselves now posted securely, and having a place to retreat to on occasion, we ventur'd out in parties to scour the adjacent country. We met with no Indians, but we found the places on the neighboring hills where they had lain to watch our proceedings. There was an art in their contrivance of those places that seems worth mention. It being winter, a fire was necessary for them; but a common fire on the surface of the ground would by its light have discover'd their position at a distance. They had therefore dug holes in the ground about three feet in diameter, and somewhat deeper; we saw where they had with their hatchets cut off the charcoal from the sides of burnt logs lying in the woods. With these coals they had made small fires in the bottom of the holes, and we observ'd among the weeds and grass the prints of their bodies, made by their laying all round, with their legs hanging down in the holes to keep their feet warm, which, with them, is an essential point. This kind of fire so manag'd, could not discover them, either by its light, flame, sparks, or even smoke: it appear'd that their number was not great, and it seems they saw we were too many to be attacked by them with prospect of advantage.

We had for our chaplain a zealous Presbyterian minister, Mr. Beatty, who complained to me that the men did not generally attend his prayers and exhortations. When they enlisted, they were promised, besides pay and provisions, a gill of rum a day, which was punctually serv'd out to them, half in the morning, and the other half in the evening; and I observ'd they were as punctual in attending to receive it; upon which I said to Mr. Beatty, "It is, perhaps, below the dignity of your profession to act as steward of the rum, but if you were to deal it out and only just after prayers, you would have them all about you." He liked the tho't, undertook the office, and, with the help of a few hands to measure out the liquor, executed it to satisfaction, and never were prayer generally and more punctually attended; so that I thought this method preferable to the punishment inflicted by some military laws for non-attendance on divine service.

I had hardly finish'd this business, and got my fort well stor'd with provisions, when I receiv'd a letter from the governor, acquainting me that he had call'd the Assembly, and wished my attendance there, if the posture of affairs on the frontiers were such that my remaining there was no longer necessary. My friends, too, of the Assembly, pressing me by their letters to be, if possible, at the meeting, and my three intended forts being now completed, and the inhabitants contented to remain on their farms under that protection, I resolved to return; the more willingly, as a New England officer, Colonel Clapham, experienced in Indian war, being on a visit to our establishment, consented to accept the command. I gave him a commission, and, parading the garrison, had it read before them, and introduc'd him to them as an officer who, from his skill in military affairs, was much more fit to command them than myself; and, giving them a little exhortation, took my leave. I was escorted as far as Bethlehem, where I rested a few days to recover from the fatigue I had undergone. The first night, being in a good bed, I could hardly sleep, it was so different from my hard lodging on the floor of our hut at Gnaden wrapt only in a blanket or two.

Part II

The Revolutionary War

Paradise anew
Shall flourish, by no second Adam lost,
No dangerous tree with deadly fruit shall grow,
No tempting serpent to allure the soul
From native innocence.

—Philip Freneau   *The Rising Glory of America*

A new creation waits the western shore,
And reason triumphs o'er the pride of power.
As the glad coast, by Heaven's supreme command,
Won from the wave, presents a new-form'd land
Yields richer fruits and spreads a kinder soil.

—Joel Barlow   *The Columbiad*

Introduction

During the American Revolution, a remarkable transformation took place. Faith in natural law and human reason replaced the Puritan confidence in a God-centered, predestined, New World Israel, and, in the fervor of emerging nationalism, the millennial golden age was no longer the prerogative of the church-elect but within the purview of an entire nation. Everyone could benefit from a struggle for freedom that became a rational rather than a theological mandate, and the war stories Americans told of the Revolution reflected this secularization and democratization of national mission.

Isaac Newton's work emphasized the discovery of immutable laws underlying observable phenomena, and with this new science came a breakdown in the widespread faith that God participated directly in the affairs of man. As in colonial times, Americans convinced themselves that they fought to usher in a millennium of peace and prosperity, but they saw themselves as soldiers of reason, fighting for the principles of natural law, fulfilling an optimistic secular dream that replaced a religious promise. Biblical typology gave way to confidence in human reason and the judicious design of ancient Greek and Roman civilization.

The architects of the American Revolution saw God as a supreme ordering force and the creator of a mechanistic universe whose laws man could discover and apply to his own progress. This new faith in the potential of man, and manmade systems, was to sustain Washington's citizen–soldiers through periods of extreme suffering, but when reason did not prevail, as it rarely does in war, individual soldier accounts also reflected the crushing frustration and black humor of failed idealism. As the following accounts demonstrate, the use of the morbid and the absurd for darkly comic purposes became the common soldier's secret weapon against despair.

Although the following first-person narratives echo the intellectual currents of the period, they do so in a different proportion and emphasis. While writers of fictional accounts of the war celebrated the idealistic potential of the new society and defined the proper role of a new citizen, those recording their personal war experiences were emotionally attached to the details they reported, and their efforts to come to terms with those details—to make "sense" out of the suffering of war—are the product of complex personal struggles for meaning.

Unlike their Puritan forefathers, whose habit was to see God's hand in everyday events, soldiers in this age of new science paid attention to the visible rather than to the invisible world: Theirs are records of the observed and felt, rather than the unseen and imagined. Thus, most soldier narratives of the period reflect that, for the participants, the war was an affair of great torment to the body. Given their odds for victory and the degree of individual sacrifice required, it is not hard to agree with them that victory was due in part to a native warrior prowess first celebrated by John Smith. The voices of the Revolution reinforced already accepted myths of American moral and physical warfighting superiority.

For some veterans like Israel Potter the war began as an innocent adventure, fraught with suffering but of little cosmic significance. He identifies himself with the farmer–soldier myth of Cincinnatus: a man of the land who rises to the challenges of war, then returns to the simplicity of pastoral life—a classical rather than Biblical allusion. Years later in his 1855 biographical narrative *Israel Potter: or, Fifty Years of Exile,* the writer Herman Melville would make Potter's experience a symbol of how an unforgiving economic system betrayed the ideals of America's revolution. Abner Stocking records his suffering with a stoic's pride: hardships and sacrifice cleanse the souls of those making the march to Quebec, proving them worthy of the blessing of freedom. In the paradoxical logic of war, the price is so great that the effort must be of great value. Jacob Francis's humorous anecdote about General Israel Putnam offers an insight into the democratic principles of leadership in the American army.

Where surgeon Albigence Waldo relies on his liberal education and identifies with Shakespeare's heroes to try to explain the suffering of soldiers in the field, Joseph Plumb Martin calls upon his ironic sense of humor to make the best of the Continental army's pathetic situation. In dark contrast to Martin's humor, Jonathan Rathbun is horrified by the details of war and, in his anger, demonizes Benedict Arnold much the same way Puritans demonized their enemies.

Another observant and literate army surgeon, James Thacher, describes the siege of Yorktown with a balance of eloquent rhetoric and realistic detail: a "furious discharge of cannon and mortar" is Cornwallis's "first salutation," and a bomb that appears "like a fiery meteor with a blazing tail" scatters "fragments of the mangled bodies and limbs of the British soldiers" when it lands.

In the years following the war, writers of fiction like William Gilmore Simms and James Fenimore Cooper, emulating Sir Walter Scott's popular literary example, romanticized the harsh details of the American Revolution, emphasized the new nation's role in history, and celebrated the inherent nobility of the American warrior. Fictional accounts helped form unrealistic notions of combat which, less than a century later, would make civil war an acceptable means of solving long-standing sectional differences. It would take the tragically obvious human suffering of Shiloh to remind America of the painful reality of war told by the common soldier during the fight for independence.

Chronology

1775

19	Apr	Battles of Lexington and Concord.
17	Jun	Battle of Bunker Hill.
3	Jul	Washington assumes command.
31	Dec	Unsuccessful attack on Quebec.

1776

17	Mar	British evacuate Boston.
21–28	Jun	British siege of Charleston.
4	Jul	Declaration of Independence.
27	Aug	British victory at Long Island.
16	Sep	Battle of Harlem Heights.
28	Oct	Battle of White Plains.
16	Nov	British capture Fort Washington.
20	Nov	British capture Fort Lee.
26	Dec	Washington takes Trenton.

1777

3	Jan	Battle of Princeton.
25–27	Apr	Tryon's Danbury raid.
5	Jul	Burgoyne takes Fort Ticonderoga.
16	Aug	Americans win Battle of Bennington.
11	Sep	British win Battle of Brandywine.
19	Sep	Burgoyne checked at Freeman's Farm.
26	Sep	Howe occupies Philadelphia.
4	Oct	British win Battle of Germantown.
7	Oct	Burgoyne defeated at Bemis Heights.
17	Oct	Burgoyne surrenders at Saratoga; France decides to enter the war.
8	Nov	British evacuate Fort Ticonderoga.
15	Nov	British capture Fort Mifflin.
	Dec–Jan	Valley Forge.

1778

| 6 | Feb | Franco-American alliance signed. |

28	Jun	Battle of Monmouth.
	Jul	Wyoming Valley massacre.
29	Dec	British occupy Savannah.

1779

8	May	Spain enters the war against England.
11	Jul	Tryon's raid on Norwalk.
15	Jul	Wayne takes Stony Point.
9	Oct	Franco-American attack on Savannah fails.

1780

12	May	Charleston falls.
20	Jun	Battle of Ramsour's Mill.
6	Aug	American victory at Hanging Rock, S.C.
16	Aug	Gates defeated at Camden, S.C.
25	Sep	Benedict Arnold deserts American cause.
2	Oct	British spy John André executed.
7	Oct	British defeated at King's Mountain.

1781

1	Jan	The Pennsylvania Line mutinies, marches on Congress.
17	Jan	Battle of Cowpens, American victory under Morgan.
20	Jan	The New Jersey Line mutinies.
23	Feb	Battle of Haw River, N.C.
15	Mar	Battle of Guilford Courthouse.
29	Jul	Loyalist victory at Deep River, N.C.
5	Sep	French fleet drives British fleet away from Chesapeake Bay.
6	Sep	Arnold's raid on New London and Fort Griswold massacre.
6–19	Oct	Siege of Yorktown.
19	Oct	Cornwallis surrenders at Yorktown.
25	Oct	Battle of Johnstown.
13	Nov	East Chester raid.

1782

4	Jun	Crawford defeated at Sandusky.
11	Jul	British evacuate Savannah.

30	Nov	Preliminary peace treaty signed in Paris.
14	Dec	British evacuate Charleston.
1783		
3	Apr	Tories attack Tuckertown, N.J.
3	Sep	Peace treaty signed.
25	Nov	British evacuate New York City.
23	Dec	Washington retires from command.

Israel Potter

(1744–1826?)

A native of Cranston, Rhode Island, Israel Potter served as an infantryman in the First Rhode Island Regiment at Bunker Hill. Wounded and subsequently captured while serving on an American ship, Potter escaped from prison in England but remained there, barely surviving in impoverished obscurity, for almost fifty years. He returned to postwar America a poor and broken man, begging a pension for his service during the Revolution. Denied a government subsidy, this real life Rip Van Winkle died an unknown pauper, a symbol, at least to Herman Melville, of how an unforgiving economic system had betrayed the ideals of America's Revolution.

Yet, Potter's own words reflect little self-pity, and in his account of his first experience under fire, we sense the spirit of high adventure that motivated the common soldier at the beginning of the war. Potter portrays himself as the ideal citizen soldier, and his language reflects his life on the frontier. The entertaining short portrait of General Israel Putnam celebrates the democracy of the revolutionary army, not the image of the gentleman–soldier portrayed in the popular drama of the time.

from "Life and Adventures of Israel R. Potter"

[Potter describes his part in the Battle of Bunker Hill in June of 1775]

By the break of day Monday morning I swung my knapsack, shouldered my musket, and with the company commenced my march with a quick step for Charleston, where we arrived about sunset and remained encamped in the vicinity until about noon on the 16th June; when, having been previously joined by the remainder of the regiment from Rhode Island, to which our company was attached, we received orders to proceed and join a detachment of about 1000 American troops, which had that morning taken possession of Bunker Hill and which we had orders immediately to fortify, in the best manner that circumstances would admit of. We laboured all night without cessation and with very little refreshment, and by the dawn of day succeeded in throwing up a redoubt of eight or nine rods square. As soon as our works were discovered by the British in the morning, they commenced a heavy fire upon us, which was supported by a fort on Copp's hill; we however (under the command of the intrepid Putnam) continued to labour like beavers until our breast-work was completed.

About noon, a number of the enemy's boats and barges, filled with troops, landed at Charlestown, and commenced a deliberate march to attack us—we were now harangued by Gen. Putnam, who reminded us, that exhausted as we were, by our incessant labour through the preceding night, the most important part of our duty was yet to be performed, and that much would be expected from so great a number of excellent marksmen—he charged us to be cool, and to reserve our fire until the enemy approached so near as to enable us to see the white of their eyes—when within about ten rods of our works we gave them the contents of our muskets, and which were aimed with so good effect, as soon to cause them to turn their backs and to retreat with a much quicker step than with what they approached us. We were now again harangued by "old General Put," as he was termed, and requested by him to aim at the officers, should the enemy renew the attack—which they did in a few moments, with a reinforcement—their approach was with a slow step, which gave us an excellent opportunity to obey the commands of our General in bringing down their officers. I feel but little disposed to boast of my own performances on this occasion and will only say, that after devoting so many months in hunting the wild animals of the wilderness, while an inhabitant of New Hampshire, the reader will not suppose me a bad or inexperienced marksman, and that such were the fare shots which the epauletted red coats presented in the two attacks, that every shot which they received from me, I am confident on another occasion would have produced me a deer skin.

So warm was the reception that the enemy met with in their second attack, that they again found it necessary to retreat, but soon after receiving a fresh reinforcement, a third assault was made, in which, in consequence of our ammunition failing, they too well succeeded—a close and bloody engagement now ensued—to fight our way through a very considerable body of the enemy, with clubbed muskets (for there were not one in twenty of us provided with bayonets) were now the only means left us to escape the conflict, which was a sharp and severe one, is still fresh in my memory, and cannot be forgotten by me while the scars of the wounds which I then received, remain to remind me of it! Fortunately for me, at this critical moment, I was armed with a cutlass, which although without an edge, and much rust-eaten, I found of infinite more service to me than my musket—in one instance I am certain it was the means of saving my life—a blow with a cutlass was aimed at my head by a British officer, which I parried and received only a slight cut with the point on my right arm near the elbow, which I was then unconscious of, but this slight wound cost my antagonist at the moment a much more serious one, which effectually *dis-armed* him, for with one well directed stroke I deprived him of the power of very soon again measuring swords with a "yankee rebel!" We finally however should have been mostly cut off, and compelled to yield to a superior and better equipped force, had not a body of three or four hundred Connecticut men formed a temporary breast work, with rails &c. and by which means held the enemy at bay until our main body had time to ascend the heights, and retreat across the neck;—in this retreat I was less fortunate than many of my comrades—I received two musket ball wounds, one in my hip and the other near the ankle of my left leg. I succeeded however without any assistance in reaching Prospect Hill, where the main body of the Americans had made a stand and commenced fortifying—from thence I was soon after conveyed to the Hospital in Cambridge, where my wounds were dressed and the bullet extracted from my hip by one of the Surgeons; the house was nearly filled with the poor fellows who like myself had received wounds in the late engagement, and presented a melancholy spectacle.

Bunker Hill fight proved a sore thing for the British, and will I doubt not be long remembered by them; while in London I heard it frequently spoken of by many who had taken an active part therein, some of whom were pensioners, and bore indelible proofs of American bravery—by them the Yankees, by whom they were opposed, were not infrequently represented as a set of infuriated beings, whom nothing could daunt or intimidate: and who, after their ammunition failed, disputed the ground, inch by inch, for a full hour with clubbed muskets, rusty swords, pitchforks and billets of wood, against the British bayonets.

Abner Stocking

(1753–?)

During the winter of 1775 following Lexington, Concord, and Bunker Hill, American forces under General Montgomery occupied Montreal and unsuccessfully attacked Quebec. A twenty-two-year-old private from Connecticut in Colonel Benedict Arnold's Third Division during the American march to Canada and attack on Quebec, Abner Stocking kept a journal that reflects the youthful confidence shared by many during the early stages of the Revolution. Where Israel Potter's narrative is an old man's remembrance of a "melancholy spectacle," Abner Stocking presents a detailed description of immediate hardship and the "melancholy issue" of the human cost of the invasion.

Although Stocking acknowledges God's providence, he does not interpret his combat experience in grand cosmic terms. It is Colonel Arnold and not God's grace who sends them beef, and Stocking is willing to suffer Arnold's more rigid discipline after he has reasoned that independence is worth the extra burden. Although they exist in his narrative, Stocking holds the signs and omens from the invisible world to a bare minimum: His journal celebrates man's will, not God's, and reinforces John Smith's romantic ideal of inborn American military prowess.

from "Journal of Abner Stocking as Kept by Himself, During His Long and Tedious March Through the Wilderness to Quebec"

November 1st. Our fatigue and anxiety were so great that we were but little refreshed the last night by sleep. We started however very early, hungry and wet. Knowing that our lives depended on our speedy arrival to an inhabited country, we marched very briskly all day and even until late in the evening. We then encamped in a fine grove, but in a starving condition. Captain Goodrich's company had the good fortune to kill a large black dog, that providentially came to them at that time. They feasted on him heartily without either bread or salt. Our hunger was so great that many offered dollars for a single mouthful of bread. Such distress I never before felt, or witnessed. I anxiously turned my thoughts back to my native land, to a country flowing with milk and honey. I was surprised that I had so lightly esteemed all the good things which I there once enjoyed. Little, thought I, do we know of the value of the common blessings of Providence, until we are deprived of them. With such reflections I laid myself down on the cold, wet ground, hungry and fatigued.

November 2d, When we arose this morning many of the company were so weak that they could hardly stand on their legs. When we attempted to march, they reeled out like drunken men, having now been without provisions five days. As I proceeded I passed many sitting, wholly drowned in sorrow, wishfully placing their eyes on every one who passed by them, hoping for some relief. Such pity-asking countenances I never before beheld. My heart was ready to burst and my eyes to overflow with tears when I witnessed distress which I could not relieve. The circumstances of a young Dutchman, and his wife, who followed him through this fatiguing march, particularly excited my sensibility. They appeared to be much interested in each others welfare and unwilling to be separated, but the husband, exhausted with fatigue and hunger fell a victim to the king of terrors. His affectionate wife tarryed by him until he died, while the rest of the company proceeded on their way. Having no implements with which she could bury him she covered him with leaves, and then took his gun and other implements and left him with a heavy heart. After traveling 20 miles she came up with us.

Just at evening this day, we met cattle coming up the river, sent us for our relief. This was the most joyful sight our eyes ever beheld. The French people who drove them informed us that Colonel Arnold had arrived in their settlement two days before, with the advance party, and had purchased cattle as soon as possible and sent them on.

A cow was immediately killed and cut open in great haste; a small calf being found in her, it was divided up and eaten without further ceremony. I got a little piece of the flesh, which I eat raw with a little oat meal wet with cold water, and thought I feasted sumptuously.

November 3d. This day we proceeded on down the river about

20 miles, wading several small rivers, some of which were up to our middles. The water was terrible cold as the ground was at this time covered with snow and ice. At evening we came in sight of a house which was the first we had seen for the space of 31 days.

Our joy was inexpressible in breaking out of that dismal wilderness in which we had been so long buried, and once more beholding a country inhabited by human beings; it was like being brought from a dungeon to behold the clear light of the sun.

The French people received us with all the kindness we could wish, they treated our sick with much tenderness, and supplied us with every thing they could for our comfort. They seemed moved with pity for us and to greatly admire our patriotism and resolution, in encountering such hardships for the good of our country. But they were too ignorant to put a just estimate on the value of freedom.

November 4. Last night we got a plenty of good beef and potatoes, but little bread could be procured. It snowed most of the night and the weather was cold. After marching down the river about 10 miles, we began to get such necessaries as we wanted; such as bread, milk, eggs, butter and most kinds of sauce. To be supplied with these articles, of which we had been so long deprived, was a great luxury.

Had we been in New-England among people of our own nation, we should not, I think, have been treated with more kindness. They readily supplied us with whatever they had to spare, and discovered much tenderness towards those of our company who were sick, or feeble. I last night lodged in a house, which I had not done before for 39 days.

Jacob Francis

(1754–1836)

Jacob Francis was one of hundreds of blacks who fought on the American side during the Revolution. Born a slave in New Jersey, Francis served five masters before he earned his freedom at age twenty-one. Later in that same year he enlisted in the Continental army at Salem, Massachusetts. After the Battle of Trenton, Francis returned to New Jersey and served short enlistments with the New Jersey militia. Captured near Newark, Francis was released and back in ranks for the Battle of Monmouth. When pensions were offered to needy veterans, he provided the following account of his Revolutionary war service and received his pension in 1836.

The following anecdote offers another brief portrait of the colorful General Israel Putnam; it is also a story within a story about the equality of man. General Putnam demonstrates that he represents a classless society, and that to win the war everyone had to contribute. Jacob Francis and many other black men like him performed regular duty in the war for that kind of freedom. At least during the struggle for independence, blacks had an equal opportunity to experience a soldier's suffering and privations.

from Francis's "Petition for Pension"

I lived in Salem and worked for different persons till the fall of 1775. In the spring of that year the war had commenced and the battles of Bunker Hill and Lexington had taken place. About the last of October, I enlisted as a soldier in the United States service for one year. I was told they were enlisting men to serve one year from the first of January, 1776, but I should receive pay from the time I enlisted, and I enlisted and entered the service about the last of October and received two months' pay for my service up to 1 January 1776. I enlisted at Cambridge, about four miles from Boston, under Capt. John Wooley, or Worley, or Whorley, in Col. Paul Dudley Sergeant's regiment (Colonel Sergeant, I understood, had lived in Cape Ann). When I left New Jersey and went with Mr. Saxton to St. John's, I did not know my family name, but called myself Jacob Gulick (or Hulic) after the Mr. Gulick I had lived with, and was enlisted by that name; but, after I returned to New Jersey, was informed by my mother that my family name was Francis, and after that time I went by the name of Jacob Francis. Captain Wooley, or Worley, as his name was called, was captain; his brother was lieutenant. His Christian name I forget, and he had two sons, one a sergeant and the other a drummer in the same company in which I enlisted. The major's name was Ashton or Aston; his Christian name I don't recollect. The lieutenant colonel's name was Jackson. I remember there was in the regiment Captains Pope, Scott, Barnes, Ferrington, and I forget the names of the others. General Putnam was the general that I first recollect being under. At the time I was enlisted, the British army lay in Boston. After that, I remained with the regiment at Cambridge and in the neighborhood of Boston until the British were driven out of Boston.

I recollect General Putnam more particularly from a circumstance that occurred when the troops were engaged in throwing up a breastwork at Lechmere Point across the river, opposite Boston, between that and Cambridge. The men were at work digging, about five hundred men on the fatigue at once. I was at work among them. They had dug up a pretty large stone which lay on the side of the ditch. The general spoke to the corporal who was standing looking at the men at work and said to him. "My lad, throw that stone up on the middle of the breastwork."

The corporal, touching his hat with his hand, said to the general, "Sir, I am a corporal."

"Oh," said the general, "I ask your pardon, sir" and immediately got off his horse and took up the stone and threw it up on the breastwork himself and then mounted his horse and rode on, giving directions.

Albigence Waldo

(1750–1794)

Albigence Waldo was a surgeon of the First Connecticut Infantry Regiment and joined Washington's army in Pennsylvania in September 1777. Waldo witnessed the Battle of Germantown and the dark days of the American cause at Valley Forge during the winter of 1777–78.

His day-to-day record is as realistic and compelling an account of soldier suffering as that of Abner Stocking. Better educated than Stocking, Waldo frequently mixes classical and biblical allusions with his observations. He tries to explain what he sees philosophically and medically, but his rational detachment surrenders to the demands of his physical deprivation and cynical sense of humor. Overall, his diary is a fascinating record of an active and representative eighteenth-century mind caught in the misery that was Valley Forge.

from Waldo's "Journal of Valley Forge"

December 14—Prisoners & Deserters are continually coming in. The Army which has been surprisingly healthy hitherto, now begins to grow sickly from the continued fatigues they have suffered this Campaign. Yet they still show a spirit of Alacrity and Contentment not to be expected from so young Troops. I am Sick-discontented and out of humor. Poor food—hard lodging—cold weather—fatigue—Nasty Cloaths—Nasty Cookery—Vomit half my time—smoak'd out of my senses—the Devil's in't—I can't Endure it—Why are we sent here to starve and freeze—What sweet Felicities have I left at home; A charming Wife—pretty Children—Good Beds—good food—good Cookery— all agreeable—all harmonious. Here all Confusion—smoke and

Cold—hunger and filthyness—A pox on my bad luck. There comes a bowl of beef soup—full of burnt leaves and dirt, sickish enough to make a Hector spue—away with it boys—I'll live like the Chameleon upon air. Poh! Poh! crys Patience within me—you talk like a fool. Your being sick Covers your mind with a Melanchollie Gloom, which makes everything about you appear gloomy. See the poor soldier, when in health—with what cheerfulness he meets his foes and encounters every hardship—if barefoot he labors thro' the Mud & every hardship—if barefoot he labors thro' the Mud & Cold with a song in his mouth extolling War & Washington—if his food be bad, he eats it notwithstanding with seeming content—blesses God for a good stomach and Whistles it into digestion. But harkee Patience, a moment—There comes a Soldier, his bare feet are seen thro' his worn out Shoes, his legs nearly naked from the tatter'd remains of an only pair of stockings, his Breeches not sufficient to cover his nakedness, his Shirt hanging in Strings, his hair disheveled, his face meager; his whole appearance pictures a person forsaken and discouraged. He comes, and crys with an air of wretchedness and despair, I am Sick, my feet lame, my legs are sore, my body cover'd with this tormenting Itch—my Cloaths are worn out, my Constitution is broken, my formed Activity is exhausted by fatigue, hunger and Cold, I fail fast. I shall soon be no more! and all the reward I shall get will be—"Poor Will is dead." People who live at home in Luxury and Ease, quietly possessing their habitation, Enjoying their Wives and Families in peace, have but a very faint idea of the unpleasing sensations, and continual Anxiety the man endures who is in a Camp, and is the husband and parent of an agreeable family. These same People are willing we should suffer every thing for their Benefit and advantage, and yet are the first to Condemn us for not doing more!!

December 15—Quit. Eat Pessimmens [persimmons], found myself better for their Lenient Operation. Went to a house, poor & small, but good food within—eat too much from being so long Abstemious, thro' want of palatables. Mankind are never truly thankfull for the Benefits of life, until they have experienced the want of them. The Man who has seen misery knows best how to enjoy good. He who is always at ease & has enough of the Blessings of common life is an Impotent Judge of the feelings of the unfortunate. . . .

December 16—Cold Rainy Day, Baggage ordered over the Gulph

of our Division, which were to march at Ten, but the baggage was order'd back and for the first time since we have been here the Tents
were pitch'd, to keep the men more comfortable. Good morning
Brother Soldier (says one to another) how are you? All wet I thank'e,
hope you are so (says the other). The Enemy have been at Chestnut
Hill Opposite to us near our last encampment the other side of Schuylkill, made some Ravages, kill'd two of our Horsemen, taken some prisoners. We have done the like by them. . . .

December 18—Universal Thanksgiving—a roasted Pig at Night.
God be thanked for my health which I have pretty well recovered. How
much better should I feel, were I assured my family were in health. But
the same good Being who graciously preserves me, is able to preserve
them & bring me to the ardently wish'd for enjoyment of them again.

Our brethren who are unfortunately Prisoners in Philadelphia
meet with the most savage and inhumane treatments that Barbarians
are capable of inflicting. Our Enemies do not knock them in the head
or burn them with torches to death, or flay them alive, or gradually
dismember them till they die, which is customary among Savages and
Barbarians. No, they are worse by far. They suffer them to starve, to
linger out their lives in extreem hunger. One of these poor unhappy
men, drove to the last extreem by the rage of hunger, eat his own
fingers up to the first joint from the hand, before he died. Others eat
the Clay, the Lime, the Stones of the Prison Walls. Several who died in
the Yard had pieces of Bark, Wood, Clay and Stones in their mouths,
which the ravings of hunger had caused them to take in for food the
last Agonies of Life! "These are thy mercies, O Britain!"

December 21—(Valley Forge) Preparations made for huts. Provisions Scarce. Mr. Ellis went homeward—sent a Letter to my Wife.
Heartily wish myself at home, my Skin & eyes are almost spoil'd with
continual smoke. A general cry thro' the Camp this Evening among
the Soldiers, "No Meat! No Meat!"—the Distant vales Echoed back the
melancholy sound—"No Meat! No Meat!" Imitating the noise of Crows
and Owls, also, made a part of the confused Musick. What have you for
your Dinner Boys? "Nothing but Fire Cake and Water, Sir." At night,
"Gentlemen the Supper is ready." What is your Supper Lads? "Fire
Cake and Water, Sir." Very poor beef has been drawn in our Camp the
greater part of this season. A Butcher bringing a Quarter of this kind
of Beef into Camp one day who had white Buttons on the knees of his

breeches, a soldier cries out—"There, there Tom is some sort of your fat Beef, by my soul I can see the Butcher's breeches buttons through it."

December 22—Lay excessive Cold and uncomfortable last Night—my eyes are started out from their Orbits like a Rabbit's eyes, occasion'd by a great Cold and Smoke. "What have you got for Breakfast, Lads? Fire Cake and Water, Sir." The Lord send our Commissary of Purchases may live (on) Fire Cake and water, 'till their glutted Gutts are turned to Pasteboard.

Our Division are under Marching Orders this morning. I am ashamed to say it, but I am tempted to steal Fowls if I could find them, or even a whole Hog, for I feel as if I could eat one, But the Impoverish'd Country about us, affords but little matter to employ a Thief, or keep a Clever Fellow in good humor. But why do I talk of hunger & hard usage, when so many in the World have not even Fire Cake & Water to eat.

The human mind is always poreing upon the gloomy side of Fortune, and while it inhabits this lump of Clay, will always be in any uneasy and fluctuating State produced by a thousand Incidents in common Life, which are deemed misfortunes, while the mind is taken off from the nobler pursuit of matters in Futurity. The sufferings of the Mind, and this Attention is more or less strong, in greater or lesser souls, althou' I believe that Ambition & a high Opinion of Fame, makes many People endure hardships and pains with that fortitude we after times Observe them to do. On the other hand, a despicable opinion of the enjoyments of this Life, by a continued series of Misfortunes, and a long acquaintance with Grief, induces others to bear afflictions with becoming serenity and Calmness.

It is not in the power of Philosophy however, to convince a man he may be happy and Contented if he will, with a Hungry Belly. Give me Food, Cloaths, Wife & Children, kind Heaven! and I'll be as contented as my Nature will permit me to be.

This Evening a Party with two field pieces were order'd out. At 12 of the Clock at Night, Providence sent us a little mutton, with which we immediately had some Broth made, and a fine Stomach for same. Ye who Eat Pumkin Pie and Roast Turkies, and yet Curse fortune for using you ill, Curse her no more, least she reduce your Allowance of her favors to a bit of Fire Cake, & a draught of Cold Water, & in Cold Weather too.

December 25—Christmas—We are still in Tents—when we ought to be in huts—the poor sick, suffer much in Tents this cold weather. But now we treat them differently from what they used to be at home, under the inspection of Old Women and Doct. Bolus Linctus [Pill and Syrup]. We give them Mutton and Grogg and a Capital Medicine once in a while, to start the Disease from its foundation at once. We avoid Piddling Pills, Powders, Bolus's Linctus Cordials and all such insignificant matters whose powers are Only render'd important by causing the Patient to vomit up his money instead of his disease. But very few of the sick Men die.

December 26—The Enemy have been some Days the west Schuylkill from Opposite the City to Derby. Their intentions not yet known. The City is at present pretty Clear of them. Why don't his Excellency [George Washington] rush in and retake the City, in which he will doubtless find much Plunder? Because he knows better than to leave his Post and be catch'd like a d———d fool cooped up in the City. He has always acted wisely hitherto. His conduct when closely scrutinised is uncensurable. Were his Inferior Generals as skillful as himself, we should have the Grandest Choir of Officers ever God made. Many Country Gentlemen in the interior parts of the States who get wrong information of the Affairs and State of our Camp, are very much Surprised at G Washington's delay to drive off the Enemy, being falsely inform'd that his Army, consists of double the Number of the Enemy-ies such wrong information serves not to keep up the spirit of the People, as they must be by and by undeceiv'd to their no small disappointment—it brings blame on his Excellency, who is deserving of the greatest encomiums; it brings disgrace on the Continental Troops, who have never evidenced the least backwardness in doing their duty, but on the contrary, have cheerfully endur'd a long and very fatiguing Campaign.

December 28—Yesterday upwards of fifty officers in Gen Greene's Division resigned their Commissions—Six or Seven of our Regiment are doing the hike to-day. All this is occasion'd by Officers Families being so much neglected at home on account of Provisions. Their Wages will not buy considerable, purchase a few trifling Comfortables here in camp, and maintain their families at home, while such extravagant prices are demanded for the common necessaries of Life—What then have they to purchase Cloaths and other necessaries with? It is a Melancholy reflection that what is of the most universal importance, is most universally neglected—I mean keeping up the Credit or Money. The present Circumstances of the Soldier is better by far than the Officers—for the family of the Soldier is provided for at the public expense if the Articles they want are above the common price—but the Officer's family, are obliged not only to beg in the most humble manner for the necessaries of Life—but also to pay for them afterwards at the most exorbitant rates—and even in this manner, many of them who depend entirely on their Money, cannot procure half the material comforts that are wanted in a family—this produces continual letters of complaint from home.

When the Officer has been fatiguing thro wet and cold and returns to his tent where he finds a letter directed to him from his Wife, fill'd with the most heart aching tender Complaints, a Woman is capable of writing. . . . What man is there—who has the least regard for his family—whose soul would not shrink within him? Who would not be disheartened?

December 29—Snow'd all day pretty briskly. . . . So much talk about discharges among the officers—and so many are discharged—his Excellency lately expressed his fears of being left Alone with the Soldiers only. Strange that our Country will not exert themselves for his support, and save so good—so great a Man from entertaining the least anxious doubt of their Virtue and perseverance in supporting a Cause of such unparallel'd importance!

Joseph Plumb Martin

(1760–1850)

A common soldier who survived the hardships of over eight years of army duty during the Revolution, Joseph Plumb Martin describes looting, the mutiny of the Connecticut line, a hanged deserter, and the near "fragging" of an unpopular officer whom soldiers planned to give "a bit of a hoist" by planting a wooden canteen filled with powder under his bunk. Martin revels in the brotherhood of arms, reports no false heroism, and laces his narrative with humor and wit that remind today's reader of Mark Twain and Will Rogers.

The son of an eccentric, Yale-educated Congregational minister turned cooper, fifteen-year-old Martin enlisted for six months in the Connecticut militia. Following service in the battles for New York and White Plains, he returned home, felt restless, and enlisted in the Continental army for the duration of the war. He campaigned in Pennsylvania, survived the winter at Valley Forge, fought at Monmouth, wintered at West Point, served as an elite light infantryman and sapper, participated in the siege of Yorktown, and finally bid farewell to the army at Newburgh, New York, in 1783. Martin's solace during these very demanding trials was his sense of humor and the intangible but important bond of comradeship with fellow soldiers.

From Martin's *Private Yankee Doodle: Being a Narrative of Some of the Adventures, Dangers and Sufferings of a Revolutionary War Soldier*

[Martin describes the Continental army's march to Valley Forge and their deprivations during that winter of 1777]

We marched from hence [Mount Holly] and crossed the Delaware again between Burlington and Bristol. Here we procured a day's ration of southern salt pork (three fourths of a pound) and a pound of sea

bread. We marched a little distance and stopped "to refresh ourselves." We kindled some fires in the road, and some broiled their
meat; as for myself, I ate mine raw. We quickly started on and marched
till evening, when we went into a wood for the night. We did not pitch
our tents, and about midnight it began to rain very hard, which soon
put out all our fires and we had to lie "and weather it out." The troops
marched again before day. I had sadly sprained my ankle the day before and it was much swelled. My lieutenant told me to stay where I
was till day and then come on. Just as I was about to start out, our
Brigadier General [James M. Varnum] and suite passed by and seeing
me there alone, stopped his horse and asked me what I did there. I
told him that Lieutenant S—ordered me to remain there till daylight.
Says he, "Lieutenant S—deserves to have his throat cut," and then
went on. I had finished my pork and bread for supper, consequently
had nothing for this day. I hobbled on as well as I could. The rain and
traveling of the troops and baggage had converted the road into perfect mortar and it was extremely difficult for me to make headway. I
worried on, however, till sometime in the afternoon, when I went into
a house where I procured a piece of a buckwheat slapjack. With this
little refreshment I proceeded on and just before night overtook the
troops. We continued our march until sometime after dark, when we
arrived in the vicinity of the main army. We again turned into a wood
for the night. The leaves and ground were as wet as water could make
them. It was then foggy and the water dropping from the trees like a
shower. We endeavored to get fire by flashing powder on the leaves,
but this and every other expedient that we could employ failing, we
were forced by our old master, Necessity, to lay down and sleep if we
could, with three others of our constant companions, Fatigue, Hunger,
and Cold.

Next morning we joined the grand army near Philadelphia, and
the heavy baggage being sent back to the rear of the army, we were
obliged to put us up huts by laying up poles and covering them with
leaves, a capital shelter from winter storms. Here we continued to fast;
indeed we kept a continual Lent as faithfully as ever any of the most
rigorous of the Roman Catholics did. But there was this exception, we
had no fish or eggs or any other substitute for our commons. Ours was
a real fast and, depend upon it, we were sufficiently mortified.

About this time the whole British army left the city, came out, and encamped, or rather lay, on Chestnut Hill in our immediate neighborhood. We hourly expected an attack from them; we had a commanding position and were very sensible of it. We were kept constantly on the alert, and wished nothing more than to have them engage us, for we were sure of giving them a drubbing, being in excellent fighting trim, as we were starved and as cross and ill-natured as ours. The British, however, thought better of the matter, and, after several days maneuvering on the hill, very civilly walked off into Philadelphia again.

Starvation seemed to be entailed upon the army and every animal connected with it. The oxen, brought from New England for draught, all died, and the southern horses fared no better; even the wild animals that had any concern with us suffered. A poor little squirrel, who had the ill luck to get cut off from the woods and fixing himself on a tree standing alone and surrounded by several of the soldier's huts, sat upon the tree till he starved to death and fell off the tree. He, however, got rid of his misery soon. He did not live to starve by piecemeal six or seven years. While we lay here, there happened very remarkable northern lights. At one time the whole visible heavens appeared for some time as if covered with crimson velvet. Some of the soldiers prognosticated a bloody battle about to be fought, but time, which always speaks the truth, proved them to be false prophets.

Soon after the British had quit their position on Chestnut Hill, we left this place and after marching and countermarching back and forward some days, we crossed the Schuylkill in a cold, rainy and snowy night [December 12] on a bridge of wagons set end to end and joined together by boards and planks. And after a few days more maneuvering we at last settled down at a place called "the Gulf" (So named on account of a remarkable chasm in the hills) and here we encamped some time, and here we had liked to have encamped forever—for starvation here rioted in its glory. But lest the reader should be disgusted at hearing so much said about "starvation," I will give him something that, perhaps, may in some measure alleviate his ill humor.

While we lay here there was a Continental Thanksgiving ordered by Congress; and as the army had all the cause in the world to be particularly thankful, if not for being well-off, at least that it was no worse, we were ordered to participate in it. We had nothing to eat for two or three days previous, except what the trees of the fields and forests afforded us. But we must now have what Congress said, a sumptuous Thanksgiving to close the year of high living we had now nearly seen brought to a close. Well, to add something extraordinary to our present stock of provisions, our country, ever mindful of its suffering army, opened her sympathizing heart so wide, upon this occasion, as to give us something to make the world stare. And what do you think it was, reader? Guess. You cannot guess, be you as much of a Yankee as you will. I will tell you; it gave each and every man half a gill [two ounces] of rice and a tablespoonful of vinegar!!

After we had made sure of this extraordinary superabundant donation, we were ordered out to attend a meeting and hear a sermon delivered upon the happy occasion. We accordingly went, for we could not help it. I heard a sermon, a "thanksgiving sermon," what sort of one I do not know now, nor did I at the time I heard it. I had something else to think upon. My belly put me in remembrance of the fine Thanksgiving dinner I was to partake of when I could get it. I remember the text, like an attentive lad at church. I can still remember that it was this, "And the soldiers said unto him, And what shall we do? And he said unto them, Do violence to no man, nor accuse anyone falsely." The preacher ought to have added the remainder of the sentence to have made it complete, "And be content with your wages." But that would not do, it would be too apropos. However, he heard it as soon as the service was over, it was shouted from a hundred tongues. Well, we had got through the services of the day and had nothing to do but to return in good order to our tents and fare as we could. As we returned to our camp, we passed by our commissary's quarters. All his stores, consisting of a barrel about two-thirds full of hocks of fresh beef, stood directly in our way, but there was a sentinel guarding even that. However, one of my messmates purloined a piece of it, four or five pounds perhaps. I was exceeding glad to see him take it; I thought it might help to eke out our Thanksgiving supper, but alas! how soon my expectations were blasted! The sentinel saw him have it as soon as I did and obliged him to return it to the barrel again. So I had nothing else to do but to go home and make out my supper as usual, upon a leg of nothing and no turnips.

The army was now not only starved but naked. The greatest part were not only shirtless and barefoot, but destitute of all other clothing, especially blankets. I procured a small piece of raw cowhide and made myself a pair of moccasins, which kept my feet (while they lasted) from the frozen ground, although, as I well remember, the hard edges so galled my ankles, while on a march, that it was with much difficulty and pain that I could wear them afterward; but the only alternative I had was to endure this inconvenience or to go barefoot, as hundreds of my companions had to, till they might be tracked by their blood upon the rough frozen ground. But hunger, nakedness and sore shins were not the only difficulties we had at that time to encounter; we had hard duty to perform and little or no strength to perform it with.

The army continued at and near the Gulf for some days, after which we marched for the Valley Forge in order to take up our winter quarters. We were now in a truly forlorn condition,—no clothing, no provisions and as disheartened as need be. We arrived, however, at our destination a few days before Christmas. Our prospect was indeed dreary. In our miserable condition, to go into the wild woods and build us habitations to stay (not to live) in, in such a weak, starved and naked condition, was appalling in the highest degree, especially to New Englanders, unaccustomed to such kind of hardships at home. However, there was no remedy, no alternative but this or dispersion. But dispersion, I believe, was not thought of, at least, I did not think of it. We had engaged in the defense of our injured country and were willing, nay, we were determined to persevere as long as such hardships were not altogether intolerable. I had experienced what I thought sufficient of the hardships of a military life the year before, although nothing in comparison to what I had suffered the present campaign, and therefore expected to meet with rubbers [misfortunes]. But we were now absolutely in danger of perishing, and that too, in the midst of a plentiful country. We then had but little and often nothing to eat for days together; but now we had nothing and saw no likelihood of any betterment of our condition. Had there fallen deep snows (and it was the time of year to expect them) or even heavy and long rainstorms, the whole army must inevitably have perished. Or had the enemy, strong and well provided as he then was, thought fit to pursue us, our poor emaciated carcasses must have strewed the plain. But a kind and holy Providence took more notice and better care of us than did the country in whose service we were wearing away our lives by piecemeal.

[Martin remained in the army until the very end of the war. In the following account of the Continental army's final encampment at West Point and New

Windsor, N.Y., he describes the sadness of breaking the bonds of comradeship that the war had formed. It was, as he says, "a serious time."]

Time thus passed on to the nineteenth of April [1783], when we had general orders read which satisfied the most skeptical, that the war was over and the prize won for which we had been contending through eight tedious years. But the soldiers said but very little about it; their chief thoughts were more closely fixed upon their situation as it respected the figure they were to exhibit upon their leaving the army and becoming citizens. Starved, ragged and meager, not a cent to help themselves with, and no means or method in view to remedy or alleviate their condition. This was appalling in the extreme. All that they could do was to make a virtue of necessity and face the threatening evils with the same resolution and fortitude that they had for so long a time faced the enemy in the field. At length the eleventh day of June, 1783, arrived. "The old man," our captain, came into our room, with his hands full of papers, and first ordered us to empty all our cartridge boxes upon the floor (this was the last order he ever gave us) and then told us that if we needed them we might take some of them again. They were all immediately gathered up and returned to our boxes. Government had given us our arms and we considered the ammunition as belonging to them, and he had neither right nor orders to take them from us. He then handed us our discharges, or rather furloughs, for they were in appearance no other than furloughs, permission to return home, but to return to the army again if required. This was policy in government; to discharge us absolutely in our present pitiful, forlorn condition, it was feared, might cause some difficulties which might be too hard for government to get easily over.

The powder in our cartridges was soon burnt. Some saluted the officers with large charges; others only squibbed them, just as each one's mind was affected toward them. Our "old man" had a number of these last-mentioned symbols of honor and affection presented him. Some of the men were not half so liberal in the use of powder as they were when they would have given him a canteenful at once.

[This refers to an earlier attempt to "frag," or kill their commander with a bomb made of a canteen filled with powder.]

I confess, after all, that my anticipation of the happiness I should experience upon such a day as this was not realized; I can assure the reader that there was as much sorrow as joy transfused on the occasion. We had lived together as a family of brothers for several years, setting aside some little family squabbles, like most other families, had shared with each other the hardships, dangers, and sufferings incident to a soldier's life; had sympathized with each other in trouble and sickness; had assisted in bearing each other's burdens or strove to make them lighter by council and advice; and endeavored to conceal each other's faults or make them appear in as good a light as they would bear. In short, the soldiers, each in his particular circle of acquaintance, were as strict a band of brotherhood as Masons and, I believe, as faithful to each other. And now we were to be, the greater part of us, parted forever; as unconditionally separated as though the grave lay between us. This, I say, was the case with the most, I will not say all; there were as many genuine misanthropists among the soldiers, according to numbers, as of any other class of people whatever, but we were young men and had warm hearts. I question if there was a corps in the army that parted with more regret than ours did, the New Englanders in particular. Ah! it was a serious time.

Some of the soldiers went off for home the same day that their fetters were knocked off; others stayed and got their final settlement certificates, which they sold to procure decent clothing and money sufficient to enable them to pass with decency through the country as to appear something like themselves when they arrived among their friends. I was among those; I went up the river to the Walkill and stayed some time. When I returned to West Point the certificates were not ready and it was uncertain when they would be. I had waited so long I was loath to leave there without them. I had a friend and acquaintance in one of the Massachusetts regiments, who had five or six months to serve in the three years service. There was also in the same regiment a man who had about the same space of time to serve and who wished to hire a man to take his place. My friend persuaded me, although against my inclinations, to take this man's place, telling me that at the expiration of our service we would go together into the western parts of the state of New York, where there was a plenty of good land to be had as cheap as the Irishman's potatoes (for nothing at all, faith, and a little farther on, cheaper nor all that) and there we would get us farms and live like heroes. The other man offering me sixteen dollars in specie, with several other small articles, I consented, and now I had got hobbled again, though but for a short time. After I had been in this regiment about a month or six weeks, this "friend of mine" told me that he had taken an affront at something, I have forgotten what, and was determined not to stay there any longer, and endeavored to persuade me to go with him. I told him I had so short a time to serve and as there was a prospect that I should not have to stay so long as I had engaged to do, I would not go off like a scoundrel, get a bad name, and subject myself to suspicion and danger. I labored to persuade him to relinquish his foolish resolution and I thought I had, but he a few days after set off with himself and I have never heard of him since. I hope he did well, for he was a worthy young man. Soon after this, an order was issued that all who had but four months to serve should, after they had cut two cords of wood near the garrison for firewood, be discharged. Accordingly, I cut my two cords of wood and obtained an honorable discharge, which the other man might have done if he had not been so hasty in his determination. I now bid a final farewell to the service.

The poor soldiers had hardships enough to endure without having to starve; the least that could be done was to give them something to eat. "The laborer is worthy of his meat" at least, and he ought to have it for his employer's interest, if nothing more. But, as I said, there were other hardships to grapple with. How many times have I had to lie down like a dumb animal in the field, and bear "the pelting of the pitiless storm," cruel enough in warm weather, but how much more so in the heart of winter. Could I have had the benefit of a little fire, it would have been deemed a luxury. But when snow or rain would fall so heavy that it was impossible to keep a spark of fire alive, to have to weather out a long, wet, cold, tedious night in the depth of winter, with scarcely clothes enough to keep one from freezing instantly, how discouraging it must be, I leave to my reader to judge.

Jonathan Rathbun

(1765–1845?)

Not many voices of any war seethe with as much anger as Jonathan Rathbun's does. His expressed purpose in writing his autobiographical narrative is to teach the younger generation to hate Benedict Arnold: "Fathers, read it to your children, and early impress on their minds a love for Freedom, and teach them to detest a traitor like Arnold, and to scorn the inhuman and dishonorable conduct of the frenzied villain who murdered our brave Ledyard with his own sword after surrendering!"

The innocence of Potter, the stoicism of Stocking, the rationalism of Waldo, and the humor of Martin were not part of Rathbun's Revolution. For him, the horror of war was the dominant theme.

from the "Narrative of Jonathan Rathbun"

I was born in Colchester, Connecticut, in 1765. When sixteen years of age, I joined as a volunteer a company of militia, belonging to my native town, and marched to the relief of New London, intelligence having just reached us of an attack on that place by the British, under the conduct of the traitor Benedict Arnold. We left home to the number of about one hundred men, early in the morning of the 7th of September, 1781, the day after the battle. On our arrival in New London we witnessed a scene of suffering and horror which surpasses description. The enemy were not to be found, but they had left behind them the marks of their barbarism and cruelty. The city was in ashes. More than one hundred and thirty naked chimneys were standing in the midst of the smoking ruins of stores and dwelling houses. Very little property had escaped the conflagration except a part of the shipping, which on the first alarm was sent up the river. But though the city was destroyed it was far from being deserted. Numerous companies of militia from the neighborhood were pouring into the town; and the inhabitants, who had fled from their burning dwellings, were returning to gaze with anguish on the worthless remains of their property. Women were seen walking with consternation and despair depicted in their countenances, leading or carrying in their arms their fatherless and houseless babes, who in a few short hours had been bereaved of all that was dear on earth. Their homes, their provisions, and even their apparel were the spoils of the enemy or lay in ashes at their feet. Some were inquiring with the deepest distress for the mangled bodies of their friends, while others were seen following the carts which bore their murdered fathers, husbands or brothers to the grave. More than forty widows were made on that fatal day. Never can I forget the tears, the sobs, the shrieks of woe which fell from the kindred of our brave countrymen, who then gave their lives to achieve our national independence. It was my melancholy duty to assist in the burial of the dead, which brought me directly into the midst of these heart-rending scenes where the wife first recognized her husband, the mother her son, the sister her brother, in the body of a mangled soldier so disfigured with wounds and clotted with blood and dust, as to be scarcely known! Often on my visits to New London have I walked near the spot where I helped to inter my slaughtered countrymen; and though many years have since rolled away the recollection is still fresh in my mind, awakening anew the strong feelings of sympathy I then felt, and rousing into activity the love of my country.

I recollect several interesting facts, connected with the capture of Fort Griswold and the burning of New London, which, I believe, are not mentioned in the narratives of Messrs. Avery and Hempstead. After the capture of the fort and the massacre which followed, the enemy laid a line of powder from the magazine of the fort to the sea, intending to blow up the fort, and complete the destruction of the wounded within and around it. Stillman Hotman, who lay not far distant, wounded by three strokes of the bayonet in his body, proposed to a wounded man near him to crawl to this line and saturate the powder with their blood, and thus save the magazine and fort, and perhaps the lives of some of their comrades, not mortally wounded. He alone succeeded in reaching the line, where he was found dead lying on the powder which was completely wet with his blood. I do not find his name among the killed in the list of Mr. Avery.

Another fact of a different character was currently reported at the time and deserves to be recorded to the deeper disgrace of the infamous Arnold. He had a sister living in New London, with whom he dined on the day of the battle, and whose house was set fire to, as is supposed, by his orders, immediately afterwards. Perhaps he found her too much of a patriot for his taste and took this step in revenge.

James Thacher
(1754–1844)

Like Albigence Waldo, James Thacher was a surgeon who served the American cause. His journal of the war records the final siege of Cornwallis's forces at Yorktown and reflects an awe of the spectacle that is war. The scenes of battle hold him in a spell, yet he does not flinch at describing the human cost of war. Thacher's language is a unique mixture of inflated imagery and realistic detail—as he puts it, "the sublime and the stupendous." He tempers his description of the "most beautifully brilliant" bombshell descent with the statistics of death and descriptions of amputations.

Thacher idealizes General Washington through portraits of the General's personal courage and reassuring calmness under fire. At the same time, he demonizes the British, especially Lord Cornwallis. Thacher's ability to describe the Battle of Yorktown in graphically realistic detail heightens the drama and irony of the chivalric trappings of the British surrender.

from Thacher's *The American Revolution from the Commencement to the Disbanding of the American Army*

October 1st and 2nd—Our troops have been engaged in throwing up two redoubts in the night time; on the discovery, the enemy commenced a furious cannonade, but it does not deter our men from going on vigorously with their work. Heavy cannon and mortars are continually arriving, and the greatest preparations are made to prosecute the siege in the most effectual manner.

3rd and 4th—A considerable cannonading from the enemy; one shot killed three men, and mortally wounded another. While the Rev. Mr. Evans, our chaplain, was standing near the commander-in-chief, a shot struck the ground so near as to cover his hat with sand. Being much agitated, he took off his hat, and said, "See here, general." "Mr. Evans," replied his excellency, with his usual composure, "you had better carry that home, and show it to your wife and children."

Two soldiers from the French, and one from us, deserted to the enemy, and two British soldiers deserted to our camp the same night. The enemy from want of forage are killing off their horses in great number; six or seven hundred of these valuable animals have been killed, and their carcasses are almost continually floating down the river. The British are in possession of a place called Glouchester, on the north side of the river, nearly opposite Yorktown; their force consists of one British Regiment, and Colonel Tarleton's legion of horse and infantry. In opposition to this force the French legion, under the command of the Duke de Luzerne, and a detachment of French infantry and militia, are posted in that vicinity. Tarleton is a bold and impetuous leader, and has spread terror through the Carolinas and Virginia for some time past. In making a sally from Glouchester yesterday, they were attacked by the French, and defeated with the loss of the commanding officer of their infantry, and almost fifty men killed and wounded; among the latter Tarleton himself. The duke lost three men killed, and two officers and eleven men wounded. It is with much concern we learn that Colonel Sammel died at Williamsburg, of the wound which he received a few days since, when he was taken prisoner; the wound was inflicted after he had surrendered. At the request of General Washington, Lord Cornwallis allowed him to be carried to Williamsburg, where he died this day, universally lamented, as he was while living universally respected and esteemed.

The British have sent from Yorktown a large number of negroes, sick with the small-pox, probably for the purpose of communicating the infection to our army. Thus our inhuman enemies resort to every method in their power, however barbarous or cruel, to injure and distress, and thus to gain an advantage over their opposers.

From the 10th to the 15th, a tremendous and incessant firing from the American and French batteries is kept up, and the enemy return the fire, but with little effect. A red-hot shell from a French Battery set fire to the *Charon*, a British 44-gun ship, and two or three smaller vessels at anchor in the river, which were consumed in the night. From the bank of the river, I had a fine view of this splendid conflagration. The ships were enwrapped in a torrent of fire, which spreading with vivid brightness among the combustible rigging, and running with amazing rapidity to the tops of the several masts, while all around was thunder and lighting from our numerous cannon and mortars, and in the darkness of night, presented one of the most sublime and magnificent spectacles which can be imagined. Some of our shells, overreaching the town, are seen to fall into the river, and bursting, throw up columns of water like the spouting of the monsters of the deep.

We have now made further approaches to the town, by throwing up a second parallel line, and batteries within about three hundred yards; this was effected in the night, and at day-light the enemy were roused to the freshest exertions; the engines of war have raged with redoubled fury and destruction on both sides, no cessation day or night.

The French had two officers wounded, and fifteen men killed or wounded, and among the Americans, two or three were wounded. I assisted in amputating a man's thigh.

The siege is daily becoming more and more formidable and alarming, and his lordship [Cornwallis] must view his situation as extremely critical, if not desperate.

Being in the trenches every other night and day, I have a fine opportunity of witnessing the sublime and stupendous scene which is continually exhibiting. The bomb-shells from the besiegers and the besieged are incessantly crossing each others' path in the air. They are clearly visible in the form of a black ball in the day, but in the night, they appear like a fiery meteor with a blazing tail, most beautifully brilliant, ascending majestically from the mortar to a certain altitude, and gradually descending to the spot where they are destined to execute their work of destruction.

It is astonishing with what accuracy an experienced gunner will make his calculations, that a shell shall fall within a few feet of a given point, and burst at the precise time, though at great distance. When a shell falls, it whirls around, burrows, and excavates the earth to a considerable extent, and bursting, makes dreadful havoc around. I have more than once witnessed fragments of the mangled bodies and limbs of the British soldiers thrown into the air by the bursting of our shells; and by one from the enemy, Captain White, of the seventh Massachusetts regiment, and one soldier were killed, and another wounded near where I was standing. About twelve or fourteen men have been killed or wounded within twenty-four hours; I attended at the hospital, amputated a man's arm, and assisted in dressing a number of wounds.

The enemy having two redoubts, about three hundred yards in front of their principal works, which enfiladed our intrenchment and impeded our approaches, it was resolved to take possession of them both by assault. The one on the left of the British garrison, bordering on the banks of the river, was assigned to our brigade of light-infantry, under the command of the Marquis de la Fayette. The advanced corps was led by the intrepid Colonel Hamilton, who had commanded a regiment of light-infantry during the campaign, and assisted by Colonel Gimat.

The assault commenced at eight o'clock in the evening, and the assailants bravely entered the fort with the point of the bayonet without firing a single gun. We suffered the loss of eight men killed, and about thirty wounded, among whom Colonel Gimat received a slight wound to his foot, and Major Gibbs, of his excellency's guard, and two other officers, were slightly wounded. Major Campbell, who commanded the fort, was wounded and taken prisoner, with about thirty soldiers, the remainder made their escape.

I was desired to visit the wounded in the fort, even before the balls had ceased whistling about my ears, and saw a sergeant and eight men dead in the ditch. A captain of our infantry, belonging to New Hampshire, threatened to take the life of Major Campbell, to avenge the death of his favorite, Colonel Sammel; but Colonel Hamilton interposed, and not a man was killed after he ceased to resist.

During the assault, the British kept up an incessant firing of cannon and musketry from their whole line. His Excellency General Washington, Generals Lincoln and Knox, with their aides, having dismounted, were standing in an exposed situation waiting the result. Colonel Cobb, one of General Washington's aides, solicitous for his safety, said to his excellency, "Sir, you are too much exposed here. Had you better not step a little back?" "Colonel Cobb," replied his excellency, "if you are afraid, you have the liberty to step back."

The other redoubt on the right of the British lines was assaulted at the same time by a detachment of the French, commanded by the gallant Baron de Viomenil. Such was the ardor displayed by the assailants, that all resistance was soon overcome, though at the expense of nearly one-hundred men killed and wounded.

[Oct.] 19th—This is to us a most glorious day; but to the English, one of bitter chagrin and disappointment. Preparations are now making to receive as captives that vindictive, haughty commander, and that victorious army, who, by their robberies and murders, have so long been a scourge to our brethren of the Southern states. Being on horseback, I anticipate a full share of satisfaction in viewing the various movements in the interesting scene.

The Americans were drawn up in a line on the right side of the road, and the French occupied the left. At the head of the former, the great American commander, mounted on his noble courser, took his station, attended by his aides. At the head of the latter was posted the excellent Count Rochambeau and his suite. The French troops, in complete uniform, displayed a martial and noble appearance, their band of music, of which the timbrel formed a part, is a delightful novelty, and produced while marching to the ground a most enchanting effect.

The Americans, though not all in uniform, nor their dress so neat, yet exhibited an erect, soldierly air, and every countenance beamed with satisfaction and joy. The concourse of spectators from the country was prodigious, in point of numbers was probably equal to the military, but universal silence and order prevailed.

It was about two o'clock when the captive army advanced through the line formed for their reception. Every eye was prepared to gaze on Lord Cornwallis, the object of peculiar interest and solicitude; but he disappointed our anxious expectations; pretending indisposition, he made General O'Hara his substitute as the leader of his army. This officer was followed by the conquered troops in a slow and solemn step, with shouldered arms, colors cased, and drums beating a British march.

Having arrived at the head of the line, General O'Hara, elegantly mounted, advanced to his excellency the commander-in-chief, taking off his hat, and apologized for the non-appearance of [Lord] Cornwallis. With his usual dignity and politeness, his excellency pointed to Major-General Lincoln for directions, by whom the British army was conducted into a spacious field, where it was intended they should ground their arms.

We are not to be surprised that the pride of the British officers is humbled on this occasion, as they have always entertained an exalted opinion of their own military prowess, and affected to view the Americans as a contemptible, undisciplined rabble. But there is no display of magnanimity when a great commander shrinks from the inevitable misfortunes of war; and when it is considered that Lord Cornwallis has frequently appeared on splendid triumph at the head of his army, by which he is almost adored, we conceive it incumbent on him cheerfully to participate in their misfortunes and degradations, however humiliating; but it is said he gives himself up entirely to vexation and despair.

James Fenimore Cooper

(1789–1851)

James Fenimore Cooper's second novel, *The Spy* (1821) tells the tale of the exploits of a brave rebel spy named Harvey Birch and the savage conflict between Tories and Whigs in the neutral ground of Westchester County, N.Y. Cooper's imagination transforms the violence and social revolution of the American War for Independence into a cavalier romance, complete with grand cavalry charges and aristocratic models of society's natural leaders.

Cooper, however, transcends conventional romance and cavalier stereotype with the creation of Harvey Birch, who is not only the model new citizen in a new country, but also the prototypical frontier hero. The following passages demonstrate the romantic license Cooper and his fellow fiction writers took with the details of the Revolutionary War and his attempts to idealize both General Washington and the common men who served the cause of freedom. In *The Spy*, Cooper portrays war as a moral crucible that separates and tempers the best and most idealistic traits of the American character.

from Cooper's *The Spy*

[In this early chapter, Cooper describes a cavalry ambush by rebel forces that bears little resemblance to the details of war described in previous personal narratives. The "chosen beasts of West Chester" would have had a difficult time avoiding the cook stoves of Albigence Waldo or Joseph Plumb Martin.]

The rough and unimproved face of the country, the frequency of covers, together with the great distance from their own country, and the facilities afforded them for rapid movements to the different points of the war, by the undisputed command of the ocean, had united to deter the English from employing a heavy force in cavalry, in their early efforts to subdue the revolted colonies.

Only one regiment of regular horse was sent from the mother country, during the struggle. But legions and independent corps were formed in different places as it best accorded with the views of the royal commanders, or suited the exigency of the times. These were not infrequently composed of men raised in the colonies, and at other times drafts were had from the regiments of the line, and the soldier was made to lay aside the musket and bayonet, and taught to wield the saber and carbine. One particular body of the subsidiary troops was included in this arrangement, and the Hessian yagers were transformed into a corps of heavy and inactive horse.

Opposed to them were the hardiest spirits of America. Most of the cavalry regiments of the continental army were led and officered by gentlemen from the south. The high and haughty courage of the commanders had communicated itself to the privates, who were men selected with care and great attention to the service they were intended to perform.

The sufferings of the line of the American army were great beyond example; but possessing the power, and feeling themselves engaged in a cause which justified severity, the cavalry officers were vigilant in providing for their wants, and the horses were well mounted, well fed, and consequently eminently effective. Perhaps the world could not furnish more brave, enterprising, and resistless corps of light cavalry, than a few that were in the continual service at the time of which we write.

Dunwoodie's men had often tried their prowess against the enemy, and they now sat panting to be led once more against foes whom they seldom charged in vain. Their wishes were soon to be gratified; for their commander had scarcely time to regain his seat in the saddle, before a body of the enemy came sweeping round the base of the hill which intersected the view of the south. . . . The column of Dunwoodie wheeled in perfect order, opened and, as the word to charge was given, the troops of Lawton [Dunwoodie's second in command] emerged from their cover, with their leader in advance, waving his sabre over his head, and shouting, in a voice that was heard above the clangor of the martial music.

The charge threatened too much for the refugee troop. They

scattered in every direction, flying from the field as fast as their horses, the chosen beasts of West Chester, could carry them. Only a few were hurt; but such as did meet the arms of their avenging countrymen never survived the blow, to tell who struck it. It was upon the poor vassals of the German tyrant that the shock fell. Disciplined to the most exact obedience, these ill-fated men met the charge bravely, but they were swept before the mettled horses and nervous arms of their antagonists like chaff before the wind. Many of them were literally ridden down, and Dunwoodie soon saw the field without an opposing foe. The proximity of the infantry prevented pursuit, and behind its column the few Hessians who escaped unhurt sought protection.

[Late in the novel, Cooper presents the following idealized portraits of selfless service on the part of the citizen soldier Harvey Birch and General George Washington.]

It was at the close of a stormy day in the month of September, that a large assemblage of officers was collected near the door of a building that was situated in the heart of the American troops, who held the Jerseys. The age, the dress, and the dignity of deportment of most of these warriors indicated them to be of high rank; but to one in particular was paid a deference and obedience that announced him to be of the highest. His dress was plain, but it bore the usual military distinctions of command. He was mounted on a noble animal of a deep bay; and a group of young men, in gayer attire, evidently awaited his pleasure, and did his bidding. Many a hat was lifted as its owner addressed this officer; and when he spoke, a profound attention, exceeding the respect of mere professional etiquette, was exhibited on every countenance. At length the general raised his own hat, and bowed gravely to all around him. The salute was returned, and the party dispersed, leaving the officer without a single attendant, except his body servants and one aide-de-camp. Dismounting, he stepped back a few paces, and for a moment viewed the condition of his horse with the eye of one who well understood the animal, and then casting a brief but expressive glance at his aide, he retired into the building, followed by that gentleman.

On entering an apartment that was apparently fitted for his reception, he took a seat, and continued for a long time in a thoughtful attitude, like one in the habit of communing much with himself. During this silence, the aide-de-camp stood in expectation of his orders. At length the general raised his eyes, and spoke in those low placid tones that seemed natural to him.

"Has the man whom I wished to see arrived, sir?"

"He waits the pleasure of your excellency."

"I will receive him here, and alone, if you please."

The aide bowed and withdrew. In a few minutes the door again opened, and a figure gliding into the apartment, stood modestly at a distance from the general, without speaking. His entrance was unheard by the officer, who sat gazing at the fire, still absorbed in his own meditations. Several minutes passed, when he spoke to himself in an under tone—

"To-morrow we must raise the curtain, and expose our plans. May heaven prosper them!"

A slight movement made by the stranger caught his ear, and he turned his head, and saw that he was not alone. He pointed silently to the fire, towards which the figure advanced, although the multitude of his garments, which seemed more calculated for disguise than comfort, rendered its warmth unnecessary. A second mild and courteous gesture motioned a vacant chair, but the stranger followed, and continued for some time. At length the officer arose, and opening a desk that was laid upon the table near which he sat, took from it a small, but apparently heavy bag.

"Harvey Birch," he said, turning to the stranger, "the time has arrived when our connection must cease; henceforth and for ever we must be strangers." The peddler dropped the folds of the great coat that concealed his features, and gazed for a moment earnestly at the face of the speaker; then dropping his head upon his bosom, he said meekly,—

"If it be your excellency's pleasure."

"It is necessary. Since I have filled the station which I now hold, it has become my duty to know many men, who like yourself, have been my instruments of procuring intelligence. You have I trusted more than all; I early saw in you a regard to truth and principle, that I am pleased to say, has never deceived me—you alone know my secret agents in the city, and on your fidelity depend, not only their fortunes, but their lives."

He paused, as if to reflect in order that full justice might be done to the peddler, and then continued,—

"I believe you are one of the very few that I have employed who have acted faithfully to our cause; and, while you have passed as a spy of the enemy, have never given intelligence that you were not permitted to divulge. To me, and to me only of all the world, you seem to have acted with a strong attachment to the liberties of America."

During this address, Harvey gradually raised his head from his bosom, until it reached the highest point of elevation; a faint tinge gathered in his cheeks, and, as the officer concluded, it was diffused over his whole countenance in a deep glow, while he stood proudly swelling with his emotions, but with eyes that sought the feet of the speaker.

"It is now my duty to pay you for these services; hitherto you have postponed receiving your reward, and the debt has become a heavy one—I wish not to undervalue your dangers; here are a hundred doubbloons; remember the poverty of our country, and attribute to it the smallness of your pay."

The peddler raised his eyes to the countenance of the speaker; but, as the other held forth the money, he moved back, as if refusing the bag.

"It is not much for your services and risks, I acknowledge," continued the general, "but it is all that I have to offer; hereafter, it may be in my power to increase it."

"Does your excellency think that I have exposed my life, and blasted my character, for money?"

"If not for money, what then?"

"What has brought your excellency into the field? For what do you daily and hourly expose your precious life to battle and the halter? What is there about me to mourn, when such men as you risk their all for our country? No, no, no—not a dollar of your gold will I touch; poor America has need of it all!"

* * *

The officer stood for a few moments in the attitude of intense thought. He then drew to him the desk, and wrote a few lines on a piece of paper, and gave it to the peddler.

"That Providence destines this country to some great and glorious fate I must believe, while I witness the patriotism that pervades the bosoms of her lowest citizens," he said.

* * *

The officer gazed at the strong emotion he exhibited with pain, and he made a slight movement toward the gold; but it was arrested by the expression of his companion's face. Harvey saw the intention, and shook his head as he continued more mildly—"It is, indeed, a treasure that your excellency gives me. . . . perhaps," he continued, with a melancholy smile, "it may be known after my death who was my friend; but if it should not, there are none to grieve for me."

"Remember," said the officer, with strong emotions, "that in me you will always have a secret friend; but openly I cannot know you."

"I know it, I know it," said Birch; "I knew it when I took the service. 'Tis probably the last time that I shall ever see your excellency. May God pour down his choicest blessings on your head!" He paused, and moved towards the door. The officer followed him with eyes that expressed deep interest. Once more the peddler turned, and seemed to gaze on the placid, but commanding features of the general with regret and reverence, and then, bowing low, he withdrew.

Part III

The War of 1812

*Oh, thus be it ever when freemen shall stand
Between their loved homes and the war's desolation;
Blest with victory and peace, may the heaven rescued land
Praise the Power that hath made and preserved us a nation!
Then conquer we must, when our cause it is just,
And this be our motto: "In God is our trust!"
And the star-spangled banner in triumph shall wave,
O'er the land of the free, and the home of the brave!*

—Francis Scott Key   "The Star-Spangled Banner"

Introduction

The divisiveness over foreign policy and the dismal combat record of Americans during the War of 1812 would have done little to enhance the new nation's patriotism or confidence in its place in history without the help of cultural myth-makers. Because the actual course of the conflict was a record of military disasters, which included the occupation and burning of the national capital, the blockade of American coasts, and British control of the northwestern frontier, the public relied on stories about individual heroism and national destiny to maintain their country's self-image.

Instead of a futile standstill in arms, the war reported in the press and recorded in contemporary accounts became a second War of Independence and a second decisive victory of unique American frontier spirit and moral character over English arrogance and tyranny.

News of the American victory at New Orleans arrived about the same time as news of the peace treaty. Although fought after the war was over, the Battle of New Orleans in memory came to symbolize American victory, and Andrew Jackson became the latest personification of the nation's ideal frontier American warrior. Henry Clay claimed that the War of 1812 achieved "the firm establishment of the American character," and as the following stories illustrate, it was a constitution enriched by the exuberance, humor, and images of the American frontier.

In the popular imagination the War of 1812 in general, and the Battle of New Orleans in particular, confirmed the innate moral and martial superiority of democracy's volunteer American militia over the best professional soldiers Europe could field. Jackson's 3,500 Americans withstood a British charge of over 6,000 disciplined veterans of the Napoleonic Wars, and inflicted over 2,000 casualties. Jackson, half landed aristocrat and half Indian killer, attributed his victory to the "untutored courage" of the American character. Military success supported by myth confirmed the virtue and strength of inherent national potential.

Romantic notions of the frontier hero and the rhetoric of a second Revolutionary War rejuvenated national pride and fortified national unity during and after the War of 1812. The collective myths of this conflict revised a humiliating military stalemate into an optimistic confirmation of the superiority of the national character and mission.

Chronology

1812

18	Jun	House of Representatives votes for war.
	Jul	Gen. William Hull marches to Detroit, invades Canada. Gen. Henry Dearborn moves up Lake Champlain, plans assault on Montreal. Gen. Stephen Van Rensselaer plans to take control of Niagara area.
17	Jul	Fort Michilimackinac surrenders to British.
16	Aug	Hull retreats from Canada, surrenders at Detroit.
19	Aug	USS *Constitution* defeats the British frigate *Guerriere*.
18	Oct	The *Wasp* captured by the *Poitiers*.
3	Dec	William Eustis resigns as secretary of war; President Monroe assumes duties.

1813

23	Jan	River Raisin massacre.
24	Feb	John Armstrong becomes secretary of war.
	Mar	Court-martial finds Hull guilty of cowardice and sentences him to be shot. Capt. David Porter sails the *Essex* into the Pacific to attack British whalers.
27	Mar	Oliver Hazard Perry assumes responsibility for construction of Lake Erie fleet.
	Mar–Dec	British forces raid Chesapeake Bay area.
15	Apr	Wilkerson occupies Mobile.
27	Apr	Americans capture York (Toronto).
1	May	Siege of Fort Meigs begins.
5	May	Americans capture Fort George. Battle of Rapids of Miami.
1	Jun	The *Shannon* defeats the *Chesapeake* under Capt. James Lawrence.
6	Jun	Americans defeated at Stoney Creek.
30	Aug	Fort Mims massacre.
10	Sep	The Battle of Lake Erie: the first British–American fleet engagement. Commodore Perry's "We have met the

enemy and they are ours" message to Gen. Harrison signals his move on land.

27	Sep	Harrison lands in Canada.
5	Oct	Harrison defeats Tecumseh at the Battle of the Thames, weakens Indian alliance with British.
	Sep–Oct	Gens. James Wilkinson and Wade Hampton are routed in their efforts to take Montreal.
	Oct	Porter takes possession of the Marquesas Islands, leaves Marine Lt. John Gamble and twenty-one men to secure first overseas American possession.
10	Dec	Fort George evacuated and Newark burned by Americans.
18	Dec	Fort Niagara occupied by British.

1814

27	Mar	Battle of Horseshoe Bend.
5	Jul	Battle of Chippewa.
25	Jul	Battle of Lundy's Lane.
13	Aug	Siege of Fort Erie begins.
24	Aug	Battle of Bladensburg.
24–25	Aug	Adm. Sir George Cockburn burns the White House and other government buildings.
28	Aug	British capture Alexandria, Va.
4	Sep	Armstrong resigns and Monroe again assumes secretary of war duties.
11	Sep	Battle of Lake Champlain. Capt. Thomas Macdonough defeats Capt. George Downie, halts Sir George Prevost's army, forces it back to Canada to winter.
13–14	Sep	Cockburn attacks Baltimore. Lt. Col. Walker Keith Armistead, the first graduate of West Point, defends Fort McHenry and forces a British withdrawal.
23	Dec	British land below New Orleans. Gen. Andrew Jackson attacks.
24	Dec	Peace of Ghent signed, ending hostilities in Europe.

1815

8	Jan	Jackson defeats British regulars under Gen. Sir Edward Pakenham; ends the land war.
17	Feb	Ratifications of peace treaty exchanged; War of 1812 ends.

James Miller

(1776–1851)

Born in Peterborough, New Hampshire, about the time of the Battle of Bunker Hill, James Miller studied at Williams College and was admitted to the bar in 1803. In 1809 he attracted the attention of General Benjamin Pierce, who appointed him a major in the 4th Regiment of the U.S. Infantry. Five years later, Colonel Miller led his regiment against the British in the Battle of Lundy's Lane, a spectacular American victory that won Miller the reputation of "New England's most distinguished soldier."

Miller later went on to serve as governor of the Arkansas Territory. His health ruined, he returned home and was elected to Congress but did not fill his seat in favor of accepting the job of collector of customs for the district of Salem, Massachusetts. It was during his twenty-four-year tenure at the Salem Customs House that American novelist Nathaniel Hawthorne got to know and respect him. Hawthorne's praise of the "Old General" in the customs-house chapter of *The Scarlet Letter* lacks the pejorative ambiguity Hawthorne usually reserves for representatives of the New England past.

Like John Smith and William Plumb Martin before him, Miller believed in the innate superiority of American warriors, and his letters reflect confidence in their success if led well.

from James Miller's Letters

Upper Canada, August 27th 1812

My Dearest Ruth,

When I last wrote you my feelings were very different from what they now are. I then thought that things appeared prosperous and flattering. I considered we had a sufficient force to bear down all opposition and I still think had we done as we ought we could [have] carried conquest to a very considerable extent, but alas times are now altered we are all Prisoners of War. Sunday on the 9th, I was on a march from Detroit to the river Reason with the 4th Regt. and a Detachment of Ohio Militia consisting of six hundred in the whole in order to guard some provisions which was coming on for our Army. About sixteen miles from Detroit at a place called Maguago near an Indian town or rather betwixt two Indian towns, I was attacked in a thick wood by a superior number of British and Indians. They made the first attack a very heavy fire upon us then the most hideous yell by the Indians. The woods appeared to be full of them. I had all my men formed to the best advantage the moment we saw their fire. I ordered a general charge which was instantly obeyed by every officer and soldier. We visited closer on them then made a general fire upon them and put them to flight. We drove them through the woods firing and charging them without a halt for more than two miles completely defeated them and drove them every devil across Detroit River home to their own Fort except those who we took prisoners and killed, which was a considerable part of them. My killed and wounded amounted to seventy five, sixteen of whom were killed dead on the ground. They took no prisoners from me. I secured the body of every man I had killed or wounded. We took five prisoners, but made no Indian prisoners. We gave them no quarters. They carried off their wounded generally from the number of the enemy found dead. Their loss of killed and wounded must have been nearly double to ours. We wounded the famous Tecumich in the neck, but not sufficiently to kill him. Lieut. Larrabee has lost his left arm in consequence of a wound in the action. No officer was killed, but five wounded. Lieut. Larrabee the worst.

Only one week after I with six hundred men completely conquered almost their whole force which they then had. They come and took Fort Detroit and made nearly two thousand of us Prisoners on Sunday the 16th. Thus being no operations going on against them below us gave them an opportunity to reinforce. The number they brot against us is yet unknown, but my humble opinion is we could have defeated them without a doubt had we attempted it, but General Hull thot differently and surrendered without making any termes of capitulation. Col. Brush and I made the best termes we could after the surrender which was but poor. The Militia they let return home by agreeing not to bare arms against his Majesty or his subjects during the War or until exchanged. All the Regulars are kept except a few Subaltirn Officers who are allowed to go home on "parole of honor" whether ever I shall get away from them, God only knows. I have been sick with the fever Ague for a long time. It takes me every other day, the intermediate day I feel very well.

I have petitioned repeatedly for leave to be paroled, but to no affect. We are now apposite Niagara on our way to Montreal. I intend to repeat my request I had thot they would let me return until I had recovered my health, but they appear to think that of little consequence to them by this capture. I have lost two horses, two saddles and two bridles. One horse was a very fine one which I gave one hundred and forty five dollars for with the saddle and bridle. The other was a low priced horse which I got for a pack horse on the march from Nineennes. I petitioned repeatedly for my clothing which was taken, my cloak I wanted very much, but they utterly refused. Well as God would have it Sgt. Gooding was there a Prisoner and my chest got wet on the passage and several others so they were delivered to Gooding to dry. Sergent[s] Furbush Tracy and Jenisong took my things to dry which took them a long time. while they were doing it, they smuggled my cloak and eight of my best shirts, my stockings, vests, pantaloons, small clothes and in fact almost every thing worth any thing and fixed them up nice when we were brot from Detroit they were brot from Malden and brot my cloaths with them and delivered them safe to me so I shall do very well for cloaths. I am sorry to inform you of the death of Doctor Foster. He died at Detroit on the 8th. Mr. Bacon is waiting the officers are hurrying him. I must leave the rest for them to tell you in Jenson Prisoners are not treated with so much indulgence I must close. You must not mention my remarks respecting our surrender to Mrs. Bacon as she will tell it to every one being all honey with G. Hull. Please to give my love to all friends, tell them I love to see them, but uncertain when. That God may bless and protect you all is the most ardent prayer my dearest Ruth of your ever affectionate and most devoted
James Miller

Fort Erie, July 28th 1814

My beloved Ruth,

I have great reason to thank God for his continued mercies and protection. On the 25th inst., at the Falls of Niagara, we met the enemy, and had, I believe, one of the most desperately fought actions ever experienced in America. It continued for three hours, stubbornly on both sides, when about ten o'clock at night we succeeded in driving them from their strong position. Our loss was very severe in killed and wounded. I have lost from my regiment, in killed and wounded and missing, one-hundred-and-twenty-six. The enemy had got their artillery posted on a height, in a very commanding position, where they could rake our columns in any part of the field, and prevented their advancing. Maj. McRee, the chief engineer, told Gen. Brown he could do no good until that height was carried and those cannon taken or driven from their position. It was then night but moonlight.

Gen. Brown turned to me and said, "Col. Miller, take your regiment, and storm that work and take it." I had short of three hundred men with me, as my regiment had been much weakened by the numerous details made from it during the day. I, however, immediately obeyed the order. We could see all their slow matches and port-fires burning and ready. I did not know what side of the work was most favorable to approach, but happened to hit upon a very favorable place, notwithstanding we advanced upon the mouths of their cannon. It happened that there was an old rail-fence on the side where we approached, with a small growth of shrubbery by the fence and within less than two rods of the cannon's mouth, undiscovered by the enemy. I then very cautiously ordered my men to rest across the fence, take good aim, fire, and rush, which was done in style. Not one man at the cannon was left to put fire to them. We got into the centre of their park before they had time to oppose us. A British line was formed, and lying in a strong position to protect their artillery. The moment we got to the centre, they opened a most destructive flank fire on us, killed a great many, and attempted to charge with their bayonets. We returned the fire so warmly they were compelled to stand; we fought hand to hand for some time, so close that the blaze of our guns crossed each other; but we compelled them to abandon their whole artillery, ammunition-wagons and all, amounting to seven pieces of elegant brass cannon, one of which was a twenty-four-pounder, with eight horses and harness, though some of the horses were killed. The British made two more attempts to charge us at close quarters, both of which we repulsed before I was reinforced, after which the 1st and 23rd Regs. came to my relief. And even after that, the British charged with their whole line there several times, and after getting within half pistol-shot of us were compelled to give way. I took, with my regiment, between thirty and forty prisoners, while taking and defending the artillery. After Generals Brown, Scott, and others were wounded, we were ordered to return back to our camp; about three miles, and preparations had not been made for taking off the cannon, as it was impossible for me to defend them and make preparations for that too, and they were all left on the ground except one beautiful six-pounder, which was presented to my regiment in testimony of their distinguished gallantry. The officers of this army all say, who saw it, that it was one of the most desperate and gallant acts ever known; the British officers whom we have prisoners say it was the most desperate thing they ever saw or heard of. Gen. Brown told me, the moment he saw me, that I had immortalized myself. "But," said he, "my dear fellow, my heart ached for you when I gave you the order, but I knew that it was the only thing that would save us." We wounded Major Gen. Druininon, took Major Gen. Null Prisoner, with betwint twenty or thirty other officers. How many non com officers and Privates I have not yet lernt as they were sent hastily across the River, but a very considerable number. I should like to fill up the paper but time will not permit. Tell Mrs Noar ———— is well was not in the fight as I had sent him back to Buffalow on business. You may direct to me at Buffalow. I hope I shall hear from you soon, if you could only be sensible how much comfort your letters afford me you would even let the children try to get time to write. I have not been well for a week or ten days, but am better, I hope you are all well. May God continue his blessings and protection to us all and return me safe to the bosom of my adored Ruth. Please to give my love sincerely to all, particularly to Catharene and the children. Tell them I want to kiss them but you must do it.

Until.

Nathan Newsom

(177?–18??)

Militiaman Nathan Newsom presents an enlisted man's view of the events leading up to Hull's surrender. His account is a celebration of the common man-turned-soldier who persevered despite harsh weather, difficult combat, and an inefficient command and supply system. However, his reports of day-to-day hardships and the effects of poor leadership reveal a class consciousness that was not present in the Revolutionary War accounts of equally horrific suffering. His distaste for overpaid officers and distrust of dishonest commissaries reflect a dissatisfaction with the social structure that goes beyond his present circumstances.

What continues to sustain him is a faith in the "fair character of the American people" and the ability of the average citizen to rise to any challenge. He does his duty; the friendly and enemy Indians are neither devils or angels—perhaps an indication that by this time in history Americans are more used to them—and there is no talk of divine mission in his narrative.

from *Diary of Nathan Newsom*

We had been at Urbana only very few days until the ever disgraceful and memorable act of Hull the traitor happened. The scene was horrid and pitiful. Some men who happened not to be convenient when Hull sold them, took their flight through the wilderness as they could, and passed by Urbana in small parties in the utmost despair. The company of Captain Brush were from the neighborhood of Chillicotyhe—they passed through Urbana to their homes in quite small parties for several successive days in the most abject appearance and lowness of spirit. Anger and indignation were apparent in the countenance of every man, at the infamous conduct of Hull, who had not only committed treason of the highest degree, but had put a blot on the fair character of the American people.

From the 20th of August to the 14th of September, nothing very extraordinary appeared—Urbana exhibited a scene of military preparation. Troops were coming and troops were going. We were daily trained to military discipline.

Oct. 1st. On the first day of Oct., about ten o'clock a.m. we struck our tents, and after some comical parade through the streets of Urbana regulating our guard in order of march, the same as we expected to do, when we arrived in the enemy's country. We pitched our tents that evening on an eastern branch of Mad river, called King's Creek, between three & four miles from Urbana. The men generally composing this army are volunteers drafted men or substitutes. An idea was held out to the volunteers when they volunteered, that so soon that they entered into the service for six months, $16 would be advanced to them for clothing; as also 2 months pay at $5 per month. But nearly two months expired before any pay could be drawn, at which time they received only two months pay. Many of the men being not prepared with winter clothing they attributed it to this disappointment, and considerable cursing and discontent was manifested by the troops.

We were somewhere about 800 men strong when we left Urbana. Desertions were frequent, but with very little or no injury to the army, as none but the most trifling characters deserted. On the night of the 3d an express arrived stating that a large body of Indians were advancing, which created a great desire in the troops to meet them. All hands rose in the night and prepared to start early in the morning. And on the 4th, it being Sunday, we marched about 5 miles, crossed Mad river and encamped on the bank.

On the 7th October we struck our tents on the banks of Mad river, and marched up the river some miles, then turned a north direction from it to M'Pherson's Block house, where we encamped; it being 21 miles from Urbana. Many Indian families arrived at M'Pherson's Block house on the same day we did, who had fled from the hostile Indians for protection to the army. Many of their warriors have turned out with our spies and participate in our victories and in our defeats. They left their squaws and children here.

Most of our officers as well as the men are as yet destitute of the qualifications requisite in military life.

On the 11th General Tupper returned to our encampment from the troops stationed under the command of Generals Harrison and Winchester. He had left us when we were stationed at Urbana to take the command of some troops in the quarter.

On the 12th, we struck our tents at McPherson's Blockhouse and marched about 6 miles to Solomon's Town, a place evacuated by the Indians.

On the 13th, an Indian came into camp. He passed the guard by leave of the officer of the guard. He made some inquiry about the number of tents &c which created some suspicion in the men. He was put under guard. The officers were obliged to put him under a strong guard, for fear the soldiers would raise a mob and kill him. On the 14th, early in the morning; the officers sent for Captain Lewis, a notorious influential Indian, who had taken as active part in favor of the Americans, and it was supposed he had a knowledge of all friendly Indians in this part of the country. Lewis appeared, attended by several distinguished personages of the savage race, as also some of their squaws, who interested, attended of the occasion. Lewis, as well as the other Chiefs and squaws, claimed the prisoner Indian as one of the friendly party. The officers of course let him go. This act exasperated some of the inferior officers as well as the soldiers; because some of the soldiers in the army who had been at Detroit and along the British line were willing to take their oath as to the identity of the before stated prisoner Indian;—and that they knew him to be a British Indian. Under these circumstances the commotions of the soldiers were such as really appeared dangerous to the army. On the 15th two men were punished. They had to ride a rail in front of the line, carried by two men. Their crime was desertion.

On the 16th, two men were marched in front of the line, in conformity with their sentence. The one for complaining that the Indians were more respected and better treated by the commanding officers, than the soldiers. The other for getting drunk and sleeping on his post.

On the night of the 21st, there were several guns fired in succession by the sentinels. It being about 9 o'clock. No individual could easy believe otherways, but that it was the beginning of a formidable attack by the Indians. Every man (some excepted) took hold of his arms, and ran with joy, thinking an opportunity was now offering to avenge himself of the savage enemies of his country. In a few minutes time every line was arrayed in battleform, and rushed on to meet the enemy; but on right examination no enemies were found. However, two or three sentinels asserted, that several men were seen by then out side of the line, and they did not answer when hailed; they fired on them conformable with their orders. On the 22d, the army was paraded in a hollow square.

Three prisoners were brought up who were substitutes for drafted men; their crime was desertion. Their sentence was read to them and put into execution immediately after. They were stripped naked, their pantaloons excepted. Their backs were daubed with tar, to make a paper stick thereon, containing their crime in very large letters. Their hands and feet were tied together; and in this position they were hung by hand and feet to a rail and carried by the front of the lines; afterwards their left eye-brows were shaved. They were afterwards ordered to be taken to the guard-house, and there left hand kuffed, and on half rations, during four days, before liberated. On Friday 23d of October all hands (the guard and sick excepted) fell to forming what they called a brestwork. This mighty fortification was made out of brush, built square;—a road left open to each guard house.

On the 24th as also the 25th, numbers of men were allowed to go into the woods with their rifles. They run over every part of the country adjacent to Soloman town in every direction a great distance. From the great similarity of the surface of the country two men were lost; one of them encamped out from the army one night; the other encamped out two nights and had altogether lost himself. On the second day he accidentally met with a friendly Indian, named Joseph Lewis, about 18 or 20 miles from the army. The Indian displayed considerable friendship towards him, and shewed him which way the army was, in fact accompanied him, until they arrived near the army. The person so lost was Ensign Nathan Burwell.

October 31st, about 8 or 9 o'clock a.m. we struck our tents and marched about 10 miles to M'Arthur's Block house.

November 1st, 2d, 3d and 4th teams were arriving every hour at M'Arthur's Blockhouse, loaded with flour, whiskey &c for the use of the army. In this time we moved about a 1/2 mile from our first encampment at the bridge, and encamped higher up on the banks of the Sciota. Here we erected a Brestwork with logs and brush. We desire to mention that a bad habit at this time actuates the guard. Guns are fired almost every night by the sentinels at something or other, supposed by them as they say, to be Indians spying out our situation. This conduct has a bad effect on the wakefulness of the army.

November 6th, 7th, 8th the fall rains continued almost without an interval. By this continuation of rain every part of our encampment and ever the surrounding country became a complete mire of stagnated water. The water forced into the tents so that no place of rest nor comfort was to be found. The men fixed puncheons into their tents to keep the floors dry, and four guard houses were erected for the safety and comfort of the guard. Agues and intermittents [fevers] became more general, and the army increased to be more unhealthy during these long and almost steady rains.

On the 9th of November our spies arrived with a British prisoner of some distinction known by the name of Captain Clarke. He was taken near a post on the rapids of the Maumee river, which was held by the British and Indians at the place corroborated with what our spies asserted. They were circumstances which moved General Tupper to apply to the army in general for volunteers to go with him, surprise them, either by night or day, whatever time might be found the most suitable and to get possession. Six-hundred-and-ninety-odd men immediately volunteered exclusive of the staff officers. In fact, the very flower of the army immediately, not withstanding the fatigue and great danger inevitable attending this expedition was fully stated to them. Every man made ready as fast as possible. The next day being the 10th of November, between 10 and 11 o'clock they paraded, formed themselves into marching order and started in high spirits amidst acclimation and shouting. There was such a prevalent certainty among some of the troops of being victorious at the rapids and thereby get in possession of provision, that one of the Captains only drew three days rations for their men to march 80 miles. The 10th we marched about fifteen miles to a block-house, known by the name of Fort Necessity or Mud fort. We took a cannon along with 6 horses hitched to the carriage on which it was mounted, but found it impossible on account of the miry road to take it along farther than the neighborhood of the blockhouse.

On the 11th, we marched about 25 miles to where Findley's Blockhouse had formerly been, but the Indians had burned it down.

On the 13th in the morning, being then on Carron river, 16 miles from the Rapids of the Maumee; The army was paraded in a suitable form, General Tupper appeared, delivered a short, but impressive, speech. The following is nearly a summary—we were now among the enemy, that our safety and the completing of our object depended on our profound silence, our perseverance, our fortitude, courage and valor. The discourse had the desired effect. Notwithstanding there were upward to seven hundred men, including officers, the most profound silence was observed. It was seldom you heard any human voice at all, louder than the breathe. About 9 o'clock p.m. we arrived at the river about one mile above the place where we intended to ford it; but thinking it too soon to cross, the army closed up, some lay down on the top of others, or made every shift to keep warm. The wind blew hard and the weather grew excessive cold. We remained in this situation some hours in the most profound silence, and then marched to the fording cross. The wind continued hard, the cold was excessive and penetrating; the river appeared full and furious.

General Tupper was one of the first men that waded into and crossed the river. This conduct had the desired effect; it animated the troops to that degree, that they marched into the river as fast as possible with an intention to cross. Some few reached the opposite shore safe, some wetted their guns and ammunition; others were swept down the river by the violent force of the stream, lost their guns, and with some difficulty their lives were saved. Under these circumstances orders were given to return and many, assisted with horses to aid them to return again to the shore from which they came. However some men stayed on the Indian side of the river that night without kindling any fire, for fear the Indians would discover them.

On the next morning early, they were assisted with horses to cross the river, when they joined the army again. It being now Saturday the 14th November, in the morning the army put itself into a suitable position, and marched down the river to get opposite the British and Indian fort, with an intention to aggravate them to give us battle. Some of our men carefully left the lines and went in quest of Indian hogs, potatoes &c. A party of Indians, mounted on horses, killed and scalped four, others escaped with their lives to the army very narrowly. So soon as the Indians rightly discovered us, their horrid yells were shortly after heard almost every direction. Many of them, both on horses and on foot crossed the river at different places, and immediate preparation was made to give us battle. Their horrid yells, firing of guns, and advancing towards us, induced us to believe that a battle would immediately take place. We formed ourselves in suitable lines, gave them the war whoop, ran forward to meet them; but they stood us no fight. We dispersed them the whole day every direction, wherever they appeared to be the most formidable. We killed and wounded many more Indians than they did our men.

Near sun down, all firing and yelling ceased, and the Indians had retreated out of sight and out of hearing:—we were entirely out of provisions. It was thought best to march homeward. The ground was covered with snow which had fell during the time we were at the rapids. The weather continued excessive cold. Many were sick and could scarcely get along. Hunger and fatigue gave the army a ghostly appearance. On Saturday morning when we left the banks to proceed down the river, three of our men were sick—two of them were so low, apparently helpless; the third was not so low, but what he might have done something towards his security. Two horses were left with them, but some unmerciful officer in the army, whether with or without authority from the general, we do not know, returned and took the horses, and left these three sick men entirely alone, exposed to the Tomahawk and scalping knife of the savages. On Sunday morning the 15th of November we started from Carron River, and on the evening we arrived at Finley's Blockhouse.

On our return we found the army in a far worse state of health than we had left it. Two men were buried in our absence, and some wagon loads of sick conveyed to the hospital at Urbana, notwithstanding great numbers remained sick in the encampment. Three more died in a few days after our return.

From our return to the 27th of November nothing very material happened, except the army grew daily more unhealthy.

November the 28th. The situation of the army at this time presents an object of charity and every species of human misery. Nearly one half of this army is reported sick, nearly the other half is known to be almost naked, notwithstanding winter is now among us with all its attendant horrors. The cold forces itself into the skin in spite of every

effort;—hundreds of young men's constitutions are about getting ruined for life. Some of the sick lay in the last pangs of death with one
bad little blanket—the amount total of all their bedding, not withstanding many of the officers markees are filled with blankets. What
cause keeps the army together under such circumstances, under such
preparations is hard to be accounted for; unless we attribute it to the
exorbitant wages, which many of our officers receive. Their number
appears entirely too great in proportion to the quantity of privates,
if even the privates were well and clothed. Whether government will
continue to be duped and imposed upon by such conduct, time only
can develop. On the night of the 28th, a volunteer soldier in the company of Captain Calvin Shepard died. He was an inoffensive, innocent
young man. He had caught a cold preceding the commencement of a
severe spell of weather, which laid him up. His clothes were intended
for summer's wear and altogether unsuitable for the inclemency of this
kind of weather. One little old blanket was the amount total of all his
bedding. In this situation he remained many days, in the most excruci-
ating agony without the requisite aid, and at last expired. His name
was John Smith. On the 29th in the evening he was buried.

December 3d. The army mostly moved to their new encampment, the encampments being mostly completed. The whole of the
day continued cloudy, and on the night of the 3d it rained excessively
the whole night, so that the water penetrated almost into every encampment. From the 7th of this month until the 10th the weather
continued cold and generally cloudy. It snowed more or less almost
every day. The cold was so penetrating that the whiskey which was
drawn by the soldiers from the commissary and not immediately drank,
but preserved during the night in canteens, froze hard, and could not
be used the next day, without the aid of fire. No thermometer was in
the army by which we can ascertain the degrees of coldness in this
climate. However, we will leave it to the reader to decide, what causes
this whiskey to freeze; if it is the intense coldness of this climate, or
whether their commissaries are committing fraud in issuing whiskey to
the soldiers of an inferior quality and almost destitute of spirits.

Joseph Valpey, Jr.
(1792–1816)

A sailor on an American privateer, Joseph Valpey had a brother serving on the *Constitution* and a father, Joseph senior, serving on the *America* under Captain James Cheever. The privateers in 1812 were not as numerous as during the Revolution, but they were more effective. In just over two years, they captured more than thirteen hundred British vessels.

Valpey's career was shortened by his capture after only six months' service aboard the schooner *Herald*. While a prisoner of war in Dartmoor, England, he wrote these reflections, which vividly capture the excitement of the sea war of 1812. His is one more narrative that celebrates the virtues of the common sailor and the American frontier spirit. He died at sea on his way home from England and was buried in Havana, Cuba.

from the *Journal of Joseph Valpey, Jr., of Salem*

On the first day of March [1814] being a pleasant Breeze from the westward we weighed our anchor and proceeded to sea having on Board one Hundred and twenty Brisk young Men for to try our Luck and fortune on Board of the Herald of Eleven Carriage gun's[.] [A]t four in the afternoon the Man at Masthead discovered a sail[.] [A]ll hands was called to Make sail in chase [and] we soon came up with her[.] [S]he proved for to be a Spanish Brig from Havannah bound to Philadelphia[.] [T]he next day we Boarded a schooner bound to Boston.

Nothing More until the thirtyeth of March when the Man at mast head Discovered land[.] [I]t proved to be the Madeira we ran down a

123

long shore under easy. Next Morning we discovered a sail in shore, chase and soon came up with her[.] [S]he proved fore to be an Portuguese brig from Madeira Bound to London[.] [A]fter taking out two Casks of wine one Cable and some Letters and Bills of Exchange to the amount of three thousand dollars and getting the Information of an English Letter of Marque in Madeira Bound to London the first wind[,] we permitted them to proceed[.] [H]ere we cruised for several day's but seeing no Letter of Marque we bore up for Cadis[.] Nothing Material Occur'd until the eighteenth of April when the Man at Mast head discovered a sail[.] [A]ll hands was called for [to] Make sail in chase [and] we soon came up with her[.] [S]he proved for to be the English Merchant Brig Signet with a cargo of wine and barley[.]

After taking our prisoners out we put a prize master and Crew on Board and ordered her for the United States[.] [O]n the twentyeth sail O again was the Cry of the Man at the Mast head [and] all hands was called for to Make sail in chase[.] [A]fter coming up with her she proved to be the English Merchant Brig Harriot in Ballast[.] [A]fter taking out the Prisoners, Sails and provisions &c we burnt her there[.] [I]t appears that the Lord does favour us[.] [W]e steering away to the Eastward under easy sail until the twenty third we discovered a Brig Endeavoring to shun us if possible but we soon in a Cloud of Sail overhauled her[.] She proved for to be the English Merchant Brig Place in Ballast[.] [A]fter taking out the Prisoners, sails provisions and four twelve Pound Cannonades we burnt her[.] [T]hat Evening We Boarded an Portuguese brig and put all of our Prisoners on Board and ordered her to Lisbon by the prisoners request.

Early in the Morning on the twenty Eighth the Man at Mast head discovered a sail[.] [O]n Boarding her we found her to be the same Brig that we ordered for the United States on the Eighteenth[.] Ins. the prize master in hope's of Making his fortune put back for Cadis but he was received on Board of the Privateer again and put on Board and ordered for the States[.] [T]hen we bore up to the Northward and eastward and on the first day of May at daylight we discovered a large Ship and a brig[.] [I]t being Moderate all Hands was immediately Called for to out sweep's [oars][.] [W]e Swept to windward of them and then Observing that they wished for to keep clear from us we in Sweeps and then went to breakfast[.] [A]fter Breakfast all Hands was called to Quarters and sweeps again and hoisting our Coleurs and then all Hands with cheerful hearts turned too and by this time the Brig had displayed the Proud British flag and began for to play upon us with her Stern Chaser's [cannons] but we took no notice of her Shot but kept sweeping until the wind dying away and a Smooth sea And we did not think it prudent for to sweep along side not knowing what she was.

We took in our sweeps and Cleared away for Action[.] [T]here Shot still flying over us with British Glory we Spliced the Main Brace and then turned too with Coolness[.] [W]e had gave her but three broadsides when she gave us an unlucky shot between wind and Water which Obliged us for to haul off as there was six feet of Water in our hole and our Powder a Considerably damaged[.] [A]ll hands then turned too our pumps and we stopt the Leak in a few Minuets[.] [O]ur eneme was by this [time] in a Crowd of sail Endeavouring to get clear of us but our Leak being stopt and we all Taking a Stiff Dram we went to our sweeps and sweept towards a Portuguese Brig who stood a Silent Spectator to our Unpleasant play.

We Boarded her and took out Several Boxes of Oranges and learnt by her that the Enemy was a Brig of war Mounting fourteen Guns and Ninety Men[.] [W]e took in our Boat and stowed her and then Opening the boxes we ate up all the Oranges and then went to our sweeps again like hardy tars and with a light breeze of wind we had the pleasure of Being along of him by dark when we began our play again and Continued it until ten at Night when it being very dark and we could not See her[.] [B]ut when she discharged her guns we thought it best for to Leave of our play until daylight but not forgetting to give her our Long two and thirty [guns] every half hour until half past one in the Morning when it being our Second Lieutenant's watch on deck and he not having a good Lookout kept she Escaped Us.

The next Morning there being several sail in sight We gave Chase to the one who was Most suspected But she proved to be an Neutral[.] [T]hen we Turned too for to Mend our sails and Rigging and the Carpenters in Repairing the shot holes and as kind heavens would have it we had no Employment for the doctor. Nothing More worth our Notice Until the eighteenth when the Man at the Mast head discried a sail[.] [A]ll hands was called to Make Sail in Chase[.] [A]t eleven in the forenoon we Came Up with her [and] she proved to be an Irish Schooner With a Cargo of Provisions Bound to Lisbon.

After taking out our prisoners we put a prize Master and Crew on

Board and ordered her for the United States[.] [T]he next day we boarded a neutral vessel and put our prisoners on Board and wished them good Luck[.] [O]n the ninth at one P M the Man at the mast gave Us the Joyful cry of sail O but as the wind was Light We Made but little progress in coming up to her[.] [A]t five in the afternoon we dispatched our Boat with the first Lieutenant and fourteen Men well arm'd for to see what She Might be[.] [A]t half past Nine the Boat Returned and gave us the Joyful Tidings that she was a Brig under Sweedish Colours with a British Cargo of dry goods and Jewlery from London.

Anonymous Soldier

This anonymous soldier's description of the Battle of New Orleans provides a ground-level view of the carnage of the fight and the state of discipline in the volunteer American force. The British were commanded by the duke of Wellington's brother-in-law, Sir Edward Pakenham, and were battle-tested soldiers fresh from the Napoleonic Wars. Andrew Jackson mustered a mixed American force of Creoles, Negroes, pirates, and Kentucky and Tennessee militiamen, and prepared a defensive position south of New Orleans.

As Captain John Derby sailed home with news that the war was over, American riflemen were cutting down Pakenham and his forces. When the smoke cleared, over two thousand British had fallen, compared to eight American dead and thirteen wounded. This anonymous eyewitness account, which describes an America in the making with its mixed force of nationalities and races, revels in morbid battlefield humor.

"An Anonymous Account of the Battle of New Orleans"

New Orleans, 14 December–8 January 1815

Colonel Smiley, from Bardstown, was the first one who gave us orders to fire from our part of the line; and then, I recon, there was a pretty considerable noise. There were also brass pieces on our right, the noisiest kind of varmints, that began blaring away as hard as they could, while the heavy iron cannon, toward the river, and some thousands of small arms, joined in the chorus and made the ground shake under our feet. I think he was from Knox County, Kentucky, but an Irishman born, came running along. He humped upon the breastwork and stopping a moment to look through the darkness as well as he could, he shouted with a broad North of Ireland brogue, "Shoot low, boys! shoot low! rake them—rake them! They're comin' on their all fours!"

It was so dark that little could be seen, until just about the time the battle ceased. The morning had dawned to be sure, but the smoke was so thick that every thing seemed to be covered up in it. Our men did not seem to apprehend any danger, but would load and fire as fast as they could, talking, swearing, and joking all the time. All ranks and sections were soon broken up. After the first shot, every one loaded and banged away on his own hook. Henry Spillman did not load and fire quite so often as some of the rest, but every time he did fire he would go up to the breastwork, look over until he could see something to shoot at, and then take deliberate aim and crack away. Lt. Ashby was as busy as a sailor and it was evident that, the River Raisin [massacre] was uppermost in his mind all the time. He kept dashing about and every now and then he would call out, with an oath, "We'll pay you now for the River Raisin! We'll give you something to remember the River Raisin!" When the British came up to the opposite side of the breastwork, having no gun, he picked up an empty barrel and flung it at them. Then finding an iron bar, he jumped up on the works and hove that at them.

It was near the close of the firing. About the time that I observed three or four men carrying [away the body of one of the men] or directly after, there was a white flag raised on the opposite side of the breastwork and the firing ceased.

The white flag, before mentioned, was raised about ten or twelve feet from where I stood, close to the breastwork and a little to the right. It was a white handkerchief, or something of the kind, on a sword or stick. It was waved several times, and as soon as it was perceived, we ceased firing. Just then the wind got up a little and blew the smoke off, so that we could see the field. It then appeared that the flag had been raised by a British Officer wearing epaulets. I was told he was a Major. He stepped over the breastwork and came into our lines. Among the Tennesseans who had got mixed up with us during the fight, there was a little fellow whose name I do not know; but he was a cadaverous looking chap and went by the name of Paleface. As the British Officer came in, Paleface demanded his sword. He hesitated about giving it to him, probably thinking it was derogatory to his dignity, to surrender to a private all over begrimed with dust and powder, and that some Officer should show him the courtesy to receive it. Just at that moment, Col. Smiley came up and cried, with a harsh oath, "Give it up—give it up to him in a minute!" The British Officer quickly handed his weapon to Paleface, holding it in both hands and making a very polite bow.

When the smoke had cleared away and we could obtain a fair view of the field, it looked, at the first glance, like a sea of blood. It was not blood itself which gave this appearance but the red coats in which the British soldiers were dressed. Straight out before our position, for about the width of space which we supposed had been occupied by the British column, the field was entirely covered with prostrate bodies. In some places they were laying in piles of several, one on the top of the other. On either side, there was a interval more thinly sprinkled with the slain; and then two other dense rows, one near the levee and the other towards the swamp. About two hundred yards off, directly in front of our position, lay a large dapple gray horse, which we understood to have been Pakenham's.

When we first got a fair view of the field in our front, individuals could be seen in every possible attitude. Some laying quite dead, others mortally wounded, pitching and tumbling about in the agonies of death. Some had their heads shot off, some their legs, some their arms. Some were laughing, some crying, some groaning, and some screaming. There was every variety of sight and sound. Among those that were on the ground however, there were some that were neither dead nor wounded. A great many had thrown themselves down behind piles of slain, for protection. As the firing ceased, these men were every now and then jumping up and either running off or coming in and giving themselves up.

Among those that were running off, we observed one stout looking fellow, in a red coat, who would every now and then stop and display some gestures toward us, that were rather the opposite of complimentary. Perhaps fifty guns were fired at him, but he was a good way off, without effect. "Hurra, Paleface! load quick and give him a shot. The infernal rascal is patting his butt at us!" Sure enough, Paleface rammed home his bullet, and taking a long sight, he let fire. The fellow, by this time was from two to three hundred yards off, and somewhat to the left of Pakenham's horse, Paleface said, as he drew sight on him and then run it along up his back until the sight was lost over his head, to allow for the sinking of the ball in so great a distance, and then let go. As soon as the gun cracked, the fellow was seen to stagger. He ran forward a few steps, and then pitched down on his head, and moved no more. As soon as he fell, George Huffman, a big stout Dutchman, belonging to our Company, asked the Captain if he might go and see where Paleface hit him. The Captain said he didn't care and George, jumping from the breastwork over the ditch, ran over the dead and wounded until he came to the place where the fellow was lying. George rolled over the body until he could see the face and then, turning round to us, shouted at the top of his voice, "Mine Gott! he is a nagar!" He was a mulatto and he was quite dead. Paleface's ball had entered between the shoulders, and passed out through his breast. George, as he came back, brought three or four muskets which he had picked up. By this time, our men were running out in all directions, picking up muskets and sometimes watches and other plunder. One man who had got a little too far out on the field was fired at from the British breastwork and wounded in the arm. He came running back a good deal faster than he had gone out. He was not much hurt but pretty well scared.

Samuel Stubbs

(1772–18??)

A sixty-three-year-old Kentucky militiaman, Samuel Stubbs left his farm seventy miles east of Boonesboro and joined the army just in time for the failed attack on Queenstown, where he was taken prisoner. Released, he followed Zebulon Pike to victory at York, then returned to tend his fields in Kentucky. In the summer of 1814, he fought in the Battle of Lundy's Lane and Fort Erie. Somehow he managed to make his way south and participate in the Battle of New Orleans.

He dictated the following account of his exploits in a letter to his brother, recorded by Captain David Copp, who was so impressed by the cockiness of the old frontiersman that he promoted him to corporal. Stubbs embodies the spirit and humor of other American soldiers before him—we can imagine him and Israel Putnam swaping humorous yarns as they prepared their kits for the next day's march—and his language is filled with the metaphors of the frontier. He personifies fully developed American frontier audacity, a state of mind and arrogance that ushered in the Jacksonian era of Davy Crockett and Mike Fink.

Samuel Stubb's "Letter to His Brother"

Brother Ephram,

I just write you to enform you that I'm still alive and in tolerable helth and choice spirits—altho as well as my brother *officers*, I have had some hair bredth escapes. Sposing that you would like to know something about my military life since I quit home, I'll give you the whole story.

When the express first came into our neighborhood, calling

upon us all to turn out and march against the Canadians, I was like another [Israel] Putnam, ploughing in my field—but I immediately unharnest the old daples, swung my napsack, shouldered my old gun that had killed me forty-five deer the three months past, and marched away for head quarters.

In four days time I joined the army with a dozen more of my neighbors, near Queenstown. The brave Col. Van Rensselare was our commander in chief, under whose command we the next day (which being the 13th day of October 1812) in boats crossed over to Canada— But, ah, in the end it liked to have proved rather a bad job for us, for the opposite shore was lined with redcoats as thick as bees upon a sugar maple—but after exchanging a few shots our brave Colonel buzzed in among them, while I and the rest followed close to his heels, and drove them all up a steep bank. We now got a fair footing and stuck up the American colours in Canada! We did not obtain this much however without some loss on our part, and what was unfortunate for us all, our Colonel was severely wounded—but he was still able to keep upon his legs and with great courage ordered us to push forward and storm their fort, and that we did, and made them one and all scamper off into the woods.

But we were now in our turn unfortunate, for one half of our army was yet on the other side of the river, nor would the cowardly dogs come over to assist us when they saw the d———d redcoats cutting us up like slain venison! The enemy now doubled their numbers while every shot diminished ours; in truth they got the better of us, and again got possession of their batteries, altho we let fly showers of ball and buck shot into their very teeth and eyes! Ah! the poor Yankee lads, this was a sorry moment for ye! They dropped my brave companions like wild pigeons, while their balls whistled like a northwest wind through a dry cane break! Our Commander ordered a retrete, but nature never formed any of our family you know for runners, so I wadled along as well as I could behind; but the redcoat villains overhaul'd me, and took me prisoner! But not until I had a fare shot at their head commander General Brock, who galloping his horse after my retreting comrads, bellowed out to 'um like a wounded buffalo to surrender; but I leveled my old fatheful Bess, which never disappointed me in so fare a mark, and I heard no more of his croaking afterwards.

Oh one thousand which crossed over, but a few escaped biting the dust! As for poor me, I expected they'd kill and scalp me, but after stareing at me as if I had been born with two heads, and enquiring of what nation I was, and from what part of the world I came, their Colonel ordered me liberated, who said to me, 'Old daddy, your age and odd appearance induces me now to set you at liberty; return home to your family and think no more of invading us!' This I promised him I would do, but I didn't mean so, for I was determined I wouldn't give up the chase so, but at 'um again.

So I hastened off and joined General Deerbon's army; and on the 27th day of April [1813] we took Little York, which is the chief town of the Upper Province. We went in boats, and the redcoats peppered a good many of us before we reeched the shore. But when we got footing, they fled before us like an affrighted flock of redwinged boblinkons. We drove 'um from their battery, and then in a powerful body of pursuing 'um, when on a sudden, as if the whole earth was paring asunder and discharging from its bowels huge rocks and stones, a dreadful exploshon took place from the maggazeen, which the arch dogs had fixed for the purpose! And a serious exploshon it proved for us, I tell ye, for it killed one hundred of our men, including our brave commander General Pike. For my own part, I scaped with just my life as you may say, for a stone as big as your fist struck me on the head, and nocked off a piece of my scalp as broad as your hand! But, faith, this I didn't mind much, but waddled on with the rest, over dead bodies as thick as cowslops, and soon got posesshon of the town. The cowerdly British chief, General Sheaff, had thought it best to scamper off with his soldiers and Indians before we entered the town, so that I got but one fare shot at one of their copper-colour'd sanups, whose heels I soon made too light for his head, and would have scalped the dog, but my captin would'nt allow it.

As all the work appeared now to be done in this quarter, I marched off. And on the 20th June [1814] joined General Browne's army, which amounting to about three thousand brave boys of us, on the 3d day of July, crossed the Niagara. General Scott commanded the first brigade, Gen. Ripley the second, Gen. Porter the militia, and Farmers' Brother the Indians, who were painted as red as maple blossums. Fort Eree surrendered to us that very day, and on the next we marched to Chippewa, driving the enemy before us like so many fire-frightened antelopes!

On the 5th, the enemy's commander, General Riall, came out upon Chippewa plain, with two thousand two hundred regelers, while my militia boys and the Indians on both sides were engaged in the woods. For my own part, I climed a sturdy oak, where I assure you I did not suffer my old Bess to grow cold, for whenever I saw an Indian creeping like an allegator upon his belly, I gave him the contents in full, and made him hug the ground to sum purpose. I'm sure I killed fifteen of 'um in fifteen minnits, and shood have been glad to have fleeced them; but the New England men don't approve of scalping. At this time our brave troops under Gen. Scott was hotly engaged with Gen. Riall's redcoats, who after an hour's hard fighting, they turn'd tail to and run in all directions, and saved their pork by gaining their works at Chippewa. We killed about five hundred of them, while our loss was three hundred twenty-nine killed wounded and prisoners. And thus ended this engagement.

On the 25th, I agin marched with Gen. Scott, who advanced with his brigade, betwixt eight and nine hundred, about a mile in the Queenstown road, where we found the enemies, and engaged 'um about sunset. The enemies were guessed to be four thousand stout, and were cummanded by Gen. Drummond. The tussel lasted til about leven a'clock, when, gad! I believe both parties were willing to quit the field. We took twenty pieces of artilary from 'um; one of 'um I took, faith, myself alone with charg'd bagnut [bayonet]! The loss on both sides was about nine hundred; the redcoats commander, Gen. Riall, and about twenty officers were taken prisoners. Our Gen. Brown and Gen. Scott were wounded. The next day, we return'd to Fort Eree, under command of Gen. Ripley.

August 15th, Gen. Drummond ordered an assalt upon our fort in three columns, consisting of the bestest men of his army, to the amount of three thousand. There was about one thousand five hundred of us, under Gen. Gaines, who took cummand of us about the first of August. We repulsed the redcoats with great loss. We killed, mangled and made prisoners of about one thousand five hundred of 'um. They lay as thick as slartered mutton around. Ha, brother Ephe, a fine picking for skelpers! Our loss was sixty killed and wounded.

I continued with the American troops until they were about to go into winter quarters, when with the thanks of my General, like another Cincinnaty, I started home, to exchange my rifle and bagnut for the ploughshare and pruning hook. But I did not get half way when I was summoned to repair to New Orlenes, where the redcoats had landed and were thretening to over run the whole country! Accordingly, I right-about-face, and with quick step steered my course for New Orlenes, where by land and water tacks I arrived in seven days.

I found the whole place in alarm. They had had some skermishing with the redcoats, but the desisive battle was yet to be fought, as you shall here. I joined capt. Copp's company, a nice man, who gladly receiv'd me, and in three days promoted me to the office of a CORPORAL! As I never held any office before, you know, it made me feel kinder queer at first; but I soon learnt my duty, and the grate responsibility attached to my office.

On the morning of the 8th, before day-light, the enemy silently drew out a large force to storm our lines, where we were entrenched up to our chins. There was a great fog, and their columns advanced unperceived to within about half a mile of our camp, and drove in our piquet [picket] guard. About the break of day, they as bold as hunger wolves advanced to our entrenchments, led on by their foolish officers up to the very muzels of our guns. I could have dropped them as easy as a flock of benumb'd wild turkeys in a frosty morning. But I picked for those who had frog paws upon their shoulders, and the most lace upon their frocks. Aye, the Corporal did his duty that day I'll warrant ye. Some of the foolish redcoats penetrated into our lines, where they were soon baganuted or taken prisoners; many fell mounting the brest works; others upon the works themselves. The roar of artillery from our lines was insessant, while an unremitted rolling fire was kept up from our muskets. Ah, *my men* performed wonders. For an hour and a quarter the enemy obstinately continued the assault; nor did they faulter until almost all their officers had fallen. They then retreted, leaving from one thousand five hundred to two thousand in killed mangled and prisoners. On our side the loss was confined to about twenty men—but I lost but one out of my company!

So I remain, yours, &c.

Corporal Samuel Stubbs

Part IV

The War with Mexico

There was never a more gallant body of officers than those who came from civil life into the army on occasion of the Mexican War. All of them, from the rank of general downward, appear to have been animated by the spirit of young knights, in times of chivalry, when fighting for their spurs.

—Nathaniel Hawthorne *The Life of Franklin Pierce*

It is by the right of our manifest destiny to overspread and to possess the whole of the continent which Providence has given us for the development of the great experiment of liberty and federated self-government entrusted to us.

—John L. O'Sullivan *New York Morning News*

Introduction

Conducted outside existing borders and fought to acquire extra territory, the War with Mexico was the first American fighting to call into question whether war was the appropriate means for pursuing the national mission. In their disagreement over the use of arms, both expansionists and the war's critics relied on notions of America's special role in history to support their positions. Expansionists claimed that God wanted His chosen nation to bring the blessing of liberty and freedom to Oregon and Texas, while outnumbered but powerful intellectual opponents, especially in the Whig northeast, argued that because Americans were God's chosen, He did not want us to use violence to bring about those ends.

On the expansionist side of the argument, poet and reporter Walt Whitman, writing in a Democratic paper in support of a Democratic president's war policy, declared—without irony—that U.S. participation would teach that "America knows how to crush, as well as how to expand." Dissenters, however, mostly New Englanders led by former president John Quincy Adams, viewed the war as simple aggression against Mexico and blatant imperialism on behalf of the slave states.

In a nation already historically conditioned to see war as God's test of Puritan theocracy and subsequently as a means to realize the promises of natural law, some critics had difficulty accepting a conflict that was, at best, necessary to the material self-interest of an expanding continental nation and, at worst, a more powerful nation's land grab.

In addition, for a society conditioned by the noble stories of citizen–soldiers bearing arms for self-defense, the reality of a very efficient, professionally led American army conducting overwhelmingly successful operations deep inside a neighboring country required revised moral justification. The War of 1812 established the backwoodsman as the prototypical American warrior, but the War with Mexico demonstrated the combat superiority of professionally led and trained regular forces. The narratives of the period reflect the tension generated by the conflict between what Americans wanted to believe about volunteer versus professional soldiering.

Many divisive complexities were at work in American society during the War with Mexico, including the rise of increasingly bitter sectionalism and the fact that two very politically ambitious generals of the antiwar party were conducting the campaign. But it was also clear that by this time in America's history, war unsupported by religion, millennial myth, or transcendent cause was, to poet James Russell Lowell's average American soldier–farmer, Hosea Biglow, "Murder,—There you hev it plain an' flat."

To counter such pragmatic skepticism over war with Mexico, expansionist Democratic magazine publisher John L. O'Sullivan appealed to a natural and native American force, which Whitman summarized as "the daring, burrowing energies of the Nation [that] will never rest till the whole of this northern section of the great West World is circled in the mighty Republic." In the December 27, 1845, issue of the *New York Morning News*, O'Sullivan argued that America's claim to disputed territories was of a higher order than international law because it "is by the right of our manifest destiny to overspread and to possess the whole of the continent which Providence has given us for the development of the great experiment of liberty and federated self-government entrusted to us." In the ensuing debate over the morality of spreading American democracy with force of arms, manifest destiny replaced the Puritan notion of mission.

Despite O'Sullivan's unconscious but effective synthesis of America's Puritan myth of divinely ordained mission, what Whitman called "masculine American becoming," manifest destiny remained for antislavery critics a controversial justification of the War with Mexico. For them, a conflict that resulted in the spread of the institution of slavery did not justify the use of arms.

In fact, critics argued that the possible spread of slavery invalidated any moral justification of the dispute with Mexico because it morally corrupted the notion of America's mission. Thus, unlike previous American armed conflicts, the Mexican War eroded rather than strengthened the conventional faith in the country's moral exceptionalism. In his memoirs, Ulysses S. Grant went so far as to say that the Civil War was punishment for America's moral transgressions in Mexico. "The Southern rebellion was largely the outgrowth of the Mexican War. Nations, like individuals, are punished for their transgressions."

If America's myth of moral exceptionalism failed to create unanimous public support for this war, however, Captain John Smith's original romantic myth, with its special appeal to the natural nobility of American character under fire, clearly inspired the contemporary imagination. In his study of popular perceptions of this conflict, *To the Halls of the Montezumas: The Mexican War in the American Imagination*, Robert W. Johannsen explains how the advent of the "penny press" helped mold popular perceptions of the romance of war and the righteousness of empire. Increased literacy brought these stories to a much larger readership and helped to whet the appetite for more. Johannsen describes a scene in which the popular writer Grace Greenwood (Sara Jane Clarke) watched a lady reader on a train devour "a miserable Mexican war story." Greenwood, an antislavery critic of the war, pondered the taste of the nation's readers and concluded that far too many had "propensities for the commonplace and the low." It might be "commonplace and low," but the myth of the noble American character, tested by fire, sold well.

Recognizing this, one of the keenest observers of this country's consciousness capitalized on the notion of the natural American warrior to help his lifelong friend and Mexican War veteran win the presidency. In his campaign biography of Franklin Pierce, Nathaniel Hawthorne wrote that "there was never a more gallant body of officers than those who came from civil life into the army on occasion of the Mexican War. All of them, from the rank of general downward, appear to have been animated by the spirit of young knights, in times of chivalry, when fighting for their spurs."

Perhaps as a corrective to those who gave too much credit for victory to West Point officers and regular army soldiers, Hawthorne claims the "valor" that wins America's battles is "not trained in the hardihood of veterans, but a native and spontaneous fire," for "there is nothing in any other country similar to what we see in our own, when the blast of the trumpet at once converts men of peace into warriors." Hawthorne and others endorsed John Smith's myth of native warrior prowess to shape the political future of the nation.

For its supporters, the conflict with Mexico reaffirmed the nation's warrior spirit and manifest destiny. According to Johannsen, for those who read the popular press, the war "offered young Americans an opportunity to reenact the scenes of chivalric conduct and to play the parts of storied knights." It also proved to the world that a democracy could successfully prosecute a foreign war.

A few years after the end of the War with Mexico, the overwhelming emotion and the rhetorical extremism of the Civil War would suspend questions on the moral efficacy of war, and not until a generation later would a foreign war with Spain and the subsequent occupation of the Philippines revive questions about the use of arms in pursuit of empire.

Chronology

1835

Stephen Austin petitions President Santa Anna for admission of Texas into the Mexican union. Battle of the Alamo, San Antonio.

1836   Texas becomes independent.

1837   Texas petition for U.S. annexation refused.

1844   Democrat James K. Polk elected president. The election was also a referendum on the annexation of Texas.

1845

Mar   President John Tyler signs Texas annexation proposal.

Mar   Polk inaugurated as tenth president.

Jul   Brig. Gen. Zachary Taylor lands near Corpus Cristi.

| | Dec | Capt. John Fremont arrives at Sutter's Fort, Calif. |

1846

Mar	Taylor arrives at Matamoros.
Apr	Captain Thorton's force ambushed at Brownsville, Tex.
May	Battle of Palo Alto. Battle of Resaca de la Palma. Congress passes War Bill.
Jun	Oregon treaty signed with Great Britain. Col. Stephen W. Kearney leaves Leavenworth, Kans. for Santa Fe.
Jul	Bear Flag Republic declared at Sonoma, Calif. Commodore John D. Sloat occupies Monterrey.
Aug	Comm. Robert F. Stockton occupies Los Angeles. Santa Anna lands at Veracruz; Kearney occupies Santa Fe.
Sep	Taylor seizes Monterrey, Nuevo Leon.
Nov	Polk appoints Gen. Winfield Scott to command expedition to Veracruz.
Dec	Battle of San Pascual, near San Diego.

1847

Jan	Battle of San Gabriel, Los Angeles.
Feb	Taylor defeats Santa Anna at Buena Vista; Col. Alexander Doniphan occupies Chihuahua.
Mar	Scott occupies Veracruz.
Apr	Battle of Cerro Gordo; occupation of Jalapa.
May	Scott moves army to Puebla.
Aug	Battles of Contreas and Churubusco lead to truce between Scott and Santa Anna.
Sep	Truce terminated, assault on Chapultepec, Scott occupies Mexico City.

1848

Feb	American emissary Nicholas P. Trist and Mexican foreign minister Manuel Peña y Peña sign Treaty of Guadalupe Hidalgo.
Mar	Treaty of Guadalupe Hidalgo ratified by U.S. and Mexican congresses.
Jul	Last U.S. troops leave Veracruz.

Napoleon J. T. Dana

(1822–189?)

Napoleon J. T. Dana graduated from the U. S. Military Academy in 1842, and was appointed a second lieutenant in the Seventh Infantry, where he began his service at Fort Pike, Louisiana. He took part in the defense of Fort Brown, the Battle of Monterrey, the Siege of Veracruz, and the Battle of Cerro Gordo, where he was severely wounded at Telegraph Hill and promoted to brevet captain for gallant and meritorious conduct. He resigned from the army in 1855 and worked as a banker in St. Paul, Minnesota. A brigadier general in the Minnesota militia, he began his Civil War service at Harper's Ferry, fought in the Shenandoah Valley, participated in the Peninsular Campaign, the Battles of Fair Oaks and Malvern Hill, and was severely wounded at Antietam. Promoted to major general, he commanded the 13th Corps in Texas and the 16th Corps in West Tennessee and Vicksburg. He resigned in 1865 and went to work on the railroads, becoming president of Montana and Union Railway Company in 1885.

In the following letters to his wife, Dana attributes military success to divine intervention and "rejoices" that all this "happened before the volunteers arrived," for "the country will see that it is the regulars which can do their business." Faith in war as God's will and victory as a token of His approval survive in Dana's letters home.

from Dana's Letters to His Wife

[Dana describes his experiences in and around Matmoros, events that led to the May 11, 1846 American declaration of war against Mexico.]

No. 11, Fort Brown, Texas
Monday night, May 11, 1846

My own dearly beloved wife:

I am now, after the labors of the day, after tattoo has sounded, and the men are all sleeping under the starry canopy on the cold ground, going to devote my first leisure and chance that I have had for the last ten days to commencing one of my regular letters. I cannot describe, my darling, all my feelings of delight at being able once more to pour my words into your ears and to tell you how dear, how doubly dear, you are to me during all my troubles, labors and occupations. Danger and death for a time no longer before me, I see with deep, deep love the guiding star which cheers me on in trying hours, and to its influence I can attribute a great share of my courage, at the same time nearly all, my dearest Sue, when the swift-winged messengers of destruction were passing in this direction, my thoughts were with you and our little one and my prayer to God was that all this day of happiness might be in store for us—and when from a sound sleep the midnight alarm would call me from my couch, to repel assaulting columns and destructions, my first thoughts were always of my chosen one and my child and my second that I would not make them ashamed of me. God has spared me, has spared us all, in many cases most miraculously, and the most skeptical can but acknowledge that He is fighting for us and that His shield covers us.

The enemy has hardly believed it true that we have escaped so well, and I am not blaming them for their doubts, for unless we had seen we would not have believed. Shells are well known to be the most deadly weapons of war, and although their batteries threw 800 of them at us, besides 2,000 shot, although they fell in our very midst at the very feet of men and burst there, but two were hurt. It is no chance but it is an overruling Providence. I wrote you, my dearest wife, on the 4th, which was the day after they had commenced bombarding us. Well they continued their games night and day for seven successive days. The third day they commenced and bombarded very hotly. Indeed, very many shells burst inside the fort. They were evidently trying their hardest then.

In the forenoon of that day a howitzer shell mounted the parapet and before he could escape took off the leg of Major Brown below the knee. An amputation was immediately performed, and he would have done well but that there was no safe place to put him in but in a magazine, where it was too hot. It was so hot he could scarcely breathe. Of course his fevers raged and he died day before yesterday, even whilst we heard the general's cannon pouring death among the enemy whilst marching to our relief. We buried the gallant major yesterday under the flag; he is a very serious loss to our regiment: one which we will not be able to replace. He was a perfect bulldog for the fight.

Well, on the third day after they had tried their best, and as they thought they had killed a great many of our men, who, by the way, they thought had got out of provisions, in the afternoon they stopped their firing and sent in to us four officers with a white flag. Soon as we heard their trumpet sound the "parley" we knew what was coming. They brought a letter from General [Mariano] Arista summoning our garrison to surrender as prisoners of war. He told us that he had a large and well appointed army between us and our supplies, that the success we were expecting could not reach us, that he had large forces in reserve, that we were reduced to the last extremity, could not possibly hold out much longer, and that circumstances of humanity dictated that we should save our men from sacrifice. He gave us an hour to consider. Captain Hawkins who was left in command immediately convened a council, who unanimously agreed that as the enemy had not hurt us and probably could not the very idea of a surrender was absurd. An answer was returned to General Arista that we begged politely to decline his invitation.

Well, that night we expected that as a matter of course we would be stormed. Our men were delighted, in the highest spirits, and highly incensed at the idea of a surrender to those "niggerly rascals". They swore they would not do it if they had a load of powder left. All made up their minds to shoot as many Mexicans as each man could. If they had only brought us their assaulting columns they would have been cut all to pieces, but they knew better than that. Mexicans cannot yet be found who will assault a work garrisoned by our troops.

Tuesday morning, May 12

A tremendous thunderstorm came up last night, my own dear wife, and I was obliged to stop writing. Everything got wet, my candle blew out, and I put things away and went to sleep. Nothing new of consequence this morning, dearest, so I will commence where I left off.

The fourth day of the bombardment was made still hotter and the shells were thrown better than on any day previous. They fell everywhere amongst us and burst in all direction in crowds of men, and still no one was hurt; a kind Providence kept us safe. A shell fell at the feet of Corporal VanVoorhies, another rolled over a man's back, and another between a man's legs whilst he was eating dinner, and although they all burst, they hurt no one. A shot went through Captain Hawkins' tent just over his head when he was eating breakfast. Two through Mr. Page's tent, two through Major Brown's. A shell fell in the chest where the band instruments were packed, burst there, and smashed every one of them. One of the shells went through three horses.

On the fifth day a man's arm and another man's leg were broken. The sixth and seventh days were kept up by the enemy as usual with just as little injury to us.

We all the time husbanded our ammunition for the assault, and only now and then threw a few 18-pound shot where we saw men, and we killed and wounded at least twenty of them. One of our shot passed through a house in the town and killed two poor women. They ought to have been out of the way. Twice a couple hundred rancheros were sent up to open musketry on our men, but they did not care to approach near enough to see any advantage and all their bullets fell short. We placed a few rifles on the parapet and killed a couple of those fellows, and they went off satisfied.

Last Friday about three o'clock in the afternoon we heard cannonading about eight miles [away], and immediately knew that the general was on the move and had met the enemy. The cannonade lasted until sundown, which showed us that the enemy had made a tolerably good stand.

Next day we heard nothing at all for so long a time that we began to be somewhat disheartened, thinking that the general had met an overpowering force and had been obliged to retire. If this had been the case, we would indeed been in a bad way. We saw columns of the enemy in the distance passing down to reinforce their army, which had been attacked. However, about three o'clock in the afternoon we again heard the cannon and musketry within four miles of us; we then knew that the enemy had retreated to a new position and that the general had advanced. We saw the retreating columns of the enemy hurrying from the field of action towards west, a perfect rout, horse and foot had thrown their arms and would plunge in [the Rio Grande River] to swim over. Many were drowned. Panic and consternation had spread through them. They were wild with fright. They knew not what to do and only sought to fly as swiftly as possible to save themselves from the terrible effect of the fire of our troops, and close upon their heels with shouts appalling to their ears came our dragoons and light artillery, dealing death around them and cutting off from many the last hopes of flight. Our fellows were perfect devils. The heat and excitement of the battle and the flush of one of the most astounding and brilliant victories on record had made them terrible in wreaking vengeance on these savage peoples. All who did not throw down their arms and ask for quarter were cut down without any hesitation.

Soon some of our dragoons came toward the fort; they swung their hats over their heads to tell of their victory. They were the first friends we had seen for eight days. Five hundred of our brave fellows mounted the parapets, threw their caps in the air, and gave them such cheers as made [the city of] Matamoros ring from the faubourg [suburb] to the square. You might have heard the cheers two miles. Those shouts told the enemy what had happened on this side. The effect was instantaneous. Their guns immediately ceased to fire upon us, and disheartened, disgusted, and appalled, they slunked from their batteries into the town to bear the terrible tidings of their disasters, not knowing what to think was the reason why their fire was not more hurtful to us.

Since then they have been perfectly quiet, doubtless dreading that at any moment we would open our batteries to take the town. We will allow them but two or three days of quiet. We will then be perfectly ready, plenty of guns and plenty of ammunition. Matamoros will then be summoned to surrender and if she refuses, which we do not anticipate, she will be forced to do so. I do not think that the Mexicans after having been so terribly cut up as they have been will be induced again to make a stand for some time to come.

May 13

I have been hard at work all before noon, my own darling Sue, and now, after dinner, I will see if I cannot get this letter ready to go by the first chance: I have to perform the duties of ordnance officer at the fort and I have been handling powder, arms, and all kinds of things which have been captured from our unfortunate and fallen enemy: I am mighty well and hardy, my beloved one, and enjoy the best spirits and you have no idea how much happier it makes me feel to hear that you are getting on so well and [in the mail] I received five letters from you. The first I had received for so long a time, and you may rest assured that I await on every word contained in them. I am delighted that you are so comfortably fixed and right proud that you are going on smoothly on your own hooks. God grant that we may not long have to live this life of separation, but that we may soon again be brought together to renew our happy life.

But—I finished telling you yesterday of the cannonade and bombardment of this fort and now I must communicate and give you some descriptions of the two battles and the most brilliant victory which has happened since the Battle of [New] Orleans.

You recollect, my darling one, that General Taylor left here on the first of the month with all the army except this garrison, to escort up the train of the army loaded with provisions, ammunition, and other miscellany. He had a double object in view in taking all the troops he had as an escort. He knew that the enemy were on this side of the river in force superior to his own. Their object was to recapture the train and attempt Point Isabel. He was to protect his train and, if he found them in his way, to give them a fair fight, if they were double his numbers, but he little knew that they were more than three to one.

He arrived at Point Isabel on the second and the first thing he heard on the morning of the third was the cannonade of our batteries. This put him in a fever at once and he wanted to start right off to return and fight the enemy if he could find them and compel them to raise the siege of this fort. Reflection, however, and advice taught him that it was useless to return, and worse than useless, without a fresh supply of provisions, arms, ammunition, and ordnance; and it was also advisable to get reinforcements if possible. He had the highest confidence in this garrison, and knew that it would hold out to the last and repel any attack which the Mexicans were able to make upon it. So he contented himself with sending to us an express of a half a dozen rangers of Texas to get information of our condition, and went to work leisurely to load up his train, and refresh his troops for the coming storm, when the Texan company returned with news of our wonderful good condition. The greatest excitement prevailed at Point Isabel and lots of champagne was wasted in health to the gallant command which so firmly held Fort Brown, our stronghold on the Mexican frontier. All the army felt the extreme of anxiety to hasten up to our relief, and they felt confidence in us and as long as they heard the firing they knew we held out.

Well, the general remained at Point Isabel until the morning of the eighth. Then, at a very line of march from this place, he marched all day until about one o'clock when evident signs of the vicinity of the enemy were seen and it was a certainty from the signs that they were in large force, with a very numerous cavalry and plenty of artillery. Soon the two opposing forces came in sight of each other.

The enemy had chosen a position which at once proved the well-known ability of their General Arista. They were very cunning and tried to get our columns within short range, by a kind of stratagem—their cannon were concealed. They held a position on the edge of the prairie at the skirts of a thick growth of chaparral, almost impassable. In this more than half their troops and nearly all their cannon were masked, and drawn up in beautiful order in battle array. Where the remainder of their battalions giving a very inviting chance as it would seem for a fair pitched battle in an open plain. They expected that we would advance heedlessly to defeat what troops they had laid out as a bait, and then they expected to astonish us by a fire from their masked batteries and a sortie from their concealed column. But the general was not in such a hurry. He meant to have his fight and as they were, in numbers, three to his one, he advanced very carefully and cautiously. Their left flank rested on the chaparral, whilst their right extended out into the plain. Our general also went to the chaparral, rested his right on it, and threw out his left into the prairie, at the same time holding it back from the enemy. The enemy were so much more numerous than ourselves that in this position they outflanked us a good deal, but Lieutenant Duncan's light battery was thrown some way out, which obviated the sum.

When all was ready, the movement commenced by the army, swinging around on the right as a pivot and throwing the left wing in advance to meet the enemy. When within long shot the enemy opened fire from his heavy cannon, which he thought much superior to ours. Since he had not heard of our having field guns heavier than sixes, whilst his were nines, you may imagine his astonishment then when two huge eighteens drawn up by six yoke of oxen each (which the general was bringing up to put in the fort) were advanced and thundered to him. Although the effect of this could not be seen, it was ascertained afterward to be terrible. The fighting continued hotly for a short time, doing some damage among our troops, but a great deal among the Mexicans. Under cover of the eighteens Lieutenant Duncan's right battery on one flank, and Major Ringold's on the other, advanced, guarded by the different regiments of infantry, to take the enemy on the flanks, or as you would call it, raking. Their effect was terrible. The enemy felt it immediately. The rancheros which composed the Mexican volunteers were not able to stand it, and 1,500 of them were put to shameful flight. The enemy's cavalry then saw that to maintain themselves at all they must charge those regiments of infantry which supported the artillery. They must charge. Eight hundred lancers formed to charge the Fifth Regiment. On they came, with the speed of the wind. Quicker than thoughts the regiment formed in square, and with bayonets awaited the charge. Our fire dashed the cavalry of the Mexicans, [who advanced] as if they would ride right over the front of the square attacked; [the regiment] poured in its volley of buckshot, and balls and horses, officers and men of the lancers were brought to the ground. Many more reeled in their saddles, wounded. Some were thrown, and the rest in confusion galloped back to their own side of the field.

The same game was tried on Colonel Childs' battalion, with pretty much the same effect.

The enemy's cavalry than made two demonstrations to charge the batteries, but all the exertions of their officers, who were beating them with their sabers, could not induce them to do it.

In the meantime our guns had been pouring in a terrific fire. The enemy fired equally fast from an equal number of pieces, and fired well too, but there as well as here a kind Providence protected us. Not so with the enemy though. The sun went down on the fight and it was supposed that both armies could sleep on their arms and renew the battle in the morning. Our fellows made the proper dispositions and went to rest. Little did they dream of the immense damage they had done the enemy in comparison to what they had received. Little did they dream of the horrible sights which were on the opposite side of the field. Little did they think that their victory was complete, and that whilst they were taking their rest, the enemy, leaving a great part of their wounded, dead, and baggage on the field, were retreating to a new and stronger position. Seven thousand men before 2,000 of our little regular army! That night more than 400 wounded were carried into Matamoros.

Next morning our army arose bright and early, ready to continue the battle, and expecting to find the enemy in the same position he had occupied the evening before, but when our fellows looked about nothing was to be seen of a foe. It was taken for granted that they were secreted in the chaparral in order to catch our men as they came on. But on reconnoitering it was discovered that the Mexicans had evidently left their position in the greatest haste during the night, having on the field a cannon which had been broken down by our shot, all their dead, unburied, a great many wounded, and considerable baggage. The battle was a horrid spectacle, corpses mangled most horribly lying where they had fallen. Our grape and canister shot had literally mowed them down. They strewed the plain, and the wounded crying for assistance and interspersed here and there among the dead. Some were cut nearly in two by large shot, some had their heads off, some had lost arms, some legs, and so forth. Many officers were among them. One officer of lancers had a daguerreotype likeness of his sister on him, another had three letters in his cap to his father, sister, and wife, in which he said that some of the regiments had suffered much for food, that on some days past a number of them had nothing but salt meat.

The general waited in the field to bury the dead of both parties, and to give attention to the wounded. None of our officers were killed in the battle of the eighth. Major Ringold, Lieutenant Blake, Captain Page, and Lieutenant Luther were wounded. The two first are since dead. There is but little hope for the third, but the last is doing well.

After the men had breakfasted the general left his train in park with a guard and continued to move on, expecting to find that the enemy had taken up a very strong position in the chaparral. Their whereabouts was found about three o'clock in the afternoon. They had chosen one of the strongest positions possible in chaparral and in a ravine. Their battery of eight guns was placed with the intention of cutting our columns all to pieces as they advanced, but they did not know then that the American soldiers would charge right up the cannon's mouth. The two light batteries were ordered forward to the attack, with the dragoons Fourth, Fifth, and Eighth infantry, the Third and Colonel Child's battalion in reserve, our men spread in the chaparral and advanced on the enemy's lines.

The determination today was to go the whole hog and charge at once, without standing off at shooting distance. As our troops advanced their fire was terrible. Our shot and ball told with wonderful effect and the grape and canister scattered death in all directions. So swift was the advance that the enemy had only time to fire two rounds from his batteries before our troops with yells and shouts charged in amongst them. Captain May's squadron of dragoons and the Fifth and Eighth infantry charged right up to the batteries. The Mexicans stood their ground for some minutes like men, fighting hand-to-hand with sword and bayonet. Now was their last chance. If they gave ground now they were lost, and they knew it. One regiment, the Garda Costa from Tampico, would not give an inch and were entirely cut to pieces. Our fellows fought like devils. The enemy was brought down on all sides. They were forced back from their guns. The determined courage and valor of our men disheartened them. A panic seized them, and throwing down their arms they broke and fled in all directions.

A total rout followed. Each fled for life. Mounted and foot sought the nearest point. Huddled together, with our dragoons at their heels, many of them plunged into the river. Some were drowned. A great portion were dispersed among the chaparral, and many of them gave themselves up as prisoners of war. They left nearly everything they had behind them. Everything fell into our hands: nine pieces of brass cannon, a large quantity of ammunition, 500 pack mules with their saddles and equipments, 500 muskets, a great deal of baggage, some wagons; all of Arista's private baggage, plate, public and private correspondence, military papers and so forth, several hundred dollars in specie, horses and saddles, and so forth, General LaVega, and twelve or fourteen officers [as] prisoners besides about 300 or 400 men. This is one of the most remarkable and brilliant victories on record. A well-appointed and well-disciplined army of 7,000 men in their own chosen positions, with eight pieces of cannon, utterly routed, with the loss of all they had, by 2,000 men, and look at the immense difference in the loss of the two armies. Our loss was about 150 men in both engagements in killed, wounded, and missing, whilst theirs was in killed, wounded, and prisoners not less than 1,400. All their rancheros dispersed to their homes, and their infantry broken up. Out of 3,600 infantry which left Matamoros, only 300 have returned as yet. Their killed alone was upwards of 500, whilst ours was only about 65.

The Mexicans don't know what to make of it. They can scarcely realize their misfortune and cannot account for the best army which ever left Mexico being thus cut up by a handful of men, and they will not believe that they did us so little danger by the bombardment.

But you don't know, my darling Sue, how much we rejoice that all this has happened before the volunteers arrived. The country will see that it is the regulars which can do their business, and had the volunteers been here they probably would have gotten all the credit for our hard fighting.

General LaVega is quite a dashing-looking fellow. I believe he is going to Washington on parole. Captain May took him from his guns. All of his men ran: he stood there and was taken a prisoner. He is astounded and he says that all Mexico will be. He says he cannot account for the decided superiority of our soldiery. He has fought Spaniards, Frenchmen, Mexicans, Texans, and Indians, but cannot understand where we can find men who will charge right up to the muzzles of a battery. He says that it is of no use to bring numbers to whip us. It can only be done by the hardest kind of courageous fighting.

In the action of the ninth, our officers suffered much more severely. Lieutenant Inge of dragoons and Lieutenant Cochrane of the Fourth and Lieutenant Chadbourne of the Eighth were killed. Colonels McIntosh and Payne, Captain Howe, and Lieutenants Seeden, Indan, Gates, Maclay, and Burbank wounded. A kind Providence has certainly protected us; when we look over the field of battle and see the large number of the enemy slain, and the number of wounded prisoners we have joined to the 670 which are in the hospital at Matamoros, and then look at our own suffering, we have abundant reason to be grateful to God for his goodness. Some officers who were badly wounded, after giving them the best medical attendance here we have sent over to Matamoros. An equal number of officers and men have been exchanged for Captains Thornton and Hardie and Lieutenant Kane and the dragoons who were captured a short time since, and they are all with us again. The former is under arrest and will be tried for the affair.

And now, my own sweet little Sue, I will bid you good night, and tomorrow if I do not have to close my letter to you of what happens here nowadays, I can get a chance to talk about other things, I've got to tell you yet all about your letters and how much I am longing to see you and everything else. I hope I shall get a chance tomorrow. It is now very late and I must go to sleep. So now good night, my dear Sue, and may Heaven forever keep you and our little one.

U. S. Grant

(1822–1885)

Ulysses S. Grant was born in Point Pleasant, Ohio, and worked on the family farm until he left for West Point in 1839. He graduated into the infantry in 1845 and joined General Zachary Taylor in Texas. Although he viewed the occupation and annexation of Texas as "a conspiracy to acquire territory out of which slave states might be formed," he served well at Palo Alto, Resaca de la Palma, and Monterrey, and under General Winfield Scott at Mexico City, he was cited for bravery. In 1854, frustrated by the lack of advancement and financial difficulties, he resigned his commission and rejoined his family in Missouri. He moved to Galena, Illinois, in 1860 and worked as a clerk in his father's leather-goods store. After the outbreak of the Civil War, he organized a militia company and quickly rose to the rank of general.

The following letters to his friend John W. Lowe reflect Grant's initial excitement in Mexico and his later disenchantment with war. An account free of references to divine intervention and manifest destiny, Grant's pragmatic evaluation of the logistic details of war and his faith in the warrior spirit of the American soldier echo Benjamin Franklin's common-sense approach to combat.

from Grant's Letters to John W. Lowe

Metamora, Mexico
June 26th, 1846.

Dear Lowe:

I have just received your letter of the 6th of June, the first I have had from you since my Regt. took the field in anticipation of the annexation of Texas. Since that time the 4th Infantry has experienced but little of that ease and luxury of which the Hon. Mr. Black speaks so much. Besides hard marching, a great part of the time we have not even been blessed with a good tent as a protection against wind and weather. At Corpus Christi our troops were much exposed last winter which the citizens say was the severest season they have had for many years. From Corpus Christi to this place (a distance of about 180 miles) they had to march through a low sandy desert covered with salt ponds and in one or two instances ponds of drinkable water were separated by a whole days march. The troops suffered much but stood it like men who were able to fight many such battles as those of the 8th & 9th of May, that is without a murmur. On our arrival at the Rio Grande we found Matamoras occupied by a force superior to ours (in numbers) who might have made our march very uncomfortable if they had had the spirit and courage to attempt it. But they confined their hostilities (except their paper ones) to small detached parties and single individuals as in the case you mention in your letter, until they had their force augmented to triple or quadruple ours and then they made the bold efforts of which the papers are so full. About the last of April we got word of the enemy crossing the river no doubt with the intention of cutting us off from our supplies at Point Isabel. On the 1st of April at three o'clock General Taylor started with about 2000 men to go after and escort the wagon train from Point Isabel and with the determination to cut his way no matter how superior their numbers. Our march on this occasion was as severe as could be made. Until 3 o'clock at night we scarcely halted, then we laid down in the grass and took a little sleep and marched the balance of the way the next morning. Our march was mostly through grass up to the waist with a wet and uneven bottom yet we made 30 miles in much less than a day. I consider my march on that occasion equal to a walk of sixty miles in one day on good roads and unencumbered with troops. The next morning after our arrival at Point Isabel we heard the enemies Artillery playing upon the little Field work which we had left garrisoned by the 7th Infy. and two companies of artillery. This bombardment was kept up for seven days with a loss of but two killed and four or five wounded on our side. The loss of the enemy was much greater though not serious. On the 7th of May General Taylor started from P.I. with his little force encumbered with a train of about 250 wagons loaded with provisions and

ammunition. Although we knew the enemy was between us and Matamoras and in large numbers too, yet I did not believe I was not able to
appreciate the possibility of an attack from them. We had heard so
much bombast and so many threats from the Mexicans that I began to
believe that they were good for paper wars alone, but they stood up to
their work manfully. On the 8th when within about 14 miles of Matamoras we found the enemy drawn up in line of battle on the edge of
the Prairie next a piece of woods called Palo Alto (which is the Spanish
for Tall Trees). Even then I did not believe they were going to give
battle. Our troops were halted out of range of Artillery and the wagons
parked and the men allowed to fill their canteens with water. All preparations being made we marched forward in line of battle until we received a few shots from the enemy and then we were halted and our
Artillery commenced. The first shot was fired about 3 o'clock p.m. and
was kept up pretty equally on both sides until sun down or after; we
then encamped on our own ground and the enemy on theirs. We supposed that the loss of the enemy had not been much greater than our
own and expected of course that the fight would be renewed in the
morning. During that night I believe all slept as soundly on the ground
at Palo Alto as if they had been in a palace. For my own part I don't
think I even dreamed of battles. During the days fight I scarcely
thought of the probability or possibility of being touched myself (although 9 lb. shots were whistling all round) until near the close of the
evening a shot struck the ranks a little ways in front of me and knocked
one man's head off, knocked the under jaw of Capt. Page entirely away
and brought several others to the ground. Although Capt. Page received so terrible a wound he is recovering from it. The under jaw is
gone to the wind pipe and the tongue hangs down upon the throat.
He will never be able to speak or eat. The next morning we found to
our surprise that the last rear guard of the enemy was just leaving
ground, the main body having left during the night. From Palo Alto to
Matamoras there is for a great part of the way a dense forest of under
growth, here called chapparel. The Mexicans after having marched a
few miles through this were reinforced by a considerable body of
troops. They chose a palace on the opposite side from us of a long but
narrow pond (called Resaca de la Palma) which gave them greatly the
advantage of position. Here they made a stand. The fight was a pell
mell affair, everybody for himself. The chapparel is so dense that you

may be within five feet of a person and not know it. Our troops rushed forward with shouts of victory and would kill and drive away the Mexicans from every piece of Artillery they could get their eyes upon. The Mexicans stood this hot work for over two hours but with a great loss. When they did retreat there was such a panic among them that they only thought of safety in flight. They made the best of their way for the river and wherever they struck it they would rush in. Many of them no doubt were drowned. Our loss in the two days was 182 killed and wounded. What the loss of the enemy was cannot be certainly ascertained but I know acres of ground was strewed with the bodies of the dead and wounded. I think it would not be an over-estimate to say that their loss from killed, wounded, taken prisoners and missing was over 2,000 and of the remainder nothing now scarcely remains. So precipitate was their flight when they found that we were going to cross the river and take the town, that sickness broke out among them and as we have understood, they had but little effective force left. News has been received that Parades is about taking the field with a very large force. Daily, volunteers are arriving to reinforce us and soon we will be able to meet them in what ever force they choose to come. What will be our course has not been announced in orders, but no doubt we will carry the war into the interior. Monterrey, distance about 300 miles from here, will no doubt be the first place where difficulties with an enemy awaits us. You want to know what my feelings were on the field of battle? I do not know that I felt any peculiar sensation. War seems much less terrible to persons engaged in it than to those who read of the battles. I forgot to tell you in the proper place the amount of property taken. We took on the 9th eight pieces of artillery with all their ammunition, something like 200 stand of arms, muskets, pistols, swords, sabres, lances, etc., 500 mules with their packs, camp equippage and provisions and in fact everything they had. When we got into camp of the enemy everything showed the great confidence they had of success. They were actually cooking their meal during the fight, and as we have since learned, the women of Matamora were making preparations for a great festival upon the return of their victorious army. The people of Mexico are a very different race of people from ours. The better class are very proud and tyrannize over the lower and much more numerous class as much as a hard master does over his negroes, and they submit to it quite as humbly. The great majority of inhabitants are either pure or more than half blooded Indians, and show but little more signs of neatness or comfort in their miserable dwellings than the uncivilized Indian,—Matamoras contains probably about 7,000 inhabitants, a great majority of them of the lower order. It is not a place of as much business importance as our little towns of 1,000. But no doubt I will have an opportunity of knowing more of Mexico and the Mexicans before I leave the country and I will take another occasion of telling you more of them.

Don't you think Mr. Polk has done the Officers of the Army injustice by filling up the new Regt. of Riflemen from citizens? It is plain to be seen that we have but little to expect from him. I have now written you a long letter; as soon as anything more is done I will write again. If you have an opportunity I wish you would let them know at home that I am well. I don't think I have written in the last four weeks. I should like very much to see you here in command of a volunteer company. I think you would not be affected by the climate. So far our troops have had their health remarkably well.

Remember me as to your own and Judge Fishback's family. I suppose Tom has grown so much that he almost thinks of volunteering for the Mexican Wars himself. I shall be pleased to hear from you as often as you will make it convenient to write and will answer all your letters.

Yours truly,
U. S. Grant
4th Inf'y

Tiping Ahualco, Mexico,
May 3rd, 1847

Dear Lowe:—

Just as the troops were leaving Vera Cruz I received a letter from my young friend Tom and yourself. Now that we will probably be stationary for four or five days, I avail myself of the opportunity of answering. I see that you have written me several letters which you have not received answers to. I always make it a point to answer all your letters and am only sorry I don't get more of them. You say you would like to hear more about the war. If you had seen as much of it as I have you would be tired of the subject. Of our success at Vera Cruz you have read everything. The strength of the town, its forts and castle the papers are full and they do not exaggerate. On the 13th of April the rear division of Gen. Scott's army left Vera Cruz to ascend the mountains and drive Santa Anna from his strong position in one of the Passes. On the night of the 15th Gen. Worth arrived at Plana del Rio three miles from the battle ground. Gen. Twiggs with his division had been there several days preparing for an attack. By the morning of the 17th the way was completed to go around the Pass, Cierra Gorda, and make the attack in the rear as well as in the front. The difficulties to surmount made the undertaking almost equal to Bonaparte's Crossing the Alps. Cierra Gorda is a long narrow Pass, the mountains towering far above the road on either side. Some five of the peaks were fortified and armed with artillery and infantry. At the outlet of the mountain gorge a strong breast-work was thrown up and 5 pieces placed in embrasure sweeping the road so that it would have been impossible for any force in the world to have advanced. Immediately behind this is a peak of the mountains several hundred feet higher than any of the others and commanding them. It was on this height that Gen. Twiggs made his attack. As soon as the Mexicans saw this height taken they knew the day was up with them. Santa Anna vamoused with a small part of his force leaving about 6000 to be taken prisoners with all their arms, supplies, etc. Santa Anna's loss could not have been less than 2,000 killed, wounded, taken prisoners and missing. The pursuit was so close upon the retreating few that Santa Anna's carriage and mules were taken and with them his wooden leg and some 20 or 30 thousand dollars in money. Between the thrashing the Mexicans have got at Buena Vista, Vera Cruz and Cierra Gorda they are so completely broken up that if we only had transportation we could go to the City of Mexico and wherever else we liked without resistance. Garrisons could be established in all the important towns and the Mexicans prevented from ever raising another army. Santa Anna is said to be at Orazaba, at the foot of a mountain always covered with snow and of the same name. He has but a small force. Orazaba looks from here as if you could almost throw a stone to it but it looked the same from Lalapa some fifty miles back and was even visible from Vera Cruz. Since we left the Sea Coast the improvement in the appearance of the people and the style of building has been very visible over anything I had seen in Mexico before. The road is one of the best in the world. The scenery is beautiful and a great deal of magnificent table land spreads out above you and below you. Lalapa is the most beautiful place that I ever saw. It is about 4,000 feet above sea and being in the Torrid Zone, they have the everlasting spring fruit and vegetables the year around. I saw there a great many handsome ladies and more well dressed men than I had ever seen before in the Republic. From Lalapa we marched to Perote and walked quietly into the Strong Castle that you no doubt have read about. It is a great work. One Brigade, the one I belong to, is now 20 miles in advance of Perote. Soon no doubt we will advance upon Pueblo. I am Regtl. Quarter Master appointed under the new law allowing one to each Regt. and giving extra allowances. Remember me to all your family and Judge Fishback's. Tell Tom he must write to me again. I will be much pleased to receive all the letters you will write to me and all that Tom will write too. I will write to Tom from Pueblo. I suppose we will be there in a few days. If you see any of the Bethel people please remember me to them. Tell them I am heartily tired of the wars. If you were to see me now you would never recognize me in the world. I have a beard more than four inches long and it is red.

Your Friend,
U. S. Grant,
4th Inf'y.

Private Carr White

(n.d.)

An unknown infantry private from Ohio, Carr White took part in the hard-fought and costly battle for Monterrey. During the fighting, he witnessed Mexican lancers killing the wounded left on the battlefield and responded with anger: "You have no idea how this galled us & excited feelings of revenge. Oh! How I could have buried the assassin's knife in their murderous breasts if I had an opportunity. I don't blame the Texans for wanting to kill every one they come across."

In the following letter to his sister, he deliberately leaves out this demonization of the enemy and the bloody details of battle and concentrates instead on the circus atmosphere of camp life and a description of his war booty. Although we do not know how old his sister is and her tender age may have something to do with the things he reports, Carr is deliberately transforming the war into child's play. This sanitized version of war is what most often makes it into the letters of soldiers writing home.

from White's Letter to His Sister

Dear Sister:

You would laugh if you could see how we soldiers live here. every felow has his knife fork Tin cup and plate. we do our own cooking. we have got a great big Bak Oven. we bake 20 Big loves at a time. we boil our victuals in a great big kettle, and every felow gows and gets his tin full of Coffee his plat full of Meat & soop. we spread a Blanket down on the ground and every felow is like a Hungry Hog. we have fine times, all we have to do is to keep our guns & swords clean, and I tell you the way they shine is a show; we muster two hours each day, and

162

then sweep up our quarters we then go and swing or play Ball or lay down in our tents and read. we have lots of fun. Oh! it is the prettiest sight you ever saw to see about two thousand soldiers all dressed alike with Bright and shining guns, swords, & belts white as snow, if you could see them marching and hear their music. we have some of the Best swings you ever saw. we have ropes fixed to the tops of trees so that we can swing 20 feet into the air. we have a circus show here too. they are performing in the camp now. there are some little felows like Gip that can stand on their feet and ride as fast as their Horses can run. we have some little felows here not much larger than Gip that can beat the drum and play the fife as good as any body.

I have got a fine silk sash to sent to you. I was gowing to send by Capt. Johnston but he had his saddle Bags so full that he could not take it. I will send it by Adam who is gowing home in the course of a week or two. it is about four yards long and a half yard wide. I gave four dollars and a half for it in the city of montarey. when you get it take good care of it. keep it as a relick of the great fight we had here. I have a fine silver mounted Bowie knife that I found on the Battle field the day of the fight. I picked up a fine sword on the Battle field which I still keep and ware every evening on dress parade. I could have picked up a dozen swords that were laying arond without scabords, but I had enough to do to handle the gun and sword I had. I shot eleven times at the Mexicans that day as deliberately as I ever shot at a squirel They shot at us all the time with their Big Canons and muskets, one poor felow by the name of Pierson was shot right by my side[.] the Ball went clar through him and within an inch of his heart. he felt as though he were dead but lived. I steped over the Bodies of a[t] least 20 men who were either dead or wounded, I would not let myself sympathize with them for fear it would tend to intimidate. If I saw anything horible I would turn my eys away but after while I got so I could look at a dead man and feel no more sympathy than I would to see a dead dog. It was a terible time the Bulets whized arond us like so many Humin Birds. But I guess we whipe them at last.

You must write to me as soon as you get this. you must study hard. I will get some good Book for you as I go home. Tell Gip that he must study hard. Lem must study too. I want him to be as great a man as his namesake. he can if he will. Tell Gip and Lem they must keep good fires for Mother & little Liz—this winter & not lit them get cold. Gip and Lem are big enough to feed the cows & horses & they ought to do it. I am going to bring a wife home with me when I come.

    Yours

    Broth Carr

Robert E. Lee

(1807–1870)

The son of famed Revolutionary War cavalry officer Henry (Light Horse Harry) Lee and a member of a family distinguished for public service, Robert E. Lee graduated from West Point in 1846 and was commissioned in the Engineer Corps. He served in Texas as an engineer on General Winfield Scott's staff and distinguished himself during the Mexican war at Veracruz, Cerro Gordo, Mexico City, Churubusco, and Chapultepec. At the end of the war he was a colonel and went on to serve as West Point's superintendent and command a cavalry regiment in Texas. In 1861, he turned down command of all federal forces and resigned his commission. He assumed command of the Army of Northern Virginia in 1862 and surrendered to Grant on April 9th, 1865.

In the following letter home, Lee acknowledges his personal good fortune, expresses his trust in an "overruling Providence," but attributes victory to the proper execution of military principles and the victor's "own resources." In his crisp professional account of the events, he deliberately ignores the bloody details of combat in favor of praising the beauty of the countryside and the efficiency of well-led American soldiers. Ben Franklin would be proud of both Grant's and Lee's analytical reporting.

from Lee's Letter to His Family

Perote, April 25, 1847

The advance of the American troops, under Generals Patterson and Twiggs, were encamped at the Plano del Rio, and three miles to their front Santa Anna and his army were intrenched in the pass at Cerro Gordo, which was remarkably strong. The right of the Mexican line rested on the river at a perpendicular rock, unscalable by man or beast, and their left on impassable ravines; the main road was defended by field works containing thirty-five cannon; in their rear was the mountain of Cerro Gordo, surrounded by intrenchments in which were cannon and crowned by a tower overlooking all—it was around this army that it was intended to lead our troops. I reconnoitered the ground in the direction of the ravines on their left, and passed around the enemy's rear.

On the 16th a party was set to work in cutting out the road, on the 17th I led General Twigg's division in the rear of a hill in front of Cerro Gordo, and in the afternoon, when it became necessary to drive them from the hill where we intended to construct a battery at night, the first intimation of our presence or intentions were known. During all that night we were at work in constructing the battery, getting up the guns, ammunition, etc., and they in strengthening their defenses on Cerro Gordo.

Soon after sunrise our batteries opened, and I started with a column to turn their left and to get on the Jalapa road. Notwithstanding their efforts to prevent us in this, we were perfectly successful, and the working party, following our footsteps, cut out the road for the artillery. In the meantime our storming party had reached the crest of Cerro Gordo, and, seeing their whole left turned and the position of our soldiers on the Jalapa road, they broke and fled. Those in the pass laid down their arms. General Pillow's attack on their right failed. All their cannon, arms, ammunition, and most of their men fell into our hands.

The papers cannot tell you what a horrible sight a field of battle is, nor will I, owing to my accompanying General Twigg's division in the pursuit, and being since constantly in the advance. I believe all our friends are safe. I think I wrote you that my friend Joe Johnston was wounded the day before I arrived at the Plano del Rio while reconnoitering. He was wounded in the arm and about the groin; both balls are out, and he was doing well and was quite comfortable when I left; the latter wound was alone troublesome. Captain Mason, of the rifles, was badly wounded in the leg, and General Shields was wounded in the chest; I have heard contradictory reports that he was doing well and that he was dead. I hope the former.

Jalapa is the most beautiful country I have seen in Mexico, and will compare with any I have seen elsewhere. I wish it was in the United States, and that I was located with you and the children around me in one of its rich, bright valleys. I can conceive nothing more beautiful in the way of landscape or mountain scenery. We ascended upwards of four thousand feet that morning, and whenever we looked back the rich valley was glittering in the morning sun and the light morning clouds flitting around us. On reaching the top, the valley appeared at intervals between the clouds which were below us, and high over all towered Orizaba, with its silver cap of snow.

The castle or fort of Perote is one of the best finished that I have ever seen—very strong, with high, thick walls, bastioned fronts, and deep, wide ditch. It is [effective?] in construction and is very spacious, covers twenty-five acres, and although there is within its walls nearly three thousand troops, it is not yet full. Within the fort is a beautiful chapel, in one corner of which is the tomb of Guadalupe Victoria. There are various skulls, images, etc., in the sanctuaries. This morning I attended the Episcopal service within the fort. It was held on the parade. The minister was a Mr. McCarty, the chaplain of the Second Brigade, First Division. Many officers and soldiers were grouped around. I endeavored to give thanks to our Heavenly Father for all his mercies to me, for all the blessings he has bestowed upon me, for I know I fall short of my obligations.

We move out tomorrow toward Pueblo. The First Brigade—Duncan's battery, light infantry and cavalry—form the advance. I accompany the advance. General Worth will remain a day or two with the remainder of his division until the Second Division, under General Twiggs, shall arrive. General Scott is still at Jalapa, Major Smith with him. I have with me Lieutenants Mason, Tower, and the Engineer Company. In advance, all is uncertain and the accounts contradictory. We must trust to an overruling Providence, by whom we will be governed for the best, and to our own resources.

Benjamin Franklin Scribner

(1826–18??)

A twenty-year-old gentleman volunteer from Indiana, Scribner was promoted to sergeant just before the battle for Buena Vista. Although his militia training had not prepared him for the harsh realities of combat, he and other outnumbered volunteers overcame romantic notions of war and fought well under the most difficult of circumstances.

In the following account of the Battle of Buena Vista, Scribner describes "what was passing immediately around him" and not the whole action, but he does have as his subtext the familiar mythic "American-warrior-fighting-outnumbered" scenario. His description has the authentic ring of one confronting the realities of war face to face and is not too far removed rhetorically from Thomas Wheeler's account of King Philip's War or the anonymous account of the Battle of Shiloh to come. After the Battle of Buena Vista, Scribner marched back to the Rio Grande and shipped out to New Orleans and home.

from Scribner's *A Campaign in Mexico or a Camp Life of a Volunteer*

28th.—During last week, I have passed through so many thrilling scenes, that I am unable to describe them in regular order. Last Sunday we received orders to strike our tents and prepare to march. Before we had formed a line, and the command given, "file left," the most of us were ignorant of our place of destination. But so soon as we commenced marching towards Saltillo, there was an end of discussion.

Traveling about sixteen miles, we arrived at Buena Vista. After pitching our tents, we lay down supperless, for we had neither wood nor provisions. Scarcely had I fallen asleep, when the news was circulated that a mail had arrived. Soon after a letter was handed me from my friend Mrs. W., but, having no light, I was forced to postpone the reading till morning.

We had scarcely finished our breakfast, when the long roll was beaten, calling us to arms, as our picket guard had just arrived with the intelligence that the Mexican army was approaching. Having packed our wagon and formed a line, we were marched one and a-half miles towards the enemy, and stationed on a ridge just behind the narrow pass in which Major Washington's battery was placed. There we waited the approach. The Mexicans had encamped the night before at Agua Nueva, causing the Kentucky and Arkansas cavalry, who were guarding some provisions, to destroy them and retreat in the night.

We were greatly indebted to Colonel May and Captain M'Cullough, who rendered us much good service as spies. The intelligence which they brought caused us to leave the plains of Agua Nueva for a very strong and advantageous position.—Whilst we were awaiting the onset, I read Mrs. W.'s letter over and over again. It was encouraging, and afforded many topics for contemplation.

Having remained in this position more than half the day, we were ordered over to another height on the left, near the foot of the mountain, where we were, during the night, occasionally receiving a shot from the enemy's battery. Toward evening, the two rifle companies, from each of the Indiana regiments, commanded by Major Gorman, who were stationed on the left, upon the side of the mountain, were fired upon by an immense body of the enemy, who had also ascended the mountain. A heavy fire was kept up till dark, when all was silent, save the echoing of the enemy's trumpets. I never shall forget the peculiar melody of those sounds as we lay upon our arms, hungry, and shivering with cold. It was a prelude to the awful din of next day.

Before hostilities commenced, a flag of truce was sent by Santa Anna with dispatches to General Taylor, stating that he was here with twenty thousand men, and to save loss of blood, demanded immediate capitulation. General Taylor is said to have replied, "If you want us, come and take us!" It looked almost like madness, with an army of four thousand five hundred men, and sixteen small pieces of cannon, to compete with force, which all our prisoners, and Santa Anna himself, agree in being twenty thousand men, and seventeen pieces of cannon—of which eight were sixteen and twenty-four pounders. What a fearful difference! Yet that small army of raw, inexperienced volunteers not only struggled against twenty thousand strong of the flower of the Mexican army, commanded by one of the ablest generals in the world, but obtained a complete victory. This I hold to be one of the greatest achievements upon record.

Before I proceed further, I must confess my inability to give an accurate description of the whole action. The excitement and interest I experienced in what was passing immediately around me, occupied all my attention. I shall, therefore, for my future perusal, detail my own feelings and actions, together with what came under my own observation during the hazardous conflict.

At sunrise, on the following day, the roaring of the enemy's cannon announced the commencement of hostilities. A heavy fire was opened upon our riflemen upon the mountain, but they returned it in a handsome style. They were reinforced by a part of the 2d Illinois regiment and Kentucky cavalry, but still the odds were greatly against them. The whole mountain side, as far as the eye could reach, glittered with the enemy's bayonets and lances.

It was about nine o'clock in the morning when our regiment and a battery of three pieces, commanded by Lieut. O'Brien, marched out towards the battery which had been playing against us during the night and morning. We formed a line in front of three regiments of Mexico's oldest soldiers. It was an awful moment to face the thousands of veterans in solid column, with their gaudy uniforms and showy banners. But we had no time for admiration; for, before our line was formed, they had fired two rounds, which we soon returned in right good earnest. I was at my post in the rank of file closers, and was urging the men to form in their proper places, when Captain Sanderson cried out, "Never mind, Frank, fire away!" which I did, with all possible haste. About this time the battery on our left, opened upon us a deadly fire of grape, which raked our flank with terrible effect; still we stood front to front, and poured our fire upon the infantry, which did us but little injury, as they shot too high. But the battery on our left galled us exceedingly. It appeared as if we had purposely halted in their exact range, and the whole atmosphere resounded with the whizzing shot that came with increasing precision. Apollos Stephens was the first of the Greys to fall. He received a grape shot in the head, and fell back almost into my arms. O, how shall I describe the horror of my feelings?

There lay quivering in death one of my comrades, with his eyes upturned, and the tears starting from them. It was a sad and touching scene—one that will never be effaced from my memory. I was loading when he fell, and compressing my lips, and smothering my emotions, I stepped over him and fired. Our captain was the next to fall, exclaiming "I've got it boys!" A grape shot had struck his scabbard, which saved his life. Being ready to fire again, I stepped into a vacant place in the ranks, where I continued to load and fire without noticing anything around. The only thought I remember to have had was, "What a wonder I did not receive Captain Sanderson's shot, as I was next to him on the same line! so the ball must have passed me before it struck him." All was hurry and excitement, each working hard and doing his best. Occasionally a cannon-ball would whistle over our heads, or strike the ground near us, throwing the rock and dirt in all directions.

We had fired about twenty-one rounds, when I heard some one say, "They are all retreating!" and turning, I saw that the right wing had gone, and the left starting. But several who had not heard Colonel Bowles's order to retreat, cried out, "Halt, men! for God's sake, stop!" At this, many of us hesitated; but the retreat was general, and the enemy fast advancing upon us, led on by a large force of lancers. At length, Lieutenant Cayre, then in command, remarked, "It's no use, boys, to stay here alone; let us retreat!" which we did, with the balls raining around us, and the lancers at our heels. We rallied, by order, on the brow of the ridge from which we started in the morning, but were told to fall back upon the ridge on which we were first formed on the morning of the 22d. Here many of us met the Mississippi regiment of riflemen, who had just arrived from their quarters in town.

The more I reflect upon our position in the opening of the conflict, the more I am at a loss to understand the policy of sending the 2d regiment against such an overpowering force. We were three-quarters of a mile from any assistance, except that of the gallant O'Brien, who with his three little pieces did such great execution.

Our field officers all deny giving the word retreat, and General Lane, they say, intended to charge. Had he given the word, the charge would have been made; but how dreadful would have been the slaughter of our troops. It is unprecedented in the annals of warfare, for eight companies to rush against a disciplined force of three thousand infantry supported by twelve hundred lancers. Had we remained fifteen minutes longer, it is thought not one half of us would have survived. Their battery was fast getting our exact range, and it is astonishing that so many of us escaped.

After many fruitless exertions to rally his men, Colonel Bowles ordered those who were near him to join the Mississippians, at the same time falling in himself. We marched along the ridge to meet a large body of lancers supported by infantry. We soon opened our fire upon them, and that, too, in a manner which forced them to retreat, and pursuing, we halted at intervals, and continued our leaden hail. Having followed them across two deep ravines, they were reinforced, and came rushing down upon us like a tremendous avalanche, pouring out upon us their incessant shot. We fell back across the two hollows, occasionally halting to fire upon our pursuers.

While in the second ravine, the sun shining with burning heat, famishing for want of water, and almost overcome with exertions, I leaned against a rocky precipice, and there made up my mind to die. Sad and hopeless were my thoughts, when, raising my head, I beheld the Mexican line firing down upon us. At this I was involuntarily aroused, and recollecting an expression in Mrs. W.'s letter, "If you should die, it would kill your mother," I made an effort for those I loved and gained the summit. But oh! God! what a merciful preservation! The balls rained around, scattering death and destruction on every side. It appeared like the bed under a shot tower, so thick and fast did the balls hail about us. A man just before me was shot down, and a brave lieutenant, who so kindly made room for me in his company, fell wounded behind me, exclaiming, "Give me water!, give me a handkerchief!" I gazed upon his supplicating countenance, but had nothing to relieve him. Rendered reckless by the sight we had just witnessed, we rallied again upon the top of the hill, and with the 2d Indiana under Lieutenant Haddon, opened a terrible fire upon our bloodthirsty enemies. They soon retreated in the utmost disorder.

Having fled beyond our fire, a detail was sent to explore the ravine for our wounded. While descending, what a shocking scene presented itself! The barbarians were cruelly butchering our wounded, and stripping them of their clothes. But our unerring rifles soon stopped these atrocious murders. Our success was but poor compensation for the blood of twenty brave comrades. The poor lieutenant was left naked with his throat cut from ear to ear.

Edmund B. Alexander

(1802–1888)

Edmund B. Alexander was born in Virginia and graduated from West Point in 1823. He served on the frontier in the 6th Infantry. In 1838 he was promoted to captain in the 3rd Infantry and entered the Mexican War at the Siege of Veracruz. Promoted to brevet major for gallant and meritorious conduct in the Battle of Cerro Gordo, he went on to participate in the Battle of Churubusco, where he was promoted to brevet lieutenant colonel; the storming of Chapaltepec; and the storming and capture of Mexico City. He was promoted to colonel in the 8th Infantry in 1855 and continued his frontier duty until the Civil War. He stayed with the Union and served as the chief mustering and disbursing officer for the state of Missouri until the end of the war, when he was promoted to brevet brigadier general.

In the following letter to his wife, Alexander attributes American victory to having "right" and the "ruler of all" on its side. Like Grant, he worries about the newspapers getting the details right and senior officers receiving too much credit for the deeds of junior officers. Alexander demonstrates supreme faith in the righteousness of his cause and confidence in his warrior prowess.

from Alexander's Letters

San Angel, New Mex
Aug 27–47

My dear beloved Pet

It is again my happy lot my dearest to be permitted to give you an account of two hard fought battles which took place on the 20th Inst & in each of which my regiment bore a conspicuous part & well

173

did it sustain itself, as usual your husband was among the foremost, now it is all over, I cannot see or account for my miraculous escape & I most sincerely offer up my thanks to the ruler of all for the protection which he has extended to me. And I know there is no one on earth who will more sincerely do the same than my beloved wife—I do assure you we had an overwhelming force opposed to us but right appeared to be on our side—and the day was ours—the enemy were sanguine and relied on superiority of numbers of both men & cannon—I will now dear give you the incidents connected with our approach to the City of Mexico. The army was halted at Ayotla distant from the city of about 12 or 15 miles for the purpose of Reconnaissance which was immediately commenced 7 or 8 miles ahead. I was sent with my Reg't to protect the engineers to El Pinzon the most advanced work of the enemy & some 6 or 7 miles from the city. This was found to be so strongly fortified & manned as to determine the Gen'l to select a differ-ent route—the first division of regulars being in rear was immediately put in motion—it being in the rear and we had to make a partial coun-termarch. This put our Division (Twiggs) in rear and we did not leave until the next morning[. W]e had not gone far when large force princi-pally lancers were discovered on our left, preparations were immedi-ately made to attack them, when a few shots from a piece of artillery dispersed the crowd, killing 5 or 6 horses & probably as many men. We encamped this night at ———— about 8 miles from Ayotla. The next morning we had not proceeded far on route towards San Augustine when we heard many discharges of cannon, which proved to be at Wor-th's division—we arrived at this latter town about 9 o'ck and were or-dered to leave our baggage train so as to turn the position toward San Antonio before which place Worth's division was then lying & which proved to be strongly fortified—we left all we had with the wagons save a blanket and two days rations—we had not proceeded over 2 1/2 miles on our route when a large force was seen immediately in our front, and to the left of a small town Contreras and immediately a heavy fire of cannon was opened upon us which did considerable execution. I ordered the reg't behind a ledge of rocks in doing which a ball passed so near my horse as to cause him to wheel immediately around & so alarmed him that he became unmanageable, in fact I did not know for some time whether the ball had passed through him or not or whether I was shot myself. I immediately abandoned him & gave him to an orderly who had my pack mule containing all my provision, blanket etc. here the Reg't marched to the right to gain a road leading from Contreras to San Angel—the ground over which we had to pass (there being no road) except directly in front of the enemys cannon was impassible for any but foot men. Consequently I left my horse & mule & all I had—provisions Blanket etc. waided a stream gained the road above mentioned & formed my regm't in line of battle immediately on the left of the rifle Reg't[. H]ere a large force variously estimated at 14 thousand and upwards under Santa Anna in person was found directly in our front and intended to reinforce Valencia then in command of about 7000 Troops in Contraros—This was near sundown, arrangements were immediately made to attack them. We were about 600 yards apart when the enemy commenced a cheering Viva etc and blowing their trumpets & playing all sorts of instruments. To all of this our Division were quiet listening and finally the enemy not contented with these demonstrations of hostilities fired two or 3 cannon shots directly at my Reg't but without effect—Night coming on put a stop to the strife for this day the 19th. I was ordered to move my Reg't in the Town of Contreros to a church the yard of which we occupied for the night—it commenced about dark and rained hard all night many of the men had early in the day thrown away their blankets and suffered much for the want of covering—As for myself I had not eaten a mouthful since early daylight. Fortunately I met Dr. Randall who gave me $1/2$ a cracker & a small piece of raw pork or bacon which I ate raw, I next went into the church & was about disposing of myself at full length on the bricks feet wet & cold when Dr. Cuyler came and offered to share his blanket—which I readily accepted & thought myself fortunate in having even this protection from the rain, my pillow was one of the Drs boots. From the excessive fatigue of the day I soon fell asleep but was woke by the Dr. saying he was very cold and told me to hug him—which I did. We had not laid long in this way when I told him I was cold & that he must hug me, we were shifting in this way the remainder of the night—until about 3 o'ck when the reg't was formed. It still raining hard and quite dark & the road over which we had to march being narrow & muddy caused much delay in getting our position which we gained about daylight[.] I took advantage in the delays on the march to have the loads drawn & the guns wiped out—we had not been long in our position when a charge was ordered which resulted in one of the most brilliant affairs of the war, or in modern warfare—this charge was in Contreros where we kill upwards of 700[,] wounding thousands & putting the whole army to flight, taking upwards of 20 pieces of large cannon with much ammunition, etc. etc. and munitions of war were taken—This was the most complete route and slaughter I had ever seen—and did not exceed over 1/2 an hour after the charge was ordered—this was termed the battle of Contreros and took place immediately after sunrise on the morning of the 20th of Aug'st—I soon reformed my Reg't and rec'd orders to march in the direction of San Angel about 3 miles—where we halted and rested. This was about 12 m. Here for the first time since last night I got a cracker and two small slices of bacon given me by Mr. Throgmerton from Louisville. We talked much about home what he would tell my friends about me etc—here I had some talk with Butler Masons fortunate friend—who in a short time after received two wounds one in the leg and the other through the head which ended his existance—here a party of lancers made their appearance directly in our front as a decoy to lead us to Churubusco a strongly fortified work having many cannon and a very large force at least 16 thousand men & probably more—the Reg't was immediately formed and marched in the direction of Churubusco 2 1/2 miles when a heavy fire of cannon & musketry was opened upon us as we halted in a road parallel to the works and again, I directed the men to lye down behind some maquay plants to protect them from the fire where we laid some considerable time, without being able to fire a shot. When the regm'nt was ordered by me to move forward and gain a position nearer the works I immediately rushed forward leading and gained a mud house some 60 or 70 yards from the enemys strongest position under the greatest fire you can imagine. Here my reg't opened a most distructive fire upon the enemy and in a short time compelled them to surrender when my Reg't had the good fortune to be the first to enter the works and raise their collers. I was detailed some little time with Lt. Buell a gallant officer who rec'd a severe wound but a short distance from the works—I found many officers of ———Gen'l Rincon who by the by resembles Genl Taylor so much that I & several other officers told him so which pleased him much. I immediately raised the flag of the 3d Infy where those officers were, saying to Genl Rincon the seignior in the excitement of the moment, that the tattered flag which I then unfurled had fought in all the battles from Palo Alto to this place—and which that day had recd two additional holes—Placed it on the walls and ordered the Regt to give it 3 cheers which they did most heartily—here the strife ended for the day, and we could then have marched in the city without the least interruption it being about 2 miles distant, in fact some did enter the gates. Capt Kearny of the Drags. who lost his left arm by so doing - Genl Scott determined to wait here and receive propositions from Santa Anna who is most anxious to come to terms—a white flag was sent out and an armistice was entered into for the purpose of giving them time to appoint commissioners to make peace[. H]ad we marched in Santa Anna with his army would have fled to some other part of the country & we should have been compelled to follow him, as it is he has the power and I think will be glad to come to terms, and now for the first time do I feel as though I should get out of the country soon[. S]hould they prove false, we have taken cannon and ammunition enough with what we had of our own to batter the city down—or to fire at least 1 month, without interruption. The 3d have been in so many battles that they know how to fight, and when to lay low. If I do not get a Brevet for each of the 2 last fights I think I will quit—for no one ever fought harder & with greater presence of mind than myself, though I say it—I find the men have great confidence in me, I will relate a little familiar conversation I had with a soldier as I rode through the ranks after the battle at Contreros on the morning of the 20—this in presence of 2 or 3 officers & many soldiers—it was immediately after a victory when great latitude was given to the men[. H]e began by saying well captain I am willing to follow you any where, Why so? was the reply from me[.] I watched you closely during the whole of the fight & I will fight for you as long as I live & will go anywhere with you, and many other such remarks[. W]hen I ordered a charge at Churubusco which I led I had to pass a wide road about 150 yards from the enemys ranks, I soon saw that a shower of musketry & grape was poured down this road at the crossing & that there was a slight intermission[.] I took advantage of this and made the men run across immediately after each fire by which means many escaped, when about $^1/_2$ were over I found the remainder a little backward in crossing I ordered the rest to follow & rushed ahead. The poor fellow who was close to me was wounded—I visited the wounded today they were pleased to see me & their being near me etc. I find if I cant get near a man in action & he does not act right I

am sure to throw a stone at him[.] I did this in the hottest of the last
when the individual thought he was struck with a cannon ball—though
I am strict with both officers & men and they accuse me of having a
temper—still they have great respect for me, and obey with prompt-
ness any order I give—and well they may for I am just in all matters
and they know I am ready to lead them into action & in the hottest of
the fight—I have given you all the incidents connected with the 2 battles as near as I can recollect them, all blunders you must excuse as I
have written in a court room being one of 13 members sitting for the
trial of deserters from our army found in the Mexican ranks fighting
against us at Churubusco—you can readily imagine that the interrup-
tions were frequent—you know I am not at liberty to tell you the sen-
tences though you will hear them in due time, you can readily imagine
they will not be very light—for it is thought their duty was to pick off
the officers—we took near 100 of them, they had formed themselves
into a corps called the legion of strangers—I refer you to the papers
where you will see the reports, many of which are much exaggerated
and in some facts are related which did not occur, and many are
lauded to the skies who are not deserving it, and those who are deserving are—I do not know whether any mention will be made of me or
not but I do assure you dear wife there is no one more deserving—or
who risked more—but a captain is small fry compared with those of
higher rank who are trying to take all praise to themselves & their
favorites[.] I gave you in my last which I wrote on the night after the
battle an account of your poor brother's death—for fear it may not
reach you I will now say he recd his death by a cannon ball striking
him sidewise under the chin taking off the entire throat but injuring
the neck bone[. H]is death was instantaneous he was a brave little fellow and had advanced near the enemys works greatly ahead of his Co.
and shown himself behind a mud house which was no protection
against cannon—I learn these facts from an officer who was with him,
he appeared anxious to gain distinction—I sent a lock of his hair for
you to send to his poor mother to whom I fear it will be a severe shock.
I send in this a lock for yourself & shall keep some to bring with me. I
saw in his bag of clothes your mothers likeness which I took out to
bring to you, but William told me he wanted it. If he insists on it, I will
give it to him—I can sympathize with you sincerely my dear Pet for his
loss. I had seen a great deal of him & liked him much & he became

quite attached to me—I have seen William, Penrose & Capt Alex'r they are all well & escaped unhurt. Johnson poor fellow of the 6th looks miserable he has not recovered his eyesight, has no pain but is compelled to were specks & a handkerchief tied around it - I pity him much—tell Cass she would have a severe time with him—my love to her when you write—I hope to get back soon thus far all negotiations I hear are progressing smoothly—rumor says the Gen'l says all the army will be at Vera Cruz by the last of October—if so the passage from there to those I so dearly love is but short—tell dear ———— she will have no trouble in feeding me, as I have learned to eat everything & have a good appetite—a big slice anywhere I like best—now that prospects of peace are near at hand I am so restless & homesick I do not know what to do with myself—I would be willing to start to-m and walk all the way to Vera Cruz—tell Bettie her pa is anxious to see— permitted to do so—if we reach Vera Cruz by the last of Oct. I shall give up the comd of the regt probably to Maj. Clark who I am told has transferred with Jewett and will only stay long enough to dress myself up a little—Give my love to Ma your Mother, the boys sister E. and all tell them I am anxious to see them I think so much of home that I am dreaming of my dear Pet all the time. Kiss little Eddy & often for his Pa and [d]o take thousands for yourself from your heart husband.

Edm

God bless you again & again your devoted

E

Part V

The Civil War

In the beauty of the lilies, Christ was born across the sea,
With a glory in His bosom that transfigures you and me;
As He died to make men holy, let us die to make men free,
While God is marching on.

—Julia Ward Howe "The Battle Hymn of the Republic"

Do not weep, babe, for war is kind.
Because your father tumbled in the yellow trenches,
Raged at his breast, gulped and died,
Do not weep, War is kind.

—Stephen Crane "Do Not Weep, Maiden, for War Is Kind"

Introduction

From the Confederate bombardment of the Federal arsenal at Fort Sumter, South Carolina on April 12, 1861, until General Lee's surrender of the Army of Northern Virginia at Appomattox Courthouse on April 9, 1865, millions of Americans from the North and South turned the nation into a deadly battlefield. America's Civil War was the conflict Henry Clay prophesied in his 1850 compromise speech: "Such a war, too, as that would be, following the dissolution of the Union! Sir, we may search the pages of history, and none so furious, so bloody, so implacable, so exterminating . . . none, none of them raged with such violence, or was ever conducted with such bloodshed and enormities, as will that war which shall follow that disastrous event . . . of dissolution."

According to conservative estimates, more than 365,000 Union soldiers and over 256,000 Confederates died from wounds and disease during the four-year conflict. On the Union side alone there were over six million recorded cases of wounds and disease, and a casual glance down the rolls of any Southern regiment reveals that about one in four men died and the total number of wounds outnumbered the men on the roster. Historian James I. Robertson reports that of the original 5,000 men who served in the Stonewall Brigade, only 210 were left to surrender at Appomattox. Five of the eight men who commanded the brigade died in combat; the remaining three were disabled by wounds. According to J.B. Polley, only 617 of the original 5,300 men of Hood's Texas Brigade survived to the end of the war.

The clash of newly recruited armies at the Battle of Shiloh, where over 23,000 men fell in two days of confusion and unparalleled bloodshed, set the tone for battle that followed. The scope of the slaughter was unprecedented. In contrast, only ten years earlier the famous Charge of the Light Brigade during the Crimean War had involved only 673 men, 40 percent of whom did not return to England from Balaclava, yet that event was celebrated as a military disaster of giant proportion. Sixty percent of the 15,000 men who took part in Pickett's charge were casualties on the battlefield at Gettysburg. Of course, battlefield casualty statistics do not reflect the horrors and indecencies suffered by the civilian population throughout the contested and conquered areas of the country, nor do they describe the cultural chaos of a nation at war with itself.

To justify the slaughter, both sides portrayed themselves as carrying out moral crusades to fulfill promises made by Pilgrim and revolutionary fathers, and both sides drafted God in their causes. In the South, the Confederacy represented itself as the champion of the idea that governments rest upon the consent of the governed and as the true representative government of the ideals of the Revolution. In his first inaugural address, Jefferson Davis declared that God, "who knows the hearts of men, will judge of the sincerity with which we labor to preserve the government of our fathers in its spirit."

In the North, the Union saw itself as God's chosen nation, punished by the conflict in order to be purged of the sin of slavery but, once cleansed, guaranteed success in its divinely covenanted role. Both sides believed they pursued America's exceptional place in history, and both relied on the nation's faith in its special mission to sustain public support for their efforts.

On a national fast day in 1863, Abraham Lincoln proclaimed that the war was "a punishment inflicted upon us for our presumptuous sins to the end that the whole people might be redeemed." Yet, as the war progressed, it seemed to exhaust even Lincoln's complex and driven mind. The fatalistic gloom of the declaration in his second inaugural address, that "the Almighty has his own purposes," signaled his resignation to let the war run its providential course.

Although many found comfort and escape from widespread suffering in their faith in providence, theocratic explanations did not satisfy all those touched by the war's tragedy. The war of words that commenced long before the first shots on Fort Sumter and continued long after the guns were silent created a multitude of complex cultural myths to explain and resolve the national tragedy.

This rhetorical process continues today because the cultural consequences of the Civil War are still at work in our society; we have not resolved its fundamental issues of individual and collective rights, society and economy, will and inevitability. Unlike the colonial wars, which myth-makers interpreted completely as God's will, or the Revolution, rewritten as an epic triumph of natural law and patriotic idealism over English tyranny, the Civil War remains a national psychotic orgy of efficient violence that no one cultural myth adequately explains. Without outside villains, we must look inward for the source of the conflict's evil, and we still dare not look too closely in fear of what we might find. It is the one war that remains central to our national consciousness, a fact underscored by the steady flow of published volume after volume searching for keys to the American character and destiny in the events of the Civil War.

In his introduction to *Patriotic Gore*, the critic Edmund Wilson asks, "Has there ever been another historical crisis of the magnitude of 1861–1865 in which so many people were so articulate?" He correctly refers to the war's remarkable legacy of speeches, private letters, diaries, personal memoirs, journalistic reports, and some official records, but not to works of great literary merit, at least those works written during and right after the war. Although most agree with poet Robert Penn Warren that the Civil War was our "Homeric period," the closest work we have to an *Iliad* is Margaret Mitchell's sentimental celebration of female manipulation of New South economics, *Gone with the Wind.*

From a war that, as the historian Daniel Aaron observed, "seemed designed for literary treatment as if history itself had assiduously collaborated with the would-be writer," American literature inherited an artistic debt, "a burden," author William Dean Howells noted, "under which it has hitherto staggered very lamely." No one American artist has synthesized the many cultural myths explaining the Civil War, nor is any one artistic vision likely to reconcile the many issues the war left unresolved.

Despite the lack of epic literature, the Civil War looms in the American consciousness as the greatest of all our wars. It does so partly because it was so violent, partly because it was a war of Americans killing Americans on local battlefields, partly because the issues over which it was fought are still unresolved within us, but mostly because its fascinating prose record has the power to recall, if not reconcile, our best and worst national self. The following selections offer glimpses over time of American Civil War memory and myth.

The selections begin with Abner Doubleday's reminiscences of Fort Sumter during the first hours of the war. His memories record a cavalier attitude toward it. The chivalric courtesies exchanged by the officers at Fort Sumter were romantic notions of civilized warfare conditioned by the popular romantic historical literature of the years leading up to the Civil War. Charles Woodward Hutson, wounded at First Manassas, exudes the same chivalric spirit in a letter home the day after the battle, but despite his use of gamesmanship language, Hutson begins to realize the cost of the war in blood. Next, Private James K. Newton's first letter home after participating in "Bloody Shiloh" portrays war as a test of character and manhood. Early in the combat, he and many others held preconceived notions of war as organized and purposeful, a misconception reflected in his request to see the newspapers in order to "see what we did do." The anonymous eyewitness who realistically describes the aftermath of the Battle of Shiloh has quickly shed myth-induced preconceptions of war and describes the scene in grisly detail.

After years of combat, John Haley accepts the chaos of war and expresses very little shock over the magnitude of violence he witnesses during the Battle of Gettysburg. An experienced veteran reporting events later in the war, Haley finds comfort and humor in the paradoxical logic of combat, makes the best of what is always a bad situation, and accepts his place in the battle with a stoic's resignation. Rice C. Bull provides a view of the bittersweet last days of the war from the victors' point of view, and his unheroic memories parallel the sad pride of Walter A. Montgomery's record of his last days as a Confederate soldier. Both accounts reflect a common war weariness far different from the confident and chivalric rhetoric of Abner Doubleday.

The selection from *A Diary from Dixie* covers a single day in the life of Mary Boykin Chesnut's fascinating society in and around the capital of the Confederacy and introduces the engaging personality of its author. Louisa May Alcott's *Hospital Sketches* is a realistic and at the same time romantic study of the wounded men she cares for. Selections of public prose follow the records of memory and reflect the many cultural myths used to make sense out of the events of the Civil War.

A popular writer who knew war firsthand, John Esten Cooke also ignored the harsher realities of combat and tried to find the "sunshine in the blood and tears." Cooke's romantic treatment of war concentrated on idealistic lessons of duty and honor; he chose not to let the nightmares of war intrude on his dreams of the mythic South. The postbellum romance myth simply picks up where its antebellum counterpart left off, with an overlay of nostalgia.

To satisfy an ever-increasing interest in the actual events of war, in 1884 *Century Magazine* began a popular illustrated series, "Battles and Leaders of the Civil War." Despite focusing attention on the war itself, the series did little to explore the harsher realities of war. Memory dressed itself up for public display, and, as Paul Buck in *The Road to Reunion* says of the series, "Not one of its varied, vivid thrilling pages told of a war where men went mad with hatred, starved in prison camps, and invoked God's aid in damnation of the enemy. The history that the veterans told was a war in which valor countered valor, and each side devotedly served the right. The blood that was shed was baptism blood, consecrating the birth of a new and greater nation." The myth of the noble American warrior embarked on a sacred mission survived to reconcile Civil War foes.

However, one veteran refused to accept such notions or tell such stories. From his extensive combat experience, Ambrose Bierce came to believe that in battle, reason and philosophy are silent. His short story, "Chickamauga," directly confronts established religious and romantic war mythology and reflects his belief that in the face of war's horrors we are all deaf and dumb.

An opposite interpretation of the Civil War helps illustrate the rift it caused in cultural consciousness. Oliver Wendell Holmes's 1895 Memorial Day address at Harvard University champions the ennobling effects of military discipline. Holmes, wounded three times in the Civil War, sees war as an inevitable and ennobling condition of human life, and, while he hated mindless patriotism, he praises war as a proving ground of character. Holmes presents a uniquely American rhetoric of war, born of deeply ingrained national mythology; it is a narrative that would soon be questioned by the experiences of World War I.

Chronology

1860

20	Dec	South Carolina legislature adopts ordinance of secession.

1861

10	Jan	Florida secedes from Union.
11	Jan	Alabama secedes from Union.
19	Jan	Georgia secedes from Union.
26	Jan	Louisiana secedes from Union.

1	Feb	Texas secedes from Union.
4	Mar	Abraham Lincoln inaugurated.
12	Apr	Confederates fire on Fort Sumter in Charleston harbor; Civil War hostilities begin.
21	Jul	First Battle of Manassas (Bull Run); Johnston and Beauregard drive Union army back to Washington.

1862

16	Feb	Union forces under Grant take Fort Donelson on the Cumberland River in Tennessee.
6–7	Apr	Battle of Shiloh, Tennessee; meeting engagement of two untrained armies. After initial Confederate success, Grant drives Beauregard back but does not pursue.
24	Apr	Farragut's warships bombard New Orleans.
	May	Peninsular Campaign.
31	May	Battle of Fair Oaks; Joe Johnston wounded; Lee takes command and blocks McClellan's drive on Richmond.
26 Jun–1 Jul		Seven Days' Battle lifts siege of Richmond; McClellan retreats.
28–30 Aug		Second Battle of Manassas (Bull Run); Lee crushes Pope. Union forces withdraw to the fortifications of Washington.
17	Sep	Battle of Antietam (Sharpsburg, Md.). Lee invades the North; McClellan hesitates; Burnside falters; and A. P. Hill rescues Lee. Lee withdraws across the Potomac, his invasion stopped. Strategic victory for the Union: France and England decide not to recognize the Confederacy.
22	Sep	Lincoln's preliminary Emancipation Proclamation.
8	Oct	Battle of Perryville; Confederate invasion in the West thwarted. Bragg bungles attack; Buell fails to capitalize on victory, replaced as commander of the Army of the Cumberland by Rosecrans.
13	Dec	Battle of Fredericksburg; Burnside defeated decisively by Lee, retreats across the Rappahannock River.
31	Dec	Battle of Murfreesboro (Stone's River); Rosecrans, with the help of Hazen's artillery, stops Bragg.

1863

1	Jan	Lincoln issues Emancipation Proclamation.
1–2	May	Battle of Chancellorsville: Army of the Potomac under Hooker crosses Rappahannock; outflanked and out-

fought by Lee and Jackson, Hooker fails. Lee's "right arm," Stonewall Jackson, killed by fire from a North Carolina regiment.

22 May–4 July	Siege of Vicksburg: Grant defeats Johnston; entire length of Mississippi is under Union control.
1–3 Jul	Battle of Gettysburg: Lee's second invasion ends in disaster and retreat to Virginia. Although Meade fails to exploit victory, tide of war turns to favor the Union.
19–20 Sep	Battle of Chickamauga: Rosecrans and Bragg meet south of Chattanooga, Tennessee; Longstreet forces Confederate victory. Union army retreats to Rossville and Chattanooga.
24–25 Nov	Battle of Chattanooga: Grant given command in the West; Thomas replaces Rosecrans and overruns Missionary Ridge; Bragg's forces flee in confusion.

1864

9	Mar	Grant given command of all Union armies.
5–7	May	Battle of the Wilderness: Grant and Lee fight to a bloody stalemate; Grant presses on toward Spotsylvania Courthouse to block Lee's route to Richmond.
8–19	May	Battle of Spotsylvania: Grant continues to press Lee despite tremendous losses.
3	Jun	Battle of Cold Harbor: Lee's lines hold and defeat Union frontal assault; Grant crosses the James River and threatens Petersburg. Siege of Petersburg lasts until April 1865.
	May	Sherman's march through Georgia and the Carolinas continues to March 1865.

1865

4	Mar	Lincoln's second inauguration.
9	Apr	Lee surrenders to Grant at Appomattox Courthouse.
14	Apr	John Wilkes Booth assassinates President Lincoln.
26	Apr	Johnston surrenders to Sherman.

Abner Doubleday

(1819–1893)

An 1842 graduate of the U. S. Military Academy and second in command at Fort Sumter, Abner Doubleday aimed the first shots against the Confederacy during the attack on Fort Sumter. A veteran of the battles of Monterrey and Buena Vista during the Mexican War, Doubleday commanded a division at Antietam and a corps at Gettysburg and rose to the rank of brevet major-general during the Civil War. He published the following *Reminiscences of Forts Sumter and Moultrie* in 1876. Later—in 1907—he would become known as the founder of the sport of baseball.

Although his account is written years after the attack on Fort Sumter, Doubleday captures the formalities and nonchalance typical of professional soldiers at the beginning of the conflict. The officers on both sides knew each other and considered the conflict a chivalric joust by noble foes. Because both sides expected the war to be over quickly, and because no one could imagine the extreme human cost the war would exact, Doubleday could afford to be cavalier in his attitudes during the attack on Fort Sumter. All would change soon enough.

from Doubleday's *Reminiscences of Forts Sumter and Moultrie*

On the 10th, Beauregard announced his personal staff to consist of Colonels Wigfall, Chesnut, Means, M Gowan, Manning, and Boyleston.

On the same day, a house directly opposite to us in Moultrieville, at the nearest point, was suddenly removed, disclosing a formidable masked battery, which effectually enfiladed two rows of our upper tier of guns in barbette [on a gun platform], and took a third tier in reverse. It was a sad surprise to us, for we had our heaviest metal there. I

189

set to work immediately to construct sand-bag traverses; but it was difficult to make much progress, as we had no bags, and were obliged to tear up sheets for the purpose, and have the pieces sewed together. This labor, however, was entirely thrown away, for Anderson ordered us to abandon all the guns on the parapet. This, of course, was much less dangerous for the men, but it deprived us of the most powerful and effective part of our armament.

About 3 p.m. of the same day, a boat came over with Colonel James Chesnut, Ex-United States Senator, and Captain Stephen D. Lee, both aids of Beauregard. They bore a demand for the surrender of the fort. Anderson politely declined to accede to this request, but stated in conversation he would soon be starved out. This gratuitous information ought never to have been given to the enemy, in view of the fact that a naval expedition was on its way to us. It was at once supposed that Anderson desired to surrender without fighting; and about 11 p.m. another boat came over, containing Colonel Chesnut, Colonel Pryor, and Captain Lee, to inquire upon what day he would be willing to evacuate the work in case he was not attacked. The answer was, on the 15th at noon, provided he did not receive fresh instructions, or was not relieved before that time. As we had pork enough on hand to last for two weeks longer, there was no necessity for fixing so early a day. It left too little margin for naval operations, as, in all probability, the vessels, in case of any accident or detention, would arrive too late to be of service. This proved to be the case.

The enemy's batteries on Sullivan's Island were so placed as to fire directly into the officers' quarters at Fort Sumter; and as our rooms would necessarily become untenable, we vacated them, and chose points that were more secure. I moved my bed into a magazine which was directly opposite to Cummings Point, and which was nearly empty. As I was sensible that the next three days would call for great physical exertion and constant wakefulness, I endeavored to get all the sleep I could on the night of the 11th. About 4 a.m. on the 12th, I was awakened by some one groping about my room in the dark and calling out my name. It proved to be Anderson, who came to announce to me that he had just received a dispatch from Beauregard, dated 3:20 a.m., to the effect that he should open fire upon us in an hour. Finding it was determined not to return the fire until after breakfast, I remained in bed. As we had no lights, we could in fact do nothing before that time, except to wander around in the darkness, and fire without an accurate view of the enemy's works.

As soon as the out line of our fort could be distinguished, the enemy carried out their programme. It had been arranged, as a special compliment to the venerable Edmund Ruffin, who might almost be called the father of secession, that he should fire the first shot against us, from the Stevens battery on Cummings Point, and I think in all the histories it is stated that he did so; but it is attested by Dr. Crawford and others who were on the parapet at the time, that the first shot really came from the mortar battery at Fort Johnson. Almost immediately afterward a ball from Cummings Point lodged in the magazine wall, and by the sound seemed to bury itself in the masonry about a foot from my head, in very unpleasant proximity to my right ear. This is the one that probably came with Mr. Ruffin's compliments. In a moment the firing burst forth in one continuous roar, and large patches of both the exterior and interior masonry began to crumble and fall in all directions. The place where I was had been used for the manufacture of cartridges, and there was still a good deal of powder there, some packed and some loose. A shell soon struck near the ventilator, and a puff of dense smoke entered the room, giving me a strong impression that there would be an immediate explosion. Fortunately, no sparks had penetrated inside.

Nineteen batteries were now hammering at us, and the balls and shells from the ten-inch columbiads, accompanied by shells from the thirteen-inch mortars which constantly bombarded us, made us feel as if the war had commenced in earnest.

When it was broad daylight, I went down to breakfast. I found the officers already assembled at one of the long tables in the mess-hall. Our party were calm, and even somewhat merry. We had retained one colored man to wait on us. He was a spruce-looking mulatto from Charleston, very active and demoralized by the thunder of the guns and crashing of the shot around us. He leaned back against the wall, almost white with fear, his eyes closed, and his whole expression one of perfect despair. Our meal was not very sumptuous. It consisted of pork and water, Dr. Crawford triumphantly brought forth a little farina, which he had found in a corner of the hospital.

When this frugal repast was over, my company was told off in three details for firing purposes, to be relieved afterward by Seymour's company. As I was the ranking officer, I took the first detachment, and marched them to the casements, which looked out upon the powerful iron-clad battery of Cummings Point.

In aiming the first gun fired against the rebellion I had no feeling of self-reproach, for I fully believed that the contest was inevitable, and was not of our seeking. The United States was called upon not only to defend its sovereignty, but its right to exist as a nation. The only alternative was to submit to a powerful oligarchy who were determined to make freedom forever subordinate to slavery. To me it was simply a contest, politically speaking, as to whether virtue or vice should rule.

My first shot bounded off from the sloping roof of the battery opposite without producing any apparent effect. It seemed useless to attempt to silence the guns there; for our metal was not heavy enough to batter the work down, and every ball glanced harmlessly off, except one, which appeared to enter an embrasure and twist the iron shutter, so as to stop the firing of that particular gun.

I observed that a group of the enemy had ventured out from their intrenchments to watch the effect of their fire, but I sent them flying back to their shelter by the aid of a forty-two-pounder ball, which appeared to strike right in among them.

Assistant-surgeon Crawford, having no sick in hospital, volunteered to take command of one of the detachments. He and Lieutenant Davis were detailed at the same time with me; and I soon heard their guns on the opposite side of the fort, echoing my own. They attacked Fort Moultrie with great vigor.

Our firing now became regular, and was answered from the rebel guns which encircled us on the four sides of the pentagon upon which the fort was built. The other side faced the open sea. Showers of balls from ten-inch columbiads and forty-two-pounders, and shells from thirteen-inch mortars poured into the fort in one incessant stream, causing great flakes of masonry to fall in all directions. When the immense mortar shells, after sailing high in the air, came down in a vertical direction, and buried themselves in the parade-ground, their explosion shook the fort like an earthquake.

After three hours' firing, my men became exhausted, and Captain Seymour came, with a fresh detachment, to relieve us. He has a great deal of humor in his composition, and said, jocosely, "Doubleday, what in the world is the matter here, and what is all this uproar about?"

I replied, "There is a trifling difference of opinion between us and our neighbors opposite, and we are trying to settle it."

"Very well," he said; "do you wish me to take a hand?"

I said, "Yes, I would like to have you go in."

"All right," he said. "What is your elevation, and range?"

I replied, "Five degrees, and twelve hundred yards."

"Well," he said, "here goes!" And he went to work with a will.

Charles Woodward Hutson

(1840–1936)

A twenty-one-year-old college graduate, Hutson enlisted in Charleston for the Washington Light Infantry, which became Company A of Wade Hampton's Legion. Hutson saw action as an infantryman during the first two years of the war and then served with the Beauford Artillery in South and North Carolina until the war ended. He was wounded at the first battle of Manassas, captured at Seven Pines, and imprisoned for three months until exchanged. After the war, he went on to a career as a college professor, writer, and painter.

The following selection from his letters home to his parents tells them of his part in the Confederate victory at Manassas. He wrote the letter the day after the battle while recovering from a wound to his head, and his lines capture the excitement of the first major battle of the Civil War. Although thrilled to have survived, Hutson begins to realize the cost modern weapons exact. Expecting a quick victory, he hopes to get back to his unit before it enters Washington, but his enthusiasm is tempered by anxiety over the fate of his many friends who participated in the battle. The thrill of victory and rhetoric about the glorious cause compete for center stage with concerns over the human cost of war in Hutson's eloquent letter.

from Hutson's Letters

22d July 1861, Monday
University at Charlottesville

Dear Mother and Father,

I have been in a great and bloody battle and am wounded. Do not be at all alarmed. It is only a flesh wound in the head and as the ball grazed the skull and glanced, there can be no danger. It is only through the Lord's great mercy that we were not cut to pieces to a man, so fearful were the odds opposed to our division. Friday night the six infantry companies of Hampton's Legion took the train for Manassas. So slowly did we travel that it was Sunday morning before we reached that point. Our breakfast was not cooked, when we heard the booming of artillery in the direction of Bull's Run. Orders presently came that we should hasten to the field as soon as we had eaten something. In fifteen minutes more we commenced our march for the field of battle. We were taken around to the left of the place where the engagement began, in order that we might secure against a surprise of the Camp at Manassas. This was evidently the game of the enemy. They played us a ruse, the heavy cannonading near Bull's Run was intended to deceive Beauregard into meeting them at that point with his whole force. Meanwhile an immense body of their troops advanced on the left with the intention of outflanking our main army, getting into our rear and seizing our fortified camp. They were held in check, however, by a few battalions, including our own and two Georgia regiments and perhaps one or two more. The whole battle was fought not far from the base of mountains, and the ground was very hilly: so that they were unable to perceive the immense disparity between their numbers and ours. Had they known how few were the forces between them and Camp Manassas, they would doubtless have advanced more confidently: and every man of us would have fallen upon the field. As it were, their movements were irresolute: they advanced and retreated alternately, and I suppose later in the day Beauregard must have come up with his main force to the assistance of our shattered columns; and then commenced the rout of the enemy. Terribly disproportioned as was our force, we held them in check for at least three hours. Nor was the disparity in numbers alone: the enemy were armed with the six-shooting revolving rifle, and their fire was incessant. Never have I conceived of such a continuous, rushing hailstorm of shot, shell and musketry as fell around and among us for hours together. We, who escaped, are constantly wondering how we could possibly have come out of the action alive. The words I used just now, "we, who escaped," have a sad, sad sound to us, for we know not yet who are to be included in that category, and are filled with terrible anxieties as to the fate of dear friends.

I must trace now to you my own course through the action, which I can or ought to do clearly enough, since I was cool and confident from first to last, knowing where my trust was placed, that no real harm could befall me and that there was a duty before me which I must perform at every hazard. All of our men behaved gallantly, though few were free from excitement.

After being marched and countermarched for some time almost within reach of the enemy's missiles, we were thrown, by order of Gen. Bee who commanded in that part of the field, to the left of a corps of Flying Artillery (I think the "Washington" of New Orleans), under shelter of a fence. Here we were first exposed to the hissing balls of the enemy, but the men took aim deliberately and stood fire beautifully. The artillery having then withdrawn from our side, we marched down the hill, unfortunately in disorder. We were halted halfway down in a hollow place, where we had the protection of a few trees and bushes. Here, seeing that our men hesitated to fire upon the force below, because doubtful whether they were not friends, I entreated the Captain to let me advance alone near enough to the ranks of those who were firing upon us to ascertain whether they were Federals or Confederates. But the Captain would not consent, and wished to go himself; this, however, Col. Hampton would not permit. Seeing I could do nothing there, I attempted to persuade our men not to dodge, satisfied that we could never keep orderly ranks as long as the men persisted in dodging. But all my efforts in this line were unavailing: the men were fearless and advanced undauntingly enough; but, I suppose they thought dodging was a "help," anyhow, to escape from the balls. Iredell Jones and the officers kept erect, and neither they nor I were any the worse for it. Our next advance was to a fence in the valley at the bottom of the hill. Here we made a stand, and here our Company fought absolutely alone, the other Legionary Companies having retreated to a yard at the top of the hill where houses gave them shelter. Here they reformed. Meanwhile, our men were subjected to a raking fire. I was the first who fell. I had put on my spectacles, taken good aim and fired my first shot. As I was in the act of re-loading, a rifle-ball struck me in the head, a little above the forehead; and the violence of the concussion felled me to the earth immediately. I drew off my spectacles and flung them aside; and not believing my wound a bad one, as it was not painful, I attempted to reload. But the blood was gushing over my face and blinding my eyes; and I found it impossible to do so. I knew pretty well the extent of my wound, as I had probed it with my finger as I fell: and as the gash seemed to be a deep one, I feared faintness would ensue from loss of blood, especially as there was a large puddle of it where I first lay. So, I put aside my gun for awhile, and put my white handkerchief inside my hat upon the wound and tied my silk one around the hat. By the time I had finished these precautions, the company were in retreat; and with Jones and a few others I made my way to the clump of trees, whence we had advanced. Here protected by the trees I squatted down, these few detached from the company continued the fire. Jones haven given me some water from his canteen, and my eyes being by this time wiped pretty dry of the blood, I again attempted to reload. But before I could do so, a ball from the enemy shattered my rifle to pieces. I now made the best of my way to the shelter of the house on the hill, the shell and the shot of the enemy ploughing up the ground at every step I took, and the musketry rattling like hail around me. I lay behind the house quite exhausted, and much pained by the sight of some of my comrades badly wounded. Dr. Taylor examined my wound here, and charged me to use all my strength to reach the Hospital. While I lay here the body of Lieut. Col. Johnson was brought into the yard and stretched at my side. He had been shot dead a few moments before, while riding fearlessly up and down the field.

I remained at this place, until the companies there began to retreat yet farther back; when, seizing my smashed gun I hurried along by the gullies and other protecting places to a field beyond the line of the missiles, which before flew so thick and fast around me. At the extremity of this field was a house used as a temporary hospital. This place I reached, and after resting awhile, walked to the wagons in the yard used to convey the wounded to the Camp.

The ride in was a long and tedious one, and I very soon became aware that had I ventured to remain longer on the field, I should soon have dropped and been only a burden to retreating friends, or else have run the risk of falling into the enemy's hands—a risk which I would have resolved, if possible, by forcing them to cut me down.

When I reached the Camp, I found many wounded comrades there, who were under treatment. As the Hospital was crowded with groaning men, some undergoing the agonies of amputation, I very gladly accepted the kind attention of a gentleman named Lamotte, who soon proved that he understood well the art of dressing wounds. He trimmed closely the hair around mine, washed out the clotted blood, bathed the wound, ascertained that there was no split in the portion of the skull exposed, and bound up my head nicely for me, strengthening me also with a glass of excellent whiskey. I felt much more comfortably, when this was done, and the encrusted blood, which stuck like a black mask to my face, was washed. Much of my hair is still clotted with blood.

After getting a little supper and having deliberated on what would be our wisest course, most of us wounded who were safe in camp concluded that, as no tents were pitched and we could not be cared for properly there, it would be best to go down on the evening train to Culpepper C. H. where the hospitals are. The cars were crowded with the wounded. At Culpepper we found that accommodations could not be found for all; and some of us came on to Charlottesville, where we already perceive that we shall not want for gentle tending. I am writing now on a marble table in a hall of the University, where the wounded are lodged. Two of my Company, Atkinson and Gardner, are with me, the former wounded like myself in the head, the latter in the wrist and side. Before we left Camp we heard that the enemy had suffered heavy loss, were in full retreat, and that Beauregard was in hot pursuit. Many regiments lost almost all their staff-officers: two Georgia ones lost all. Col. Hampton was, by one report, dangerously wounded; by another, dead. Our Adjutant, Barker, was also said to be dead. The Legionary infantry was certainly much cut to pieces. Our cavalry and artillery were not in the action, not having arrived yet. All the forces, on both sides, must have been engaged; and if the enemy have met with a serious defeat, I imagine it will be the last general engagement. Patterson was taken and Col. Scott killed. Many prisoners were taken. Before we left, fifty eight were brought into the camp at Manassas. The battle lasted all day, and was very bloody. Early as it was when I was forced to retire, I met few who were not hurt.

I brought off my knapsack with me, and will be quite comfortable. We are very uneasy about our friends yet unheard from. Many, I fear, whom I care greatly for are now mangled or dead. At the last accounts, Conner was leading our shattered Legion and perhaps other officerless battalions, and pressing on the rear of the enemy within two miles of Centreville. I trust he yet survives. I long to hear how the Carolina regiments fared. Kershaw's was in the battle, and you know I have many friends among them.

As soon as my wound permits, I intend returning to Manassas and making every effort to rejoin the Army, wherever it may be. I hope to be able to bear arms again, before we enter Washington. You will see, by my writing so long a letter that I am in no danger from my wound. My head feels heavy, and the place throbs—that is all. I hope you are not too much troubled. My love to sisters and all the dear kinsfolk and friends.

Your Ever Loving Son
C. Woodward Hutson

How we ought continually to thank God for the mercies which he does so unceasingly show us!

The Dr. here has just dressed my wound, says it is an inch and a half long and would have gone deeper had it not struck the bone, says I am a very hard-headed fellow. He is a kindly, merry gentleman, and I like him much. He asked me if I was not related to Willy Wigg, knowing him well and knowing his middle name.

James K. Newton

(1843–1892)

Born and raised on a farm in DePere, Wisconsin, James K. Newton left his job as a schoolteacher and enlisted in Company F of the 14th Wisconsin Volunteer Infantry. He emerges from his letters as an articulate, intelligent, and independent American voice. Although he supported Lincoln, he remained anti-abolitionist. He had pride in his unit and faith in the cause of the Union, but he disliked the army and did not want to see the South devastated.

During his service, he was captured at Corinth, Mississippi, and paroled in time to take part in the Vicksburg campaign. Reenlisting in 1863, he marched in General Banks's plagued Louisiana and Texas campaign and fought in Arkansas and Missouri against Sterling Price. Shortly before his muster out of service in 1865, he was commissioned a lieutenant. He returned to teaching first at Ripon, then Oberlin College, where he became a full professor of languages in 1875.

His first battle was Shiloh, and in the following letter, he describes the shock of battle on the citizen-turned-soldier to his parents. His request for newspapers is an example of our need for words and stories to make sense out of the chaos of combat.

Newton's "A Letter to Family, 12 April 1862"

Pittsburgh Landing
Somewhere in the wilderness in west Tennessee
Saturday April 12, 1862

Dear Father & Mother
& all the Family

It is with a feeling of thankfulness that I sit down to write these few lines; to think that I have been spared when so many others have fallen. I suppose by the time you receive this that you will have heard all about the battle of Pittsburgh Landing (as I suppose it will be called). All that I need say about the 14th is that they didn't run.

Last Sunday morning about daylight the cannon began to boom up the river about ten miles & every one began to speculate as to what was the matter up there. In a few hours all sorts of rumors reached the camp but from what source I dont know. One report was that the 18th Wis was all cut to pieces & that report was as near true as it could be. The next report was that our men were completely whipped out & that they were running in every direction & after we got up here we found it just about so. About 4 o'clock in the afternoon there came an order for us to get ready to march in half an hour to reinforce our men up the river. We dropped everything at once and started for the boat taking nothing with us but our arms & blankets. After we got down to the boat we found that we would have to wait for more men to come because they wouldn't let one Regt go up the river alone, so we waited until about 9 o'clock in the evening when they got together 17,000 men & we came up the river in company. While we lay at the dock in Savanna a boat came down the river with the Col & Lieut Col of the 18th Wis, both of them badly wounded. The Col has since died.

When we reached Pittsburgh which we did about 11 o'clock that night, we found that our force still held the bank of the river where they were formed in line of battle, while the Secesh had formed another line of battle about 100 rods in front of us. Our Regt was formed on the right of the line where we stood all night while it rained like shot all the time, we didn't think until then what good service our India rubber blankets would do us. As it was we kept ourselves comparatively dry though we had to stand up all the time to do so.

Well daylight came at last but it was an awful long time coming. As soon as our pickets could see the Secesh pickets they began to fire into them. They returned the fire for a while but finally retired. Our pickets then fell back upon the main body. In a few minutes our whole line began to move toward the enemy. Our Regt was held back as a reserve for a while & there we lay right in the mud while a perfect storm of shot and shell grape & canister flew by in the air over our heads.

A battery of artillery soon came to our assistance & opened on the Rebels, they kept it up nearly half an hour before our battery silenced theirs, when all at once a lot of Secesh who had advanced under cover of their battery opened fire right in our faces. The order was then given for us to advance & then we found out what it was to fight a battle. The first man that was wounded in our company was Chas Vincent; he was shot through the leg. All that I remember for a while after that was that I loaded as fast as possible and wherever I saw a Secesh I shot at him, & that was what every one there did.

There is no use in trying to describe the battle because I can not do it. All I know about it is that we drove the rebels & they drove us & then we would drive them again. We charged on one of their batteries and took it & then they charged in their turn and we couldn't hold it so we spiked the guns & set fire to their cartridges so that They couldn't use it on us any more. The next time we charged on that battery we were supported & kept it. We were advancing & retreating all the time until afternoon, before we got the upper hand of the Secesh but when we once got it we drove them rapidly until 4 o'clock in [the] afternoon when our Cavalry & artillery came in ahead of us and pursued them until after dark while we fell back to the river and got together as well as possible.

It rained that night and the next night & we stood out in line both nights & then the worst of it was that we couldn't get any thing to eat but hard bread and not much of that. The morning after the fight the Regt was got together and it was found that we had lost between 20 & 30 killed and somewhere about 100 wounded. One Co lost 5 killed. Our Co lost two killed & five wounded.

As for myself I came off without a scratch and I am sure I don't know why it was for I stood as good a chance as any of them to get hurt. A good many of the boys came to the conclusion after the battle that the Secesh shot awful careless with their guns, and I guess all of the Co are perfectly satisfied as to what war is & they would be willing to have the war brought to an end so they could be discharged and sent home.

Dennis Murphy distinguished himself considerably on the field, in fact he behaved nobly. He was the one who avenged poor Putnam. Dennis shot down the rebel who murdered Putnam before he could take his gun from his face. I hear that his name was sent in the report to Washington for brave conduct on the field.

Our Capt behaved as brave as any of them. There was a good deal of speculation as to how he would behave on the field of battle. A good many folks thought that he wouldn't "stand fire" but he did a good deal better than others that were thought to be so brave but when they came to be tried it was found they were not made of the right stuff. . . .

Uncle's advice to us boys was to put our trust in the Lord and "give them Jesse." I guess by the time that you receive this he will have found out that we followed his advice before he gave it. If you get hold of a paper with the particulars of the battle in it I wish you would send it down here. All we know about the battle is what we saw & that wasn't much, so I would like to see a paper if possible to see what we did do.

I suppose you are making sugar "like everything" nowadays. How I would like to call in and see you about this time and get some to eat. I got a piece of soft bread yesterday for the first time since I left St. Louis. I needn't tell you, I guess, that I could eat it without butter. Give my respects to all enquiring friends with much love,

I remain
Your Affectionate Son
James

An Anonymous Eyewitness
at Shiloh

This anonymous account of the Battle of Shiloh graphically describes a soldier's view of the battlefield. One of many random newspaper and periodical clippings collected and published by an unknown anthologist named Frank Moore, this report is not at all typical of the majority of sentimental and anecdotal pieces that make up his collection, *The Civil War in Song and Story: 1860–1865*. Overall, Moore's collection of "tragic incidents, humorous episodes, and brilliant and heroic adventures of the conflict," as he calls his book in the introduction, makes the Civil War more a good-natured outdoor adventure than a national tragedy. Every so often, however, the reader comes across a graphic description of war's carnage.

The author of the Shiloh piece obviously exaggerates the ironic distance between normal civilian life and the brutal scene before him. He contrasts the social coffee break in the warm Tennessee sunshine with the aftermath of the battle; he enjoys the peace of sleep only to wake and find himself among mutilated corpses; and he takes his midday meal midst the pieces of an enemy soldier. Exaggerated irony, his chosen rhetorical means of sharing a new-found awareness of the horrors of battle, registers his shock at the brutality.

from (Anon.) *"Reminiscences of Shiloh"*

[An eyewitness gives the following pictures of the battlefield of Shiloh]:

"On that peaceful Sunday morning of April 6, 1862, the sun was rising with splendor. I had walked out to enjoy the fresh air, and, returning by my friend Lieut. D's tent, I called upon him. Said he, 'H, take a cup of coffee; I have found some milk.' 'Don't care if I do,' said I. 'I always write home on Sunday morning, and like to do it over a good cup of coffee.' 'Yes, I mean to write my little wife,' said D. 'I expect to resign soon. Don't you want a pair of new shoulder-straps, H., and brand new pair of gauntlets?' I told D. I would take them; and in a moment left his tent, after making him promise to take tea with me.

"But how were things at tea time? D. was mangled and dead, lying by the roadside, at the hospital by the Landing, with hundreds of others, and I had passed the most momentous day of my life—had participated (I am since told creditably) in one of the greatest battles, exceeding in fury, courage, waste, stupendousness, and gallantry, the wildest dreams of my youth. Should your happy city, on some bright Sunday morning, be sunk, with all its life, by an earthquake, and the cold waves rolling over it in eternal solitude before night, the change could be no more unexpected, nor could it come upon you with more bewildering and stunning suddenness and awfulness. On the evening of the 5th, the 18th Wisconsin infantry arrived, and were assigned to General Prentiss's division, on the front. Said Colonel ———, who had preceded them, looking for the General's quarters, 'Here they come— the bully boys—they weigh just 166 pounds apiece. Just left home six days ago.' The 18th Wisconsin cooked their first suppers in the field that night at nine o'clock, and wrapped themselves in their blankets, to be awakened by the roar of battle, and receive, thus early, their bloody baptism. Before they had been on the field one day, their magnificent corps was decimated, most of the officers killed—the proud and exultant Colonel among the dead.

"I saw an intelligent looking man with his whole diaphragm torn off. He was holding nearly all his viscera with both hands and arms. His face expressed a longing for assistance and an apprehension of fatality.

"On going to the field the second day, our regiment strode on the line over wounded, dying, and dead. My office detaching me from the lines, I had the opportunity to notice incidents about the field. The regiment halted amidst a gory, ghastly scene. I heard a voice calling, 'Ho, friend! ho! for God's sake, come here.' I went to a gory pile of dead human forms in every kind of stiff contortion; I saw one arm raised, beckoning me. I found there a rebel, covered with clotted blood, pillowing his head on the dead body of a comrade. Both were red from head to foot. The dead man's brains had gushed out in a reddish and grayish mass over his face. The live one had lain across him all that horrible, long night in the storm. The first thing he said to me was, 'Give me some water. Send me a surgeon—won't you! O God! What made you come down here to fight us? We never would have come up there.' And then he affectionately put one arm over the form, and laid his bloody face against the cold, clammy, bloody face of his dead friend. I filled his canteen nearly—reserving some for myself—knowing I might be in the same sad condition. I told him we had no surgeon in our regiment, and that we would have to suffer, if wounded, the same as he; that other regiments were coming, and to call on them for a surgeon; that they were humane. 'Forward!' shouted the Colonel; and 'Forward!' was repeated by the officers. I left him.

"The above recalls to mind one of the hardest principles in warfare—where your sympathy and humanity are appealed to, and from sense of expediency you are forbidden to exercise it. After our regiment had been nearly annihilated, and were compelled to retreat under a galling fire, a boy was supporting his dying brother on one arm, and trying to drag him from the field and the advancing foe. He looked at me imploringly, and said: 'Captain, help him—won't you? Do, Captain; he'll live.' I said: 'He's shot through the head; don't you see? and can't live—he's dying now.' 'O, no, he ain't, Captain. Don't leave me.' I was forced to reply: 'The rebels won't hurt him. Lay him down and come, or both you and I will be lost.' The rush of bullets and the yells of the approaching demons hurried me away—leaving the young soldier over his dying brother.

"Nearly every rebel's face turned black immediately after death. Union men's faces retained their natural pallor two or three days.

"I ate my dinner on Monday within six paces of a rebel in four pieces. Both legs were blown off. His pelvis was the third piece, and his head and chest were the fourth piece. Those four pieces occupied a space of twelve feet square. I saw five dead rebels in a row, with their heads knocked off by a round shot. Myself and other amateur anatomists, when the regiment was resting temporarily on arms, would leave to examine the internal structure of man. We would examine brains, heart, stomach, layers of muscles, structure of bones, &c,. for there was every form of mutilation. At home I used to wince at the sight of a wound or of a corpse; but here, in one day, I learned to be among the scenes I am describing without emotion—as perfectly cool as I am now.

My friend, Adjutant ———, and myself, on the second night, looking in the dark for a place to lie down, he said, 'Let's lie down here. Here's some fellows sleeping.' We slept in quiet until dawn revealed that we had passed a night among sprawling, stiffened, ghastly corpses.

"I saw one of our dead soldiers with his mouth crammed full of cartridges until the cheeks were bulged out. Several protruded from his mouth. This was done by the rebels.

"On the third day most of our time was employed in burying the dead. Shallow pits were dug, which would soon fill with water. Into these we threw our comrades with a heavy splash, or a dump against solid bottom. Many a hopeful, promising youth thus indecently ended his career. Some of our boys were disposed to kick the Secesh into these pits. One fell in with a heavy dump on his face. The more humane proposed to turn him over. 'O, that'll do, ' said a Union Missourian, 'for when he scratches, he'll scratch nearer hell.' This is a hard story, I know, but I want you to see real war.

"I stood in one place in the woods near the spot of the engagement of the 57th Illinois, and counted eighty-one dead rebels. There I saw one tree, seven inches in diameter, with thirty-one bullet holes. Such had been death's storm. Near the scenes of the last of the fighting, where the rebels precipitately retreated, I saw one grave containing one hundred and thirty-seven dead rebels, and one side of it another grave containing forty-one dead Federals. Several of the trenches were in view from that spot.

"One dead and uniformed officer lay covered with a little housing of rails. On it was a fly-leaf of a memorandum-book with the pencil-writing: 'Federals, respect my father's corpse.' Many of our boys wanted to cut off his buttons and gold cord; but our Colonel had the body religiously guarded.

"Many of our regiments were paid off just previously to the battle, and our dead comrades were robbed of hundreds of thousands of dollars. The rebels were surprised and abashed at the apparent wealth of our army. They attired themselves in our uniforms, and rifled from officers' trunks tens of thousands of dollars worth of fine clothing, toilet articles, and interesting souvenirs of every man's trunk. They made themselves stupid and drunk over our fine victuals and wines. They seem to have gone mad with the lust of plunder.

"To show how complete and successful was the advance of the

enemy, their advance guard lay in the woods on the 5th, witnessing our parades and reviews. One of our returned paroled prisoners, a mule-driver, who was captured two days before the battle, had told me that he was taken through their whole army, which was camped three miles from ours, the night before the attack.

"A resident here told me that on the retreat of the rebel army from Shiloh, it was utterly routed and demoralized.

"After the battle was over, we, formerly citizens who had never seen or heard the hiss of bullet, gathered the mangled corpses of those we had known at home and joked with the day before—friends who were as full of life, hope, and ambition as ourselves—and buried them in blankets, or sent them home in boxes, with as little concern as possible, and went immediately to joking and preparing to fight again. What spirit or principle was it that in one day gave us all the indifference and stoicism of veterans?

"Two women, laundresses in the 16th Wisconsin, running to the rear when the attack was commenced, were killed.

"My poor friend Carson—the scout—after having fought, and worked, and slaved for the beginning of the war, unrequited, comparatively, and after passing hundreds of hair-breadth escapes, and through this wild battle, was killed by almost the last shot. A round shot took off his whole face and fore part of his head. Poor Carson! We all remember your patriotism, your courage, your devotion. We will cheer all we can, the bereaved and dear ones you have left.

"Surgeons on the field would halt officers and order them to strip off their white shirts for bandages. Many an officer, halted on the field tore off his accouterments and uniform to provide the necessary bandages."

John Haley

(1840–1921)

An independent-minded enlisted man from Maine, John Haley served in Company I, 17th Maine Volunteer Regiment, from August 7, 1862, the day the regiment was formed, until June 10, 1865, the day it was mustered out. He characterized himself as a "poor fighter" and his army career as "successful mediocrity," but his combat record belies his modest assessment. He fought in more than his share of battles, including Po River, Fredericksburg, Chancellorsville, Gettysburg, Wilderness, Spotsylvania, Cold Harbor, and Petersburg. Recording most of his experiences within twenty-four hours of the events described, he also kept a thorough diary.

After the war, he transcribed his war notebooks into what he called "Haley's Chronicles, 1862–1865 with Some Observations and Comments Thereon, Some Wise, Some Otherwise, All True." They reflect his disdain for the Irish and Negro, his dislike of officers, and his protests of the horrors of war. In the following selection, Haley talks about the incongruity of "political arguments" and the horrible effects of battle. He quotes poetry and talks about how the "very elements" stood still. His view that war is a perversion of nature and that it has nothing to do with politics is a far cry from Oliver Wendell Holmes, Jr's., which we read at the end of this chapter. Haley's description of the Battle of Gettysburg provides a revealing glimpse of an American consciousness dismayed by the harsh realities of combat.

from Haley's Civil War Journal

July 1st.

We made no move until noon, when we bivouacked near the college grounds. Close by is a gap in the mountains where it was feared the

Rebel cavalry might make a dash and get in the rear of our army. We could guard this gap with a small force, so two brigades of Birney's division were left and the rest of the corps moved on to Gettysburg. The 1st Corps (Reynolds's) and the 11th Corps (Howard's) met the enemy there early in the morning and, with Buford's cavalry, kept them at bay. Reynolds was killed in the early part of the day and the command devolved on Howard's unit until the arrival of Hancock about 4 p.m. (There seems to be a disposition on the part of some to overlook the fact that General Howard is entitled to a portion of the credit for securing the position of defense on Cemetery Hill and for holding it several hours.)

The brigades of de Trobriand and Ward passed the night here. We threw out pickets and then laid us down to dream and to dread the morrow. Now that we have encountered Lee's army, we expect a battle no less spirited than that of Antietam.

July 2nd.

We are turned out about 3 o'clock and ordered to get breakfast though we hadn't a solitary thing to lay our jaws to except coffee. Some hadn't even this. The first order was followed by another to move immediately, so we started and marched until we hauled up for coffee. Before the water was even warm, an aide came from General Birney telling us to move right on. No delay must be allowed as we were in danger of being cut off from the rest of the army.

Lee's army was extending to the left and wheeling around so as to envelop our left and cover the road we were then on. We moved with all diligence and marched four or five miles, halting again, by General de Trobriand's order, to make coffee. The same result as before: another imperative to move right away. Not a moment too soon was this order obeyed; less than fifteen minutes after we passed, the Rebels swung around across the Emmettsburg Road in rear of our column. It is a wonder that we were not treated to a demoralizing flank fire. Nothing but ignorance of our presence explains this lack of attention on the part of the Confederates. As we came up the Emmettsburg Road, we had an army on each side of us. There was considerable firing going on, with the bullets whistling over our heads, and we seemed to be in considerable danger.

We met a large number of citizens coming from Gettysburg and going toward the Rebels. They were loaded down with bedding and clothing, probably all that some of them saved from their burning houses. About two miles from the town, we turned off to the right into the fields and moved to the rear some distance. We came to a lane and turned to the right near to what was called the Peach Orchard and also near the house of one Rose. It was about 10 a.m. when we arrived and commenced maneuvering, but we didn't settle into position until 3 p.m., when we finally got into line in rear of a strip of woods not far from the Emmettsburg Road, slightly to the right of Sherfy's Peach Orchard.

Our line had been formed less than an hour when the picket firing, until now quite slack, became exceedingly lively and gave evidence of something of a more serious character. We double-quicked down to the left, across a wheat field, and came to a front in rear of a stone wall. The right of the regiment was protected only by a rail fence bordering a piece of woods through which the Rebels were rapidly advancing. Aided by the stone wall, we opposed ourselves to their further progress and, for a time, were quite successful. The Confederate advance was very impetuous, and our skirmish line, although exceptionally heavy, was brushed away as chaff before a wind. This was due to no fault on the part of the skirmishers, but to the size and momentum of the attacking column, which comprised nearly one-half of Lee's army—the flower of it at that. By the time our line was formed, the Rebel column had arrived at the opposite edge of the woods, and although we opened a brisk fire on them from behind the wall, it didn't seem to check them much. As they drew nearer, our fire began to tell on their ranks, which were more dense than usual. We peppered them well with musketry while Randolph's battery, which was on a gentle rise in rear of us, served a dose of grape and canister every few seconds.

There was a dreadful buzzing of bullets and other missiles, highly suggestive of an obituary notice for a goodly number of Johnny Rebs, and we could see them tumbling around right lively. A great number of our own men were sharing the same fate. I'm confident that we could have held a reasonable force at bay, but they were strongly reinforced. Our ammunition now began to run low and the troops on our right, being flanked, gave way, exposing us to a heavy flank fire. The troops who gave way had only a rail fence in front of them, while we had a stone wall, which sheltered us well until our flank was uncovered. Even then we didn't hurry about leaving. The batteries in our rear still continued to pour destruction into the Rebel ranks, and it seemed nothing short of annihilation would stop them.

At this point, while shot, shell, spherical case, and canister filled the air, General de Trobriand, our brigade commander, rode down into the wheat field and inquired, "What troops are those holding the stone wall so stubbornly?" On learning it was the 17th Maine, one of his regiments, he ordered us to "Fall back, right away!" But we didn't hear the order. It isn't often that an order to fall back in a battlefield is disregarded. The old fellow didn't quite comprehend this state of ours. We had good reason for our action. This stone wall was a great protection and the Rebels were straining every nerve to get possession of it for the same purpose. So, we held it till our ammunition was exhausted and we had used all we could find on the dead and wounded. If we could hold on until reinforcements or a supply of ammunition came, all would be well. Otherwise, no one could tell what direful woes might befall us. We knew the fate of the army hung on the result.

General Birney, our division commander, next came down and ordered us away from the wall, saying we were in grave danger of capture. We knew that the moment we abandoned our position the Rebels would seize it. But we couldn't hold it without ammunition, and as the troops on our right gave way, we saw it was now time for us to go. We fell back a short distance, and as we ceased firing the Rebs advanced to the wall. Some of them climbed over it and began to press us so hard General de Trobriand ordered us to make a stand. We told him we were destitute of ammunition.

"Then you must hold them with the bayonet," said he.

We halted and formed under his direction. This checked them momentarily, but only a moment, for they saw our condition and knew they had the field unless someone came to our aid. One other thing gave them great confidence: They had been told that the Army of the Potomac had not yet arrived and that they were facing only raw troops.

At this time a portion of the 5th Corps was thrown in to reinforce or relieve us. No sooner did they encounter the enemy than they broke, and the first thing we knew they were running past us to the rear and leaving us to the Rebels closing in on three sides. The battery on the knoll poured the grape and canister into their ranks but some of them came up to the guns and were literally blown from their muzzles. Blood poured out like water. Both sides understood the value of this position: If the enemy could take it, they would have the key to our line and would be between us and Washington. Nothing seemed to stop them, and it was a foregone conclusion that the game was nearly up. Some of our men cried as they beheld the victorious Rebels advancing and no resistance being offered.

We had hoped for victory. Had we been properly supported and supplied, it is morally certain that things would not have gone this way. Now it looked decidedly black, but in the midst of our gloom and despondency, a gleam of hope and light darted across our line of vision. A cheer rent the air and was heard above the din of battle and the Rebel yell. The 6th Corps, or a portion of it, had just arrived from Westminster, thirty-six miles away, in time to swing into line and give the exultant Rebels a volley in the face and eyes, which staggered them. It was our turn to show the Johnnies that they had met something more than the "raw militia of Pennsylvania," and they fell back to the region of the wheat field. We bivouacked near the Taneytown Road for the night. How any of us escaped is a mystery that eternity alone can unravel.

Soon after the arrival of the 6th Corps, General Sickles lost his leg and was carried off the field in a ambulance. He was smoking, as coolly as if nothing had happened. General Birney assumed immediate command of the corps, which, with the 2nd, was under command of General Hancock.

Sickles is a great favorite with this corps. The men fairly worship him. He is every inch a soldier and looks like a game cock. No one questions his bravery or patriotism. Before the war he killed a man who had seduced his wife. A person who has the nerve to do that might be expected to show good qualities as a general where daredeviltry is a factor.

But I must continue my account of the deeds of this day and the effects thereof. The 6th Corps relieved us about 6 o'clock. An injured companion and myself were very nearly surrounded by the Rebs when, at this point, we encountered the division of the 6th Corps coming into line. They checked the advancing foe and saved the day. The last wave of Rebel aggression was stayed and began to recede from the ridge in rear of the wheat field. We fell back near the Baltimore Pike and bivouacked, tired and hungry, for no rations had yet appeared.

Company I suffered as little as any in the battle: We lost two non-commissioned officers, corporals Mitchell and Robertson, mortally wounded. Privates Stacy, Jordan, Kimball, Roberts, and Brand were treated to Rebel mementoes in various parts of their anatomies. Lieutenant Adams had his finger torn off, and Tasker's gun had a Rebel bullet welded into it.

Other companies suffered greater losses. Those on the right, in rear of the rail fence, had it much worse. On our left, at the Devil's Den and near Round Top, there were some hand-to-hand encounters, sticks and stones doing valiant service. The 20th Maine saved Round Top, while the 3d, 4th, 16th, and 17th did their share in the day's work. Our gain was slight, but we have prevented Lee's forces from carrying out their design. Lee threw in half of his army, so a repulse was more than we had any reason even to hope for. Thus, we feel much cause for congratulation ourselves.

July 3rd.

We turned out early. Hunger had such a grip on us that it dragged us forth. Most had not eaten in thirty-six hours and felt we could devour a horse or a mule, provided it hadn't been too long defunct. The teams with rations didn't arrive until 9 o'clock. After filling up, we had orders to take position in rear of the 6th Corps, somewhat to the right of where we were engaged yesterday. During the forenoon there was nothing but an occasional crack of the pickets' rifles, and we rested on our arms.

Shortly after noon there were signs of activity in the Confederate lines. Artillery was being massed on Seminary Ridge and the same was true of infantry, although the woods concealed them. About 1 o'clock the Rebel cannon opened on us, and ours were soon replying. For two hours there was probably the greatest artillery duel ever fought on this planet. The air seethed with old iron. Death and destruction were everywhere. Men and horses mangled and bleeding; trees, rocks, and fences ripped and torn. Shells, solid shot, and spherical case shot screamed, hissed, and rattled in every direction. Men hugged the ground and sought safety behind hillocks, boulders, ledges, stone walls, bags of grain—anything that could give or suggest shelter from this storm of death.

We hardly knew what it meant, but some of our generals did, and preparations were made accordingly. General Hunt, chief of artillery, ordered our gunners to cease firing in order to cool the guns. No sooner was this done than the Rebels, supposing they had silenced us, began to come out of the woods and form in line of battle.

As soon as all was ready, the column commenced the march. Our guns opened on them with solid shot and shells as soon as they were within range. This had no effect except to huddle them closer. As they drew nearer, our guns increased the havoc in their ranks. Solid shot and shell, then grape, canister, and spherical case ploughed through their lines and rattled in their midst, sweeping them by the hundreds from the field. But on they pressed, bravely and firmly, closing up on the colors as gap after gap opened in their ranks.

A 32-pounder on Round Top fired down the line obliquely and took out as many as twenty files. Even this didn't arrest their progress. Just before the charge, while the air was reeking with death, General Hancock, whose front Longstreet was covering, rode slowly from right to left of his line and encouraged his men to hold.

At this time the Confederates had reached the Emmettsburg road and, having two fences to climb, all suggestion of alignment was lost. They were now little other than a mob, but they came on and on. They were determined to come in spite of grape, canister, and bullets. Our division and many others hastened to the scene to take part in the closing act of this drama.

On they pushed, delivering a withering fire. But our fire was equally destructive, and they soon presented a bloody and desperate appearance. No troops could resist the awful attack to which they were exposed. It was a sheet of fire, backed by a wall of steel. They couldn't reach the wall and live.

The Confederates were now treated to a heavy flank fire, and this seemed to take all the gimp out of them. Many fled in confusion to the rear, pursued by the troops of Hay's division. Hundreds, aye thousands, threw down their arms and came in as prisoners where they had vainly sought to come as victors. Most of those on the left of the Rebel column remained—dead, and wounded, or prisoner. The Union troops, by a simultaneous attack, now closed in on them, capturing all who did not seek safety in flight. Many threw themselves on the ground to escape the merciless storm of missiles hurled at them; others held up their hands in token of surrender. "He that outlives this day, and comes safe home,/ Will stand a tiptoe when this day is named."

By 4 o'clock the repulse was complete, the victory won. Thousands who two hours before were in the flush of manhood now lay dead, dying, or prisoners. The Confederates staked all and lost.

No one can describe the scenes of this day. We who were participants were in such a maddening whirl that we can give but little that is intelligible. Babel was perfect order compared to the confusion of these two hours of bloody encounter. Then all was still, the carnival of death was done, and we took a breathing spell.

At the close of the charge General Hancock fell, severely wounded. He sent word to General Meade of the repulse and advised an immediate pursuit, but nothing was done.

This was Lee's third attempt to pierce our lines. July 1st on our right, July 2nd on our left, and today our center. On each of these days success seemed to perch on the Rebel banners at first, but was wrested from them. It is certain that General Lee regards this action as a crisis in the affairs of the Confederacy. He would never have made this charge, putting his best troops into the venture, had he not felt certain of success. His feelings as he saw his troops mowed down must have been quite indescribable.

His admirers claim that Lee is very humane. This may be so, but he witnessed the slaughter of his men from the cupola of the seminary and, from the very first, it must have been plain to him that if any of his men reached the Union line, they could never hold it for an instant. Lee's troops learned the folly of attempting to charge across a mile of open country against an army quite as large as their own, more or less protected by embankments, stone walls, and boulders, and with a superabundance of artillery.

As soon as this charge ended, silence settled over the scene. A painful silence, broken only by the sigh or groan of some poor mangled victim. Where but a few moments before the smoke of battle, the cannon's roar, the rattle of musketry, the groan, the cheer, the prayer, the curse had filled the air, there was now profound stillness as though the very elements were appalled and stood mute. A fitting climax to this dreadful struggle, the details of which are indeed sickening. "O stay not to recount the tale./ 'Twas bloody, and 'tis past./ The fairest cheek might well grow pale,/ To hear it to the last." How many firesides in the North and South are plunged today into deepest sorrow? Just a few short hours, and thousands are torn and mangled, better dead than living.

I imagine from my own feelings that every one of these cherished the hope that he would come out all right, or at least alive, and prayed that this might be the last struggle. It was the last for many of them.

About dark our division was sent out on picket in the field in front. It has never been my lot to see and experience such things as on this occasion. The dead lay everywhere, and although not a half day has passed since they died, the stench is so great that we can neither eat, drink, nor sleep. Decomposition commences as soon as life is extinct. As we cannot sleep, we pass the time bringing in the wounded and caring for them. The dead are frightfully smashed, which is not to be wondered at when we consider how they crowded up onto our guns, a mass of humanity, only to be hurled back an indistinguishable pile of mutilated flesh, rolling and writhing in death.

No tongue can depict the carnage, and I cannot make it seem real: men's heads blown off or split open; horrible gashes cut; some split from the top of the head to the extremities, as butchers split beef. Some of the Rebels are very bitter toward us although we do all in our power to alleviate their sufferings, even exposing ourselves to danger to do so. One of our officers crawled on his hands and knees to give a wounded Rebel a drink, and came near paying for it with his life when another Rebel, near the wounded man, fired at him.

It pains me to state that some of our own men taunt these wounded with their lack of success and engage in political arguments, apparently forgetting how incongruous that business is. This custom is by no means monopolized on our side. It is to be deprecated, however, as it in no wise softens the asperities of war and helps keep alive sectional hate. The men who indulge in this kind of lingo soon learn that the characters and sentiments of their opponents haven't changed with their condition, and though the Rebels acknowledge our kindness in caring for them, they still claim that they are right in their attempt to destroy this government.

Among the wounded is a little, flaxen-haired boy from North Carolina who is only fourteen years old, giving credence to the report that the Confeds rob the cradle and the grave. To keep the ranks full, they take old men beyond the military age and young ones who haven't reached it, and hustle them to the front.

July 4th

Morning found us still busy bringing in the dying and dead. Soon after daylight we advanced our pickets and found that the enemy had departed. Finding the Rebel works vacated, we fell back to a hill where the air wasn't so thick from the smoke of battle. We had scarce taken off our knapsacks when it rained like a sieve. We should have been prepared, for we know that all heavy cannonading is followed by violent rain. Many of our wounded, whom we had placed on the banks of the stream because water was handy, came near being drowned.

July 5th

We laid here all day, watching to insure that the enemy didn't make a backward spring. Knowing his desperate condition, we suspect that Lee might turn on us and by a flank movement, secure this much-coveted situation. The 6th Corps started off on their flank to intercept the flying enemy, if indeed he is flying. We should be quite pleased to know for certain, as we have some fears. It seems incredible that we have whipped them. It hasn't been customary to let this army whip anything. The last three days have been a trifle more to our taste than were Peninsula, Fredericksburg, or Chancellorsville. This new experience for Lee's army must be demoralizing, and a vigorous push at this moment might result in their destruction or capture.

The general belief among our army is that one day of honest endeavor could wipe out Lee's army and practically end the Rebellion. It was a foregone conclusion that success here for Lee would have meant the downfall of the Union; his defeat means a Rebel collapse.

At night we received news of the fall of Vicksburg. This sent a thrill down our spines and helped raise our spirits, for we have suffered such an appalling loss of generals in this encounter that we feel quite blue. General Reynolds, Hancock, Sickles, Webb, Weed, Vincent, Hazlett, and Graham, besides many lesser officers, have been killed, wounded, or taken prisoner.

But the fall of Vicksburg and the defeat of Lee here at Gettysburg must make the Confederacy tremble to its foundation.

July 6th

We moved back into a pine grove on the hill and laid there all day. My impression concerning this section is by no means flattering to the inhabitants. A Rebel victory would have left these people at the mercy of Jeff Davis's minions and it would have been eminently just and right.

After all we have sacrificed for them, the women have the contemptible meanness to charge us two dollars for a loaf of bread that could be bought for seventy-five cents in Rebel Maryland. Even the proverbially mean New England Yankee would blush to ask twenty-five cents for it. One old female sauerkraut had the sublime and crowning cheek to cut a loaf into twelve slices and ask twenty-five cents a slice. If it be asked why we allow ourselves to be so swindled, the querist must put himself in our place and he will very soon understand that there are circumstances where money does not occupy the first place in one's affections.

The town isn't entirely destitute of patriotism, for here dwelt old John Burns, who, when battle was imminent, put on his "store clothes," picked up his old musket, and sought the post of danger. He is over seventy-six years of age and quite infirm, but contrived to knock several Confederates off their pins. He was wounded twice and run over by both armies, but contrived to reach home at night. In contrast to his patriotism is one of the wealthy citizens, who harnessed his span of horses and rode out to meet General Lee as he approached the town. He invited the general to his home when he (Lee) should occupy the place. General Lee gave him a look of ineffable disgust, delivered a lecture on patriotism, and wound up by ordering one of his aides to confiscate the horses. General Lee is a traitor to the government that educated him and to which he once promised allegiance, but he cannot tolerate a recreant to one's state, claiming that allegiance to the state is first.

Rice C. Bull

(1842–1930)

Born in northeastern New York's Washington County, Rice C. Bull enlisted in the 123rd New York Volunteer Infantry during the spring of 1862. He was not motivated by a desire for worldly fame or money but by a sense of duty and a wish to "finish the work begun by the country's forefathers." His diary is a simple view from the ranks and expresses few romantic or sentimental notions of war. He has a farmer's appreciation of the land through which he fights, and he captures the small details of a soldier's life.

The following passage describes the final days of the war and is typical of Bull's detached but sensitive view of the events. The simplicity and objectivity of his account make it all the more moving. The tone of Bull's narrative is similar to the tone of the narrative to follow by Walter Montgomery about the end of the war from the loser's perspective. Bull's observation that many veterans "faced the future with the handicap of physical weakness, ignorance and lost opportunities" falls far short of the chivalric glory sought by some at the beginning of the war. Veterans like Bull seemed to value most the bonds of comradeship forged under the hardship and privation of war.

from Bull's *Civil War Diary*

[While participating in Sherman's march through the Carolinas, Bull's 123rd New York Infantry hears the news of the end of the war.]

The morning of the 12th of April 1865 proved to be a time that would never be forgotten by us. We were out early, soon after breakfast had been eaten, and we were waiting orders to fall in; a courier riding in great haste came and left orders at the Headquarters of every Regiment. Then the Regiments were ordered into line; as our Division was camped in an open field it looked as though we were forming a line of battle to make ready for an advance. After the formation was completed Colonel Rogers rode to the center, remained sitting on his horse and then taking a paper in his hand read loudly so all could hear a short order from General Sherman. It announced that on April 9th General Lee had surrendered the Army of Northern Virginia to General Grant at Appomattox Court House. It would be impossible for me to describe the scene that followed. The men went wild, ranks were broken, and shouting and crying, the men in their joy hugged and kissed each other. Never have I witnessed such happiness. The news seemed too good to be true. We felt that the great hour that for three years we had looked for, fought for and prayed for, had come. We could see the end for a certainty, as we knew that after the surrender of General Lee there could be no effective opposition by General Johnston. The shouting did not cease until we had to stop from sheer exhaustion. Then we reformed and took up the march. A happier one was never made by the 123rd New York Infantry than the one on April 12th as we hastened on toward Raleigh.

Early on the 13th, we reached Raleigh, capital of North Carolina. There was no opposition made by the enemy. The city as we found it was not large, but it was a fine town with outstanding buildings and churches. It showed none of the effects of war as most of the southern towns we had passed enroute for the reason that Raleigh had been far removed from any zone of strife. After we went through the town we made our camp near the State Lunatic Asylum. It was filled with demented people who rejoiced to see us, thinking that we would let them out. They filled the windows shouting for us to set them free. One of the inmates made a great plea, saying he was sane and had been placed in the asylum by the secessionists because he was a Union man. Our officers who looked into the matter found he was one of the most violent inmates in the institution. We left him there but he did make a good plea.

As negotiations were going on with General Johnston for the surrender of his Army, we were held at Raleigh until they could be completed. While waiting we had little to do but rest. On April 22nd we were reviewed by General Sherman after we had marched through the streets of Raleigh. April 25th, negotiations having come to a halt because of some misunderstanding, the Army was ordered forward to compel by force what had failed by peaceful methods. At seven in the morning we marched and at night halted near the town of Hillsboro, which was not far from Johnston's Army which was in its entrenchments. We remained here until April 28th, during which time Johnston surrendered. Then we started on our return to Raleigh.

When we were halfway there, we were halted so another announcement could be made. This told us of the assassination of President Lincoln. The sorrow of our men was as great as had been their joy when we heard of the surrender of General Lee. President Lincoln was the idol of the men in the service, everyone reverenced him and they could not have felt greater grief had they heard of the death of some near relative. The remainder of the march to Raleigh was made in almost complete silence. When remarks were made they were curses against the murderers of the President.

It was days before the Army recovered from the sorrow it felt at the death of Lincoln but time rolled on and then came the word that we were soon to begin our Homeward March. We remained in Raleigh until April 30th, only two days but they were busy days, as during that time all preparations had to be made for the march on to Washington. As no transportation could be had, the long journey was to be made on foot. This was no hardship to us who had already marched so many miles in the face of the enemy. Now home was in sight, a march of only three hundred miles through a peaceful land would be just a pleasure trip.

April 30th, 1865, we began the "Homeward March" from Raleigh, N. C. the last, and to me, I can truly say, the happiest made by Sherman's Army. It was to differ greatly from any made by us that preceded it. As in our other marches we were to carry our usual load of goods and equipment but our cartridge boxes were emptied of all but five cartridges. We were to go through the country from Raleigh to Washington in an orderly manner, no straggling would be allowed; there were to be no foragers to gather food from the area through which we passed and no destruction of property of any kind would be permitted.

Every consideration was to be given to the people we met on our line of march who were to be no longer regarded as enemies but as friends. It was to be, indeed, a peaceful march through a peaceful country. All were cautioned to conduct themselves in as friendly a way as though they were marching through Pennsylvania or New York. The usual army ration was to be issued us; food other than that, when needed, was to be paid for when acquired. Everything connected with the Army, as when on a war basis, was to accompany us. Our trains, our ambulances, our pontoons, our artillery were all to go with us. Happily on this march not many guards were required to protect the property. We were to take the most direct route, first to Richmond and from there to Washington.

Our march to Richmond was made in eleven days. Some days we went as far as twenty miles; on others, when we were delayed by bad roads or had to lay our pontoons across rivers, not more than ten miles. The bridges over many streams had been destroyed during the war. It seemed to be a land of rivers. I noted in my diary that May 1st we crossed the Tar River; May 2nd, Flat Creek; May 3rd, Roanoke; May 4th, Meherrin; May 5th, Nottoway; May 6th, Little Nottoway; May 7th, Appomattox; and May 11th, the James River. A river was crossed nearly every day until we reached Richmond.

The country from Raleigh to Richmond did not appeal strongly to us northern people. It was mostly wooded, and where farms were cultivated, they did not look prosperous. Nearly all buildings were poor and ill-kept. On the way to Richmond we saw many ex-Confederates who had returned to their homes; and they were at work in their fields, plowing and preparing for spring planting. We could honestly confess and acknowledge to them, and to ourselves, that we would much rather meet them under these peaceful conditions than face them in the line of battle. Upon reaching Manchester, on the south side of the James River opposite Richmond, we found a division of Union troops lined up to receive us. We braced up, got into step, and made as good a showing as we could when we passed them. At Richmond we paraded through the principal streets, past Libby Prison and the Capitol Building on the hill. On the 11th we camped north of the city.

Three days later we reached Spotsylvania and there the column halted for a time to allow the men to visit the famous battlefield. I went to the Bloody Angle where just a year before the fierce engagement had taken place. Hardly anything had apparently been changed or disturbed. The double-faced entrenchments that had been occupied on one side by Union troops and six feet away on the other side by the Confederates still stood as at the time of the battle. I saw the famous tree that had been shot down by bullets fired in the action. It lay lengthwise of the trench on the Confederate side. The tree had been not more than ten feet from the Union line; it was nearly eighteen inches in diameter and was cut down by Minie bullets. Around the foot of the tree were many chips, and I placed several in my knapsack. On the south side of the trench the Confederate dead had been given scant burial; as many as one hundred skeletons were counted in a distance of not more than two hundred feet. On the northern side the dead were buried behind and facing the trench. There were very many graves, each marked with a wooden headboard. On many parts of the field the dead had not been buried; and as we looked over the ground where the charges had been made by our forces, we saw many places where there were growths of grass in the almost barren field. They marked the remains of Union soldiers, only a skeleton, encased in a mouldy uniform of blue with rusty gun and equipment at the side. It was a gruesome sight and made us all the more thankful that the war was at last ended. That night our column camped on Brook Road, a memorable place in the Great Wilderness Battle.

About noon, May 15th, we reached Chancellorsville. The column halted for three hours to give the 20th Corps men a chance to visit the battlefield where two years before they fought and suffered so severely. I was glad to see the field again, which to me had been a place of trial, and to renew my acquaintance with its familiar surroundings. But what a contrast it presented to what was there two years before. Then it was the scene of fiercest battle, the air filled with smoke, with shrieking, bursting shells and hissing minies that were bringing wounds and death to thousands. But now what a change! Everything was quiet and peaceful. The day was bright and beautiful, with no powder fumes filling the air. Almost the only sound, other than our excited words, was the singing of the birds, perhaps a requiem to the dead, who in thousands all around us lay in unmarked and many in unmade graves. In the natural surroundings there seemed to be little change since two years ago. The low hill with our earthworks where our batteries had stood during the battle looked very natural to me. Back of where our guns had stood during the action was still the old graveyard with its whitewashed fence, now showing signs of neglect for it did not look so white. The Chancellor House had evidently not been touched since it was burned on that memorable 3rd of May 1863.

We marched to the place we had formed our line that fatal morning where many laid down their lives. There was little change there. The trees we had cut and felled in our front as protection still lay as they had fallen, but were now dead and leafless. I could locate the exact spot in our line where I had been wounded and place by the little run in the rear where I had been carried. I went to the old log house around which hundreds of us wounded had been gathered after the retreat of our Army. I lived over again in my memory the awful eleven days spent there where such suffering was endured. I felt a great sense of gratitude to God that I had not only survived my wounds at Chancellorsville but during the two years of active service since that time I had escaped unscathed, and rejoiced that I was alive and homeward bound. After three hours on the battlefield we resumed our march and camped about two miles from the Chancellor House on the road leading to United States Ford.

On May 16th we crossed the Rappahannock at the Ford and marched toward Aquia Creek and Dumfries. On the 18th we crossed Bull Run near the old battleground and camped near Fairfax. On the 19th, the last day of our journey, we reached Alexandria, and passed on toward Washington and camped that night within a mile of our old Arlington Heights Camp where we received our first training of September 1862.

When we halted on the Heights with Washington almost at our feet, we knew that our Homeward March was not only finished but that, except for the coming Grand Review, our marching days were over. I know a sigh of relief and feeling of satisfaction came to all our boys. The work they had started out to do was done, the Rebellion over and the Union saved. The men of our Regiment who had survived had completed a circuit through an enemy's country and were back again to the spot from where they started. What had we not experienced in that record-making time. When we marched away from Arlington, raw recruits, in 1862, hardly an inroad had been made by our armies into the Confederate States. Now, upon our return, every part of the South had been recovered by our forces. In accomplishing this work, without reflecting on the campaigns of other Armies, all of whom did their share, it may be said that no Army conquered more territory, suffered greater hardships, fought harder battles, or marched more miles, than the Army of General Sherman that looked down on Washington from Arlington Heights.

Our war service was to end with the Grand Review in Washington May 24th. When we reached Arlington after our long march from Raleigh we were very weary, but we were so well satisfied with what we had done and there were such bright prospects ahead of us that we gave little heed to any feeling of fatigue. We knew then that to us an end of future marches had come; that our weary shoulders would no longer be burdened by our heavy knapsacks, our guns would be racked, and we would be freed from the routine of military life. Hardly any of us were soldiers from choice. We did not like the discipline required by the duties called for by military action. For three long years we had been in the Army from a sense of obligation to our country; now the war was over we longed to return to civil life. Certainly we had reason to rejoice that our lives had been spared and we had been able to endure the hardships and privations of the service to the end.

We remained at Arlington until May 23rd and during the time had nothing to do but prepare for the Grand Review. We had only our old uniforms that had lasted through our long marches so we could not hope to make a dress parade, but we brushed and cleaned them, burnished our buttons, blackened our old worn shoes as much as we could, for they were the color of the mud through which we had tramped. We cleaned our muskets until they shone. Our guns, which were our pride, could not have looked better.

No one slept the night of the 23rd. We were to break camp at midnight and everything was to be packed and carried as we were not to return to Arlington. We took great pains in packing our knapsacks to make them look as uniform as possible so they would not disfigure us as we paraded. At midnight we had our breakfast as there would be no opportunity after we started to prepare a meal. About two in the morning we were called into line and soon after, our Division leading the Corps, our Brigade leading the Division, and our own Regiment leading the Brigade, started slowly on the march to Washington. We had been camped some three miles from the long bridge spanning the Potomac River. There were many halts as the whole Corps behind us was forming for the parade and we were not to cross the bridge until every organization was in its proper place. It was nearly daybreak when we reached and crossed the Long Bridge for the last time. How much shorter our regimental line was than it had been on September 29th, 1862 when we crossed on our way to Harpers Ferry to join and become part of the old 12th Corps. At that time there were a thousand men in line, now only a scant four hundred. The dead from disease and those killed in action, the wounded and incapacitated told the story of the missing six hundred. It was only the remnant left that crossed the bridge to take part in the review.

A description of the Review cannot be made by me. I was only a participant and able to see only a small part of the Army that followed us. I know that we leading the 20th Corps were given great applause by the hundreds of thousands of spectators who lined the streets of Washington for miles. We marched in company front the whole distance and I am sure our marching was good. There were thousands of soldiers of the Army of the Potomac who had marched the day before on the streets; they shouted themselves hoarse in welcoming our return, as the old 12th Corps of which we had been a part before going west had for two years been with them in the great campaigns of the Army of the Potomac. It was a proud day for all of us, and the Review was a fitting ending of our long service.

At the conclusion of the Review, we were marched to the north of the city, just outside of the fortified line, there to camp until we were discharged and transportation and service papers prepared for us to return home. We were in this camp until June 8th 1865, and that day received our discharges. Within a few days we were taken by rail to Albany, New York, and there encamped in the fields about two miles north of the city.

We marched to the little hillside where we were to make our last camp; where we halted. We came to a front, then the order "stack arms" was given. Our guns, that we had carried for so many miles in attack and defense and by most of the boys so carefully handled and so lovingly regarded, were stacked for the last time. Their deadly work in our hands was over, they were ready for the ordnance to take them over.

Within a week all matters pertaining to our discharge and pay had been settled, our camp was to be broken up, and we were at liberty to return to our homes, there to take up the active duties of civil life, that would of necessity come to us all. Looking back now I realize, far more than I did then, how unprepared we were to meet the life conditions that faced us, not alone from wounds or broken health but from the greater reason that our long absence during the years of life when we would have fitted ourselves by education and experience for a successful effort were years gone. Many faced the future with the handicap of physical weakness, ignorance and lost opportunities.

I shall never forget the last meeting our Company had before we separated to go home. Our tents had been taken down, our knapsacks packed, and we were breaking up for the last time. When we were finished, our greatly respected and much loved Company Commander, Captain Anderson, gave his last "fall in" command to his men. Without arms or equipment and some in civilian clothes that had replaced their faded uniforms we formed in line. The Captain in a broken voice, for he could not control his emotions, bid us farewell and Godspeed. When he had finished, we men crowded about him to shake his hand and each others.

Surely we all rejoiced that the end had come, that victory was ours and that home was near. But there was after all a sadness deep down in our hearts in this parting hour. We boys had been together for three years; we had formed close friendships; we had slept under the same blanket; we had faced the enemy shoulder to shoulder on the firing line; we had marched side by side; we had borne danger, hardship, and privation alike; thus a comradeship had grown as only such conditions could form. So it was hard to separate and say goodby, one with the other; but we shook hands all around, and laughed and seemed to make merry, while our hearts were heavy and our eyes ready to shed tears.

Walter A. Montgomery
(1845–1921)

A native of Warrenton, North Carolina, Walter A. Montgomery was sixteen when he enlisted in the 12th North Carolina Infantry. He was wounded at Chancellorsville but returned to duty a month before Gettysburg, where he was wounded a second time. During his four years of service, he rose through the ranks, was promoted to sergeant in 1862, and commissioned a second lieutenant in 1864. Montgomery was paroled at Appomattox Courthouse on April 9, 1865. He returned to Warrenton and practiced law until his election to the North Carolina Supreme Court in 1895.

His account of his march home appeared as an appendix to a 1901 state-published volume on North Carolina regiments. Montgomery's tone is one of war-weariness and resignation, and free from the polemics of war; however, his account of the kindness of Southern blacks "whose refined feelings and delicate sensibilities . . . made up a beautiful picture of Southern life" echoes the mythology of the lost cause. Nevertheless, upon arriving home he notes that many of his townsmen wanted to "continue the struggle," but he comments, with a soldier's experience, "they were non-combatants."

from Montgomery's *"Appomattox and the Return Home"*

The first few hours were spent in uncertainty. We could not know that the terms would be of such a nature as to be accepted. When that suspense was quieted by the announcement that the terms were satisfactory and had been accepted by General Lee, a feeling of collapse, mental and physical, succeeded. For some hours very little was said by men or officers. They sat, or lay on the ground in reflective mood, overcome by a flood of sad recollections. Few were to be seen away from their camps, and no life was there; in fact, on that day there were more Union troops to be seen on the road and in the fields within our line than Confederates.

During the afternoon rations of bread were issued to us, but no meat until the next day, and then in small quantities. The animals were entirely without long food, and they could be seen about in the fields in favorable spots trying to find the first grass and weeds of the season. It was understood that it was a matter of difficulty for the Union commissariat to get provisions for men and horses; and we had very little for several days.

On the next day (Monday) the men began to recover themselves. They realized, not fully, it is true, but measurably, the tremendous importance of the event, and began to take thought for the future. Of course their first thought was to reach their homes as soon as possible, for their services were, in most cases, sorely needed there. Crops could be planted and cultivated by those whose lives had been formerly on the farms, and the others, in some indefinite way, hoped for something to do. Then, they wished to get through with the trying ordeal of the act of surrender, for they did not know what the formalities might be, and in spite of their great deeds of the past, and consciences at rest on the score of duty performed to the last, they yet felt that it would be to them a humiliating scene. There was no personal bitterness in their hearts, little or no profane language, no curses upon their enemies. Their conduct was equal to the occasion.

I heard no word of ill-will against the National Government in the future, no suggestions of guerrilla warfare. The universal sentiment was that the questions in dispute had been fought to a finish, and that was the end of it. Their confidence in their general officers was unshaken, and for General Lee their affection and their esteem amounted to adoration. They knew he was heartbroken. In discussing the incidents which produced the most harmful effects upon the fortunes of the army, they mentioned the death of General Jackson, and the failure to occupy the heights at Gettysburg at the conclusion of the first day's battle. They also talked freely of the injustice of the conscript law, with its permission of substitutes and twenty-negro exemption, but I heard no breath of censure for the President who recommended those laws. On Monday two matters of diversion occurred. General Gordon had the Second Corps, without arms, of course, assembled in massed columns, and from a central position, on horseback, delivered to them a farewell address. He spoke of their great and heroic achievements, of their privations and their sufferings, and their unselfish devotion to duty, and advised them to return to their homes to be as good citizens as they had been soldiers. He opened his speech with these word: "Soldiers of the Second Army Corps! No mathematician can compute the odds against which you have contended," and he entered into an exhortation that they maintain their principles and their courage, with the assurance on his part that in all future emergencies, if the contest should be renewed, they would find him ready to lead them again; that "the blood of the martyrs was the seed of the church." We heard that the tenor of the address was not much relished at the Federal headquarters.

Gordon was a good soldier throughout his entire service, and if, at the Wilderness on the evening of 6 May, 1864, when he struck Sedgwick, he had been in command of a corps, he would have rolled up Grant's right like a scroll. He was the most dashing of all the Confederates at Appomattox.

Just after the speaking, or while it was going on, a number of Federal cavalrymen, who had been riding about our camps, one of them being under the influence of strong drink, gave us some trouble. The man in his cups, in spinning some yarns about his performances of the day before, mentioned that one of his number was captured by some of General Longstreet's men, and that some of the General's staff had taken from the prisoner his "housewife" (thread and needle case), when a Georgian standing by, not being familiar with the name of the article alleged to have been taken—housewife—picked up a stone, and throwing it, brought his man to the ground. Considerable confusion ensued, and because of that circumstance, an order was issued from Federal headquarters that no Union soldiers should be allowed to visit the Confederate camps without written permission.

On that day, also, General Custer rode over to Johnston's Brigade to see his friend and classmate at West Point, John W. Lea, who was Colonel of the Fifth North Carolina Regiment, and then in command of the brigade. They had met the day before at General Custer's quarters. General Custer brought with him an orderly with a basket of provisions and a flask of whiskey. Upon invitation of Colonel Lea, several of the officers of the brigade joined General Custer and himself in the luncheon. Custer was of a most cheerful disposition and very handsome in personal appearance. He told us that the honors of the 9th were really with the Confederates, all things considered; that he took no glory to himself when he ascertained the numbers of the Confederate army. On Monday also the paroles were printed and sent around to regimental headquarters—mine is now before me and is dated 10 April, and signed by P. Durham, Captain Commanding Regiment.

We kept no guard around the camp and had no duties of any kind to perform; nor did we see a Union soldier with arms in his hands until the very moment at which our men, early on Wednesday morning, stacked their guns in front of the Federal Corps detailed to received them. That was a most simple ceremony. In a line north and south, in a field, a Federal Corps was standing with arms at shoulder waiting to receive the Confederates and their arms. We filed, in fours, just in front of them, and ten feet off came to a halt and faced to the left; the guns were then stacked and the flags laid on the stacks.

The officers were allowed, under the terms of the surrender, to keep their side arms. Not a word was spoken; we did not even look into each others' faces. We were marched from the spot to the road and, without returning to camp, turned our faces toward the South, toward our homes—and as I looked back for the last time the Federal Corps had not moved from its tracks, nor had a gun or a flag been touched, and we had not yet opened our lips.

It soon became apparent that there was no system, or plan, about the march of the troops homeward. Somehow or other it became understood that General Grimes would conduct the North Carolinians on their way; anyhow a considerable number of them were under his directions, and he ordered the march toward Campbell Court House, with the intention to go from there to Danville. For two or three miles everything passed off smoothly. When, however, we came to a point where there was a divergent road leading in a more southerly direction, Private Thomas Royster, from Granville County, saluted the General and said, "General, you are a good officer and you know the road to take a good many of these boys to their homes, but I live lower down the Roanoke than Danville and it seems to me all who want to go to counties east of Granville should take this road; anyhow I am going to try it and all who want to follow me can come on."

Royster was a splendid soldier, considerably over six feet tall, symmetrical in form, with one of the best and kindliest faces I ever saw and a most intelligent and expressive eye. We never saw Royster after ten minutes from the time we left the main column, for he with his strong body and long legs, had soon distanced us. A considerable number followed him. Amongst the number T. B. Watson, Austin Allen, R. H. Gilliland, Jas. M. Bobbitt, P. A. Bobbitt, J. H. Duke, Robert C. Montgomery, my brother, and myself. We soon formed a party, for the men, as if by instinct, broke up into small squads, and we eight continued together until we reached our homes in Warren County. We started off with a small quantity of bread and coffee, but with no meat; but on our way, with one exception, we met with kindness and consideration from the residents. We had no conversation with any other soldier on our journey except a young man whom we found in a barn on a bed of straw on a plantation, near Rough Creek Church, our first night's camping ground. At that home there were only a mother and daughter, the male members of the household being in their places in the army. At dark we walked up to the house and informed them of our condition and our desire to be allowed to use the barn for lodgings and to have the privilege of getting water from the well in the yard. They received us not only with politeness, but with kindness. They also added to our bread and coffee a piece of bacon and some sorghum molasses. In front of the barn we made a live coal fire and soon had our supper prepared. When the meal was over we filled our pipes with "Zephyr Puff," a brand of smoking tobacco, several packages of which I had taken from a burning pile in the streets of Petersburg, the night of the evacuation, and for the time we forgot our troubles.

About 9 o'clock we went again to the house and inquired of the two householders if they would like to hear some music, and upon the response, of course in the affirmative, Watson, who was a musician, leading with his cornet, and accompanied by the voices of the two Bobbitts, my brother and myself, all of us having belonged to a glee club in the army, we entertained them for half an hour.

On retiring to the barn and making our beds upon the straw, we stumbled upon our only acquaintance on the way, who was in a helpless condition, and who could not tell us how he came to be there. He only said that he could go no further and had lain down there to die. He was merely exhausted from fatigue and want of food, and upon our preparing for him something to eat and a strong pot of coffee, his strength was revived. We left him in fair condition. He reached his home in Warren County and is now a well-to-do farmer and the head of a large family.

We heard of General Ransom along our route as helping along the tired and foot-sore by often dismounting and placing such in his saddle, and speaking to them words of hope and cheer. We greatly wished to come up with him, and to talk with him, for we had great interest and pride in him; his people and ours having been for generations connected by ties of friendship. We had watched his career as a soldier, which had reflected honor on his State and upon the South, and especially his strikingly brilliant conduct at Five Forks, a few days before.

We spent the next night (Thursday) near the town of Chase City, then called Christiansburg. In passing through Charlotte Court House, on that day, we called at a large well-appointed home in the midst of extensive grounds, and at once were asked into the family living room, the family consisting entirely of ladies and children, and at once were made to feel at ease. An invitation, heartily pressed upon us, to dine, we, of course, accepted. In the interval the cornet and the voices added interest to the occasion, delighting young and old, who had heard no sound of music for months. The war songs and old Southern ballads we had practiced, and often along the Shenandoah and Rappahannock we had given solace and pleasure to our friends and companions; but unfortunately on the present occasion we, without proper forethought, began "There Will Be One Vacant Chair," when the younger lady commenced to weep.

At once we knew the cause. We were thoughtless because there were so many vacant chairs in Southern households. In that particular case it was the husband's. But the elder lady made everything so easy and so delicately explained the situation that it passed off without further embarrassment, and we left their home after dinner with their thanks and prayers, as if we had conferred a favor upon them.

Our last night was spent near the Roanoke at the hospitable home of Colonel Eaton, the uncle of Captain M. F. Taylor, who was mortally wounded on the retreat from Gettysburg. The nephew was, in truth, a most estimable gentleman and capable officer, and a great favorite with the whole regiment. He was the idol of the uncle, and we all could, sitting around that hearthstone, with truth and propriety join in honoring the dead hero and kinsman. The host was of large means, given to hospitality, and until a late hour we grieved over our losses, celebrated our victories, and mourned over the disappointment of our hopes. On rising the next morning for an early breakfast, had at our request, we found our shoes cleaned, our tattered uniforms brushed and hung on chairs. After the meal we left our kind entertainer standing on the front portico and almost overcome by his feelings, watching us as we disappeared forever from his sight, down the road that led us to our own beloved and bereaved ones.

All along our route we met with only kindness and consideration, with one exception. That was at the house of a man who was formerly a resident of our own county. He refused us water from his well, and a rest upon the steps of his house, although we informed him who we were, and he knew the families of us all. We shook the dust of his premises from our feet and renewed our journey. Before we had gotten out of sight one of his old negro slaves, who had heard the conversation between us, followed with his wife and, soon overtaking us, introduced himself as an old acquaintance of the father of each one of us whom he had known in Warren. He made apologies for the conduct of his master. He brought along with him a pair of chickens, some corn meal, and a bucket of water, and in a short while the old man and his wife had prepared for us a feast.

The old colored man said to us that when the female members of his master's family protested against his refusal to give to a Confederate soldier a cup of cold water he replied that he was afraid that they might have some contagious disease or depredate upon his poultry during the night. To the credit of humanity it may be said that we had few of such in the South. The refined feelings and delicate sensibilities of those old colored people, manifested so strikingly in such substantial sympathy, made up a beautiful picture of Southern life; and wherever we eight have been we have told it as an ever-lasting memorial of them. On our last day's journey, at a fork of the Ridgeway and Alexander Ferry road, our party broke up, Watson, Allen and Gilliland continuing their way to their homes in the same neighborhood and we, the other five, to ours in Warrenton. We are all still living except Gilliland, and all bear upon our bodies lasting signs of those days. Upon our arrival at Warrenton the streets were alive with the inhabitants anxiously waiting for the particulars of the surrender of which they had heard only vague reports. They were astonished at the news, and many of them expressed themselves in favor of "continuing the struggle," as they expressed it; but they were non-combatants.

Mary Chesnut

(1825–1886)

The daughter of a South Carolina governor and the wife of the first Southern U.S. senator to resign, Mary Boykin Chesnut was, by virtue of her husband's position as President Jefferson Davis's advisor, at the center of the social and political life of the Confederacy. She was an intelligent and independent observer of the major personalities directing the Southern cause and kept a diary of her experiences during the war. She later tried to shape her diaries into romantic fiction but, thankfully, gave up that exercise in favor of revising and expanding them. The end product is a literate and fascinating personal narrative free of sentiment and full of the atmosphere and fervor of the Confederacy.

The following passage, covering one June day in 1862, touches on a range of experience and events broader than that found in any Civil War fiction. She bounces from gossip to battles to fashion to affairs of state and back. The entry reveals, too, in her cameo of herself on the porch surrounded by flowers in "a living wall of everything beautiful and sweet," the romantic myth of the old South, a fiction that would help this region cope with defeat.

from Chesnut's *A Diary from Dixie*

June 16th. [1862] Felt suddenly ill in church. As I tried to slip by Mr. Preston unperceived, he looked up, and in his deepest tragic tones asked "Shall I go with you?" "No," I snapped in a sharp treble. After service, they came to see why I had forsaken them. The heat was so oppressive I should certainly have fainted.

Stuart's cavalry have rushed through McClellan's lines and burned five of his transports. Jackson has been reinforced by 16,000 men, and they hope the enemy will be drawn from around Richmond, and the Valley be the new seat of war. John Chesnut is in Whiting's brigade, which has been sent to Stonewall. Mem's son is with the Boykin Rangers, and she had persistently wept ever since she heard the news. It is no child's play, she says, when you are with Stonewall. He doesn't play at soldiering, doesn't take care of his men at all. He only goes to kill the Yankees.

Somebody rushed in to tell us that Wade Hampton, who came home last night, says France has recognized us. Now that is a sure thing. Louis Napoleon does not stop at trifles. He never botches his work, he is thorough; so we hope he will not help us with a half-hand.

June 16th.—(Later) And now not a word of all this is true. Wade Hampton is here, shot in the foot, but he knows no more about France than he does about the man in the moon. A wet blanket he is, just now; Johnston is badly wounded. Lee is called King of Spades, because he has them all once more digging for dear life. Unless we can reinforce Stonewall, the game is up. Our chiefs contrive to dampen and destroy the enthusiasm of all who go near them. So much entrenching and falling back destroys the morale of any army. This ever-lasting retreating, it kills the hearts of the men. Then we are scant of powder, etc. My husband is awfully proud of Le Conte's powder manufacturing here. Le Conte knows how to do it, and Mr. Chesnut provides him the means to carry out his plans.

The Hampton girls have asked their father's friends, Mr. and Mrs. Rose, and Mr. and Mrs. Alfred Huger to stay with them at Millwood; to spend the summer at any rate. An anecdote of Mrs. Huger, nee Rutledge: She was proud of her exquisite figure, and the fashion of the day enabled ladies to appear in next to nothing, pink stockinet and a book muslin, classically cut gown, nothing more. It was this liberal display of herself as nature made her that put the final stroke to Jerome Napoleon.

Mr. Venable don't mince matters. "If we do not deal a blow, a blow that will be felt, it will be soon all up with us. The Southwest will be lost to us. We cannot afford to shilly-shally much longer. Thousands are enlisting on the other side in New Orleans. Butler holds out inducements. To be sure, they are principally foreigners who want to escape starvation. Tennessee we may count as gone, since we abandoned her at Corinth, at Fort Pillow and at Memphis. A real man must be sent there, or it is all gone." In my heart I feel: "All is gone now."

They call Mars' Robert "Ole Spade Lee," he keeps them digging so. Mr. Venable said: "General Lee is a noble Virginian. Respect something in this world! As a soldier, he was as much above suspicion as Caesar required his wife to be. If I remember Caesar's Commentaries, he owns up to a lot of entrenching. You let Mars' Robert alone; he knows what he is about."

"How did the Creoles take the fall of New Orleans?" "Men, women, and children ran around distracted, screaming, chattering, gesticulating. There was no head, no order. All was mere confusion and despair." Then he defended Lovell valiantly, for he charged with all our chivalry. "Lovell had only twenty-five hundred regulars to follow him when he left New Orleans. The crack regiments of New Orleans remained. Butler captured twenty thousand men capable of bearing arms, and now they are spading for Butler at Fort Jackson. Many of the wealthiest citizens are there in their shirt sleeves, spade in hand."

"Tell us of the womenfolk. How did they take it?" "They are an excitable race. As I was standing on the levee, a daintily dressed lady picked her way, parasol in hand, toward me. She accosted me with great politeness and her face was as placid and unmoved as in antebellum days. Her first question. "Will you be so kind as to tell me what is the last general order?" "No order that I know of, Madam. General disorder prevails now." "Ah, I see. And why are those persons flying and yelling so noisily, and racing in the streets in that unseemly way?" "They are looking for a shell to burst over their heads at any moment." "Ah!" Then, with a curtsey full of dignity and grace, she waved her parasol and departed, but stopped to arrange her parasol at a proper angle to protect her face from the sun. There was no vulgar haste in her movements. She tripped away as gracefully as she came. She was the one self-possessed soul I saw there in New Orleans; but I saw another woman so overheated and out of breath she had barely time to say she had run miles when a sudden shower came up. In a second she was cool and calm. "My bonnet—I must save it at any sacrifice." So she turned her dress over her head and went off, forgetting her country's troubles and screaming for a cab."

At Secessionville, we went to drive the Yankees out, and we were surprised ourselves. We lost one hundred, the Yankees four hundred.

They lost more men than we had in the engagement. Fair shooting that! As they say in the West, "We whipped our weight in wildcats" and some to spare. Henry King was killed. He died as a brave man would like to die. From all accounts, they say he had not found this world a bed of roses.

I went to see Mrs. Burroughs at the old de Saussure house. She has such a sweet face, such soft, kind, beautiful, dark grey eyes. Such eyes are a poem. No wonder she had a long love story. We sat in the piazza at twelve o'clock of a June day, the glorious southern sun shining his very hottest; but we were in a dense shade. Magnolias were in full bloom; ivy, vines of I know not what, and roses in profusion closed us in. It was a living wall of everything beautiful and sweet. I have been thinking of it ever since. In all this flower garden of a Columbia, this is the most delicious corner I have been in yet.

More talk of Secessionville. Dr. Tennent proved himself a crack shot. They handed him rifles, ready loaded, in rapid succession; and at the point he aimed were found thirty dead men. Scotchmen in a regiment of Federals at Secessionville were madly intoxicated. They had poured out whiskey for them like water.

I got from the Prestons' French library "Fanny," with a brilliant preface by Jules Janin. Now then, I have come to the worst! There can be no worse book than "Fanny." The lover is jealous of her husband. The woman is for the polyandry rule of life; she cheats both and refuses to break with either. But to criticize it, one must be as shameless as the book itself. Of course it is clever to the last degree, or it would be kicked into the gutter. It is not nastier, or coarser, than Mrs. Stowe; but then it is not written in the interest of philanthropy.

Louisa May Alcott

(1832–1888)

Most famous as the author of *Little Women* (1868–69), her autobiographical
account of a happy New England childhood, Louisa May Alcott also served as
a nurse in a Union hospital in Georgetown until poor health forced her to
leave. The daughters of famed transcendentalist and Concord, Massachusetts,
intellectual, Bronson Alcott, Louisa and her sisters received instruction and
guidance from their father's friends, including Ralph Waldo Emerson and
Henry David Thoreau. She brought to her service as a nurse her family's and
region's enthusiasm for the Union cause, and her letters from the period,
collected in *Hospital Sketches* (1863), reflect a sentimentalism tempered by the
authentic observations of personal experience.

In the following excerpt, Alcott describes the death of "John," an unknown Virginia blacksmith. Although she sees war as a holy crusade (God is a
"divine commander" and men like John are "knights" and "soldiers of the
Lord"), Alcott is too close to the human suffering of the hospital ward to
ignore it. This account is a unique and interesting combination of the realistic
details of John's agony and the trappings and themes of domestic romance.

from Alcott's *Hospital Sketches*

At this juncture, the delirious man began to snort; the one-legged rose
up in his bed, as if preparing for another dart; Teddy bewailed himself
more piteously than before: and if ever a woman was at her wit's end,
that distracted female was Nurse Periwinkle, during the space of two or
three minutes, as she vibrated between the three beds, like an agitated
pendulum. Like a most opportune reinforcement, Dan, the bandy
[bowlegged] appeared, and devoted himself to the lively party, leaving

me free to return to my post; for the Prussian, with a nod and a smile, took the lad away to his own bed, and lulled him to sleep with a soothing murmur, like a mammoth bumble bee. I liked that in Fritz, and if he ever wondered afterward at the dainties which sometime found their way into his rations, or the extra comforts of his bed, he might have found a solution of the mystery in sundry persons' knowledge of the fatherly action of that night.

Hardly was I settled again, when the inevitable bowl appeared, and its bearer delivered a message I had expected, yet dreaded to receive:

"John is going, ma'am, and wants to see you, if you can come."

"The moment this boy is asleep; tell him so, and let me know if I am in danger of being too late."

My Ganymede departed, and while I quieted poor Shaw, I thought of John. He came in a day or two after the others; and, one evening, when I entered my "pathetic room," I found a lately emptied bed occupied by a large, fair man, with a fine face, and the serenest eyes I ever met. One of the earlier comers had often spoken of a friend, who had remained behind, that those apparently worse wounded than himself might reach a shelter first. It seemed a David and Jonathan sort of friendship. The man fretted for his mate, and was never tired of praising John—his courage, sobriety, self-denial, and unfailing kindliness of heart; always winding up with: "He's an out an' out fine feller, ma'am; you see if he aint."

I had some curiosity to behold this piece of excellence, and when he came, watched him for a night or two, before I made friends with him; for, to tell the truth, I was a little afraid of the stately looking man, whose bed had to be lengthened to accommodate his commanding stature; who seldom spoke, uttered no complaint, asked no sympathy, but tranquilly observed what went on about him; and, as he lay high upon his pillows, no picture of dying statesman or warrior was ever fuller of real dignity than this Virginia blacksmith. A most attractive face he had, framed in brown hair and beard, comely featured and full of vigor, as yet unsubdued by pain; thoughtful and often beautifully mild while watching the afflictions of others, as if entirely forgetful of his own. His mouth was grave and firm, with plenty of will and courage in its lines, but a smile could make it as sweet as any woman's; and his eyes were child's eyes, looking one fairly in the face, with a clear, straightforward glance, which promised well for such as placed their faith in him. He seemed to cling to life, as if it were rich in duties and delights, and he had learned the secret of content. The only time I saw his composure disturbed, was when my surgeon brought another to examine John, who scrutinized their faces with an anxious look, asking of the elder: "Do you think I shall pull through, sir?" "I hope so, my man." And, as the two passed on, John's eye still followed them, with an intentness which would have won a clearer answer from them, had they seen it. A momentary shadow flitted over his face; then came the usual serenity, as if, in that brief eclipse, he had acknowledged the existence of some hard possibility, and, asking nothing yet hoping all things, left the issue in God's hands, with that submission which is true piety. The next night, as I went my rounds with Dr. P., I happened to ask which man in the room probably suffered most; and, to my great surprise, he glanced at John:

"Every breath he draws is like a stab; for the ball pierced the left lung, broke a rib, and did no end of damage here and there; so the poor lad can find neither forgetfulness nor ease, because he must lie on his wounded back or suffocate. It will be a hard struggle, and a long one, for he possesses great vitality; but even his temperate life can't save him; I wish it could."

"You don't mean he must die, Doctor?"

"Bless you, there's not the slightest hope for him; and you'd better tell him so before long; women have a way of doing such things comfortably, so I leave it to you. He won't last more than a day or two, at furthest."

I could have sat down on the spot and cried heartily, if I had not learned the wisdom of bottling up one's tears for leisure moments. Such an end seemed very hard for such a man, when half a dozen worn out, worthless bodies round him, were gathering up the remnants of wasted lives, to linger on for years perhaps burdens to others, daily reproaches to themselves. The army needed men like John, earnest, brave, and faithful; fighting for liberty and justice with both heart and hand, true soldiers of the Lord. I could not give him up so soon, or think with any patience of so excellent a nature robbed of its fulfillment, and blundered into eternity by the rashness or stupidity of those at whose hands so many lives may be required. It was an easy thing for Dr. P. to say: "Tell him he must die," but a cruelly hard thing to do, and by no means as "comfortable" as he politely suggested. I had not the heart to do it then, and privately indulged the hope that some change for the better might take place, in spite of gloomy prophesies; so, rendering my task unnecessary. A few minutes later, as I came in again, with fresh rollers, I saw John sitting erect, with no one to support him, while the surgeon dressed his back. I had never hitherto seen it done; for, having simpler wounds to attend to, and knowing the fidelity of the attendant, I had left John to him, thinking it might be more agreeable and safe; for both strength and experience were needed in his case. I had forgotten that the strong man might long for the gentler tendance of a woman's hands, the sympathetic magnetism of a woman's presence, as well as the feebler souls about him. The Doctor's words caused me to reproach myself with neglect, not of any real duty perhaps, but of those little cares and kindnesses that solace homesick spirits, and make the heavy hours pass easier. John looked lonely and forsaken just then, as he sat with bent head, hands folded on his knee, and no outward sign of suffering, till, looking nearer, I saw great tears roll down and drop upon the floor. It was a new sight there; for, though I had seen many suffer, some swore, some groaned, most endured silently, but none wept. Yet his did not seem weak, only very touching, and straightway my fear vanished, my heart opened wide and took him in, as, gathering the bent head in my arms, as freely as if he had been a little child, I said, "Let me help you bear it, John."

Never, on any human countenance, have I seen so swift and beautiful a look of gratitude, surprise and comfort, as that which answered me more eloquently than the whispered—

"Thank you, ma'am, this is right good! this is what I wanted!"

"Then why not ask for it before?"

"I didn't like to be a trouble; you seemed so busy, and I could manage to get on alone."

"You shall not want it any more, John."

Nor did he; for now I understood the wistful look that sometimes followed me, as I went out, after a brief pause beside his bed, or merely a passing nod, while busied with those who seemed to need me more than he, because more urgent in their demands; not that I knew that to him, as to so many, I was the poor substitute for mother, wife, or sister, and in his eyes no stranger, but a friend who hitherto had seemed neglectful; for, in his modesty, he had never guessed the truth.

This was changed now; and, through the tedious operation of probing, bathing, and dressing his wounds, he leaned against me, holding my hand fast, and, if pain wrung further tears from him, no one saw them fall but me. When he was laid down again, I hovered about him, in a remorseful state of mind that would not let me rest, till I had bathed his face, brushed his "bonny brown hair," set all things smooth about him, and laid a knot of heath and heliotrope on his clean pillow. While doing this, he watched me with the satisfied expression I so like to see; and when I offered the little nosegay, held it carefully in his great hand, smoothed a ruffled leaf or two, surveyed and smelt it with an air of genuine delight, and lay contentedly regarding the glimmer of the sunshine on the green. Although the manliest man among my forty, he said, "Yes, ma'am," like a little boy; received suggestions for his comfort with the quick smile that brightened his whole face; and now and then, as I stood tidying the table by his bed, I felt him softly touch my gown, as if to assure himself that I was there. Anything more natural and frank I never saw, and found this brave John as bashful as brave, yet full of excellencies and fine aspirations, which having no power to express themselves in words, seemed to have bloomed into his character and made him what he was.

After that night, an hour of each evening that remained to him was devoted to his ease or pleasure. He could not talk much, for breath was precious, and he spoke in whispers; but from occasional conversations, I gleaned scraps of private history which only added to the affection and respect I felt for him. Once he asked me to write a letter, and as I settled pen and paper, I said, with an irrepressible glimmer of feminine curiosity, "Shall it be addressed to wife, or mother John?"

"Neither, ma'am; I've got no wife, and will write to mother myself when I get better. Did you think I was married because of this?" he asked, touching a plain ring he wore, and often turned thoughtfully on his finger when he lay alone.

"Partly that, but more from a settled sort of look you have, a look which young men seldom get until they marry."

"I don't know that; but I'm not so very young, ma'am, thirty in May, and have been what you might call settled this ten years; for mother's a widow, I'm the oldest child she has, and it wouldn't do for me to marry until Lizzy has a home of her own, and Laurie's learned his trade; for we're not rich, and I must be father to the children and husband to the dear old woman, if I can."

"No doubt but you are both, John; yet how came you to go to war, if you felt so? Wasn't enlisting as bad as marrying?"

"No, ma'am, not as I see it, for one is helping my neighbor, the other pleasing myself. I went because I couldn't help it. I didn't want the glory or the pay; I wanted the right thing done, and people kept saying the men who were in earnest ought to fight. I was in earnest, the Lord knows! but I held off as long as I could, not knowing which was my duty; mother saw the case, gave me her ring to keep me steady, and said 'Go:' so I went."

A short story and a simple one, but the man and the mother were portrayed better than pages of fine writing could have done it.

"Do you ever regret that you came, when you lie here suffering so much?"

"Never, ma'am; I haven't helped a great deal, but I've shown I was willing to give my life, and perhaps I've got to; but I don't blame anybody, and if it was to do over again, I'd do it. I'm a little sorry I wasn't wounded in front; it looks cowardly to be hit in the back, but I obeyed orders, and it don't matter in the end, I know."

Poor John! it did not matter now, except that a shot in front might have spared the long agony in store for him. He seemed to read the thought that troubled me, as he spoke so hopefully when there was no hope, for he suddenly added:

"This is my first battle; do they think it's going to be my last?"

"I'm afraid they do, John."

It was the hardest question I had ever been called upon to answer; doubly hard with those clear eyes fixed on mine, forcing a truthful answer by their own truth. He seemed a little startled at first, pondered over the fateful fact a moment then shook his head, with a glance at the broad chest and muscular limbs stretched out before him:

"I'm not afraid, but it's difficult to believe all at once. I'm so strong it don't seem possible for such a little wound to kill me."

Merry Mercutio's dying words glanced through my memory as he spoke: " 'Tis not so deep as a well, nor so wide as a church door, but 'tis enough." And John would have said the same could he have seen the ominous black holes between his shoulders, he never had; and, seeing the ghastly sights about him, could not believe his own wound more fatal than these, for all the suffering it caused him.

"Shall I write your mother, now?" I asked, thinking that these sudden tidings might change all plans and purposes; but they did not; for the man received the order of the Divine Commander to march with the same unquestioning obedience with which the soldier had received that of the human one, doubtless remembering that the first led him to life, and the last to death.

"No, ma'am; to Laurie just the same; he'll break it to her best, and I'll add a line to her myself when you get done."

So I wrote the letter which he dictated, finding it better than any I had sent; for, though here and there a little ungrammatical or inelegant, each sentence came to me briefly worded, but most expressive; full of excellent counsel to the boy, tenderly bequeathing "mother and Lizzie" to his care, and bidding him good bye in words the sadder for their simplicity. He added a few lines, with steady hand, and, as I sealed it, said, with a patient sort of sigh, "I hope the answer will come in time for me to see it;" then, turning away his face, laid the flowers against his lips, as if to hide some quiver of emotion at the thought of such a sudden sundering of all the dear home ties.

These things had happened two days before; now John was dying, and the letter had not come. I had been summoned to many death beds in my life, but to none that made my heart ache as it did then, since my mother called to watch the departure of a spirit akin to this in its gentleness and patient strength. As I went in, John stretched out both hands:

"I knew you'd come! I guess I'm moving on, ma'am."

He was; and so rapidly that, even while he spoke, over his face I saw the grey veil falling that no human hand can lift. I sat down by him, wiped the drops from his forehead, stirred the air about him with the slow wave of a fan, and waited to help him die. He stood in sore need of help and I could do so little; for, as the doctor had foretold, the strong body rebelled against death, and fought every inch of the way, forcing him to draw each breath with a spasm, and clench his hands with an imploring look, as if he asked, "How long must I endure this, and be still!" For hours he suffered dumbly, without a moment's respite, or a moment's murmuring; his limbs grew cold, his face damp, his lips white, and, again and again, he tore the covering off his breast, as if the lightest weight added to his agony; yet through it all, his eyes never lost their perfect serenity, and the man's soul seemed to sit therein, undaunted by the ills that vexed his flesh.

One by one, the men woke, and round the room appeared a circle of pale faces and watchful eyes, full of awe and pity; for, though a stranger, John was beloved by all. Each man there had wondered at his patience, respected his piety, admired his fortitude, and now lamented his hard death; for the influence of an upright nature had made itself deeply felt, even in one little week. Presently, the Jonathan who so loved this comely David, came creeping from his bed for a last look or word. The kind soul was full of trouble, as the choke in his voice, the grasp of his hand, betrayed; but there were no tears, and the farewell of the friends was the more touching for its brevity.

"Old boy, how are you?" faltered the one.

"Most through, thank heaven!" whispered the other.

"Can I say or do anything for you anywheres?"

"Take my things home, and tell them that I did my best."

"I will! I will!"

"Good bye, Ned."

"Good bye, John, good bye!"

They kissed each other, tenderly as women, and so parted, for poor Ned could not stay to see his comrade die. For a little while, there was no sound in the room but the drip of water, from a stump or two, and John's distressful gasps, as he slowly breathed his life away. I thought him nearly gone, and had just laid down the fan, believing its help to be no longer needed, when suddenly he rose up in his bed, and cried out with a bitter cry that broke the silence, sharply startling every one with its agonized appeal:

"For God's sake, give me air!"

It was the only cry pain or death had wrung from him, the only boon he had asked; and none of us could grant it, for all the airs that blew were useless now. Dan flung up the window. The first red streak of dawn was warming the grey east, a herald of the coming sun; John saw it, and with the love of light which lingers in us to the end, seemed to read in it a sign of hope of help, for, over his whole face there broke that mysterious expression, brighter than any smile, which often comes to eyes that look their last. He laid himself gently down; and, stretching out his strong right arm, as if to grasp and bring the blessed air to his lips in a fuller flow, lapsed into a merciful unconsciousness, which assured us that for him suffering was forever past. He died then; for, though the heavy breaths still tore way up for a little longer, they were but the waves of an ebbing tide that bat unfelt against the wreck, which an immortal voyager had deserted with a smile. He never spoke again, but to the end held my hand close, so close that when he was asleep at last, I could not draw it away. Dan helped me, warning me as he did so that it was unsafe for dead and living flesh to lie so long together; but though my hand was strangely cold and stiff, and four white marks remained across its back, even when warmth and color had returned elsewhere, I could not but be glad that, through its touch, the presence of human sympathy, perhaps, had lightened that hard hour.

When they had made him ready for the grave, John lay in state for half an hour, a thing which seldom happened in that busy place; but a universal sentiment of reverence and affection seemed to fill the hearts of all who had known or heard of him; and when the rumor of his death went through the house, always astir, many came to see him, and I felt a tender sort of pride in my lost patient; for he looked a most heroic figure, lying there stately and still as the statue of some young knight asleep upon his tomb. The lovely expression which so often beautifies dead faces, soon replaced the marks of pain, and I longed for those who loved him best to see him when half an hour's acquaintance with Death had made them friends. As we stood looking at him, the ward master handed me a letter, saying it had been forgotten the night before. It was John's letter, come just an hour too late to gladden the eyes that had longed and looked for it so eagerly: yet he had it; for, after I had cut some brown locks for his mother, and taken off the ring to send her, telling how well the talisman had done its work, I kissed this good son for her sake, and laid the letter in his hand, still folded as when I drew my own away, feeling that its place was there, and making myself happy with the thought, that, even in his solitary place in the "Government Lot," he would not be without some token of the love which makes life beautiful and outlives death. Then I left him, glad to have known so genuine a man, and carrying with me an enduring memory of the brave Virginia blacksmith, as he lay serenely waiting for the dawn of that long day which knows no night.

John Esten Cooke

(1830–1886)

Born in Winchester, Virginia, and raised on his mother's plantation in the Shenandoah Valley, John Esten Cooke celebrated Virginia by blending romance with history and highlighting his region's Cavalier heritage. Before the war, he wrote two novels that idealized old Virginia and depicted "the curiously graded Virginia society."

During the Civil War, Cooke served in the Army of Northern Virginia on J.E.B. Stuart's staff and found time to write a biography of Stonewall Jackson (1863) that was read in the North as well as the South. His novel *Surrey of Eagle's Nest* (1866) follows Jackson to Chancellorsville, and its sequel, *Mohun* (1869) traces Stuart's campaigns. Both books present romantic pictures of the battles and their leaders, and reflect Cooke's desire to escape the realities of the war by continuing where his antebellum fiction left off. In the following passage from *Mohun*, the slaughter on the third day of the Battle of Gettysburg becomes a "magnificent spectacle," and the details of human suffering present in Haley's account are replaced with "faces thrust into the muzzles of muskets spouting flame" and Pickett's Virginians "passing into eternity."

from Cooke's *Mohun*, "The Charge of the Virginians"

Lee's great blow at the enemy's left had failed. He had thrown his entire right wing, under Longstreet, against it. The enemy had been driven; victory seemed achieved;—but suddenly the blue lines had rallied, they had returned to the struggle, their huge masses had rolled forward, thrown Longstreet back in turn, and now the pale moon looked down on the battle-field where some of the bravest souls of the South had poured out their blood in vain.

Lee had accomplished nothing, and one of his great corps was panting and bleeding. It was not shattered or even shaken. The iron fiber would stand any thing almost. But the somber result remained—Longstreet had attacked and had been repulsed.

What course would Lee now pursue? Would he retire?

Retire? The army of Northern Virginia lose heart at a mere rebuff? Lee's veteran army give up the great invasion, after a mere repulse? Troops and commander alike shrunk from the very thought. One more trial of arms—something—an attack somewhere—not a *retreat*!

That was the spirit of the army on the night of the second of July.

A flanking movement to draw the enemy out of their works, or a second attack remained.

Lee determined to attack.

Longstreet and Ewell had accomplished nothing by assailing the right and left of the enemy. Lee resolved now to throw a column against its center—to split the stubborn obstacle, and pour into the gap with the whole army, when all would be over.

That was hazardous, you will say perhaps to-day, reader. And you have this immense argument to advance, that it failed. Ah! these arguments *after the event!* they are so fatal, and so very easy.

Right or wrong, Lee resolved to make the attack; and on the third of July he carried out his resolution.

If the writer of the South shrinks from describing the bloody repulse of Longstreet, much more gloomy is the task of painting that last charge at Gettysburg. It is one of those scenes which Lee's old soldiers approach with repugnance. That thunder of the guns which comes back to memory seems to issue, hollow and lugubrious, from a thousand tombs.

Let us pass over that tragedy rapidly. It must be touched on in these memoirs—but I leave it soon.

It is the third of July, 1863. Lee's line of battle, stretching along the crest of Seminary Ridge, awaits the signal for a new conflict with a carelessness as great as on the preceding day. The infantry are laughing, jesting, cooking their rations, and smoking their pipes. The ragged cannoneers, with flashing eyes, smiling lips, and faces blackened with powder, are standing in groups, or lying down around the pieces of artillery. Near the center of the line a gray-headed officer, in plain uniform, and entirely unattended, has dismounted, and is reconnoitering the Federal position through a pair of field-glasses.

It is Lee, and he is looking toward Cemetery Heights, the Mount St. Jeau of the new Waterloo—on whose slopes the immense conflict is going to be decided.

Lee gazes for some moments through his glasses at the long range bristling with bayonets. Not a muscle moves; he resembles a statue. Then he lowers the glasses, closes them thoughtfully, and his calm glance passes along the lines of his army. You would say that this glance penetrates the forest; that he sees his old soldiers, gay, unshrinking, unmoved by the reverses of Longstreet, and believing in themselves and him! The blood of the soldier responds to that thought. The face of the great commander suddenly flushes. He summons a staff officer and utters a few words in calm and measured tones. The order is given. The grand assault is about to begin.

That assault is going to be one of the most desperate in all history. Longstreet's has been fierce—this will be mad and full of headlong fury. At Round Top blood flowed—here the earth is going to be soaked with it. Gettysburg is to witness a charge recalling that of the six hundred horsemen at Balaklava. Each soldier will feel that the fate of the South depends on him, perhaps. If the wedge splits the tough grain, cracking it from end to end, the ax will enter after it—the work will be finished—the red flag of the South will float in triumph over a last and decisive field.

Pickett's division of Virginia troops has been selected for the hazardous venture, and they prepare for the ordeal in the midst of a profound silence. Since the morning scarce a gunshot has been heard. Now and then only, a single cannon, like a signal-gun, sends its growl through the hills.

Those two tigers, the army of Northern Virginia and the army of the Potomac, are crouching, and about to spring.

At one o'clock the moment seems to have arrived. Along the whole front of Hill and Longstreet, the Southern artillery all at once bursts forth. One hundred and forty-five cannon send their threatening thunder across the peaceful valley. From Cemetery Heights eighty pieces reply to them; and for more than an hour these two hundred and twenty-five cannon tear the air with their harsh roar, hurled back in crash after crash from the rocky ramparts. That thunder is the most terrible yet heard in the war. It stirs the coolest veterans. General Hancock, the composed and unexcitable soldier, is going to say of it, "Their artillery fire was most terrific; . . . it was the most terrific cannonade I ever witnessed, and the most prolonged. . . . It was a most terrific and appalling cannonade, one possibly hardly ever equaled."

For nearly two hours Lee continues this "terrific" fire. The Federal guns reply—shot and shell crossing each other; racing across the blue sky; battering the rocks; or bursting in showers of iron fragments.

Suddenly the Federal fire slackens, and then ceases. Their ammunition has run low or they are silenced by the Southern fire. Lee's guns also cease firing. The hour has come.

The Virginians, under Pickett, form in double line at the edge of the woods, where Lee's center is posted. These men are ragged and travel-worn, but their bayonets and gun-barrels shine like silver. From the steel hedge, the men move, dart lightnings.

From the Cemetery Heights the enemy watch that ominous apparition—the gray line of Virginians drawn up for the charge.

At the word, they move out, shoulder to shoulder, at common time. Descending the slope, they enter on the valley, and move steadily toward the heights.

The advance of the column, with its battle-flags floating proudly, and its ranks closed up and dressed with the precision of troops on parade, is a magnificent spectacle. Old soldiers, hardened in the fires of battle, and not given to emotion, lean forward watching the advance of the Virginians with fiery eyes. You would say, from the fierce clutch of the gaunt hands on the muskets, that they wish to follow; and many wish that.

The column is midway across the valley, and beginning to move more rapidly, when suddenly the Federal artillery opens. The ranks are swept by round shot, shell, and canister. Bloody gaps appear, but the line closes up, and continues to advance. The fire of the Federal artillery redoubles. All the demons of the pit seem howling, roaring, yelling, and screaming. The assaulting column is torn by a whirlwind of canister, before which men fall in heaps mangled, streaming with blood, their bosoms torn to pieces, their hands clutching the grass, their teeth biting the earth. The ranks, however, close up as before, and the Virginians continue to advance.

From common time, they have passed to quick time—now they

march at the double-quick. That is to say, they run. They have reached the slope; the enemy's breastworks are right before them; and they dash at them with wild cheers.

They are still three hundred yards from the Federal works, when the real conflict commences, to which the cannonade was but child's play. Artillery has thundered, but something more deadly succeeds it—the sudden crash of musketry. From behind a stone wall the Federal infantry rise up and pour a galling fire into the charge column. It has been accompanied to this moment by a body of other troops, but those troops now disappear, like dry leaves swept off by the wind. The Virginians still advance.

Amid a concentrated fire of infantry and artillery, in their front and on both flanks, they pass over the ground between themselves; storm them; strike their bayonets into the enemy, who recoil before them, and a wild cheer rises, making the blood leap in the veins of a hundred thousand men.

The Federal works are carried, and the troops are wild with enthusiasm. With a thunder of cheers they press upon the flying enemy toward the crest.

Alas! as the smoke drifts, they see what is enough to dishearten the bravest. They have stormed the first line of works only! Beyond, is another and stronger line still. Behind it swarm the heavy reserves of the enemy, ready for the death struggle. But the column can not pause. It is "do or die." In their faces are thrust the muzzles of muskets spouting flame. Whole ranks go down in the fire. The survivors close up, utter a fierce cheer, and rush straight at the second tier of works.

Then is seen a spectacle which will long be remembered within the heart by many. The thinned ranks of the Virginians are advancing, unmoved, into the very jaws of death. They go forward and are annihilated. At every step death meets them. The furious fire of the enemy, on both flanks and in their front, hurls them back, mangled and dying. The brave Garnett is killed while leading on his men. Kemper is lying on the earth maimed for life. Armistead is mortally wounded at the moment when he leaps upon the breastworks:—he waves his hat on the point of his sword, and staggers, and falls. Of fifteen field officers, fourteen have fallen. Three-fourths of the men are dead, wounded, or prisoners. The Federal infantry has closed in on the flanks and rear of the Virginians—whole corps assault the handful—the little band is enveloped, and cut off from succor—they turn and face the enemy, bayonet to bayonet, and die.

When the smoke drifts away, all is seen to be over. It is a panting, staggering, bleeding remnant only of the brave division that is coming back slowly to yonder. They are swept from the fatal hill—pursued by yells, cheers, cannon-shot, musket-balls, and canister. As they doggedly retire before the howling hurricane, the wounded are seen to stagger and fall. Over the dead and dying sweeps the canister. Amid volleys of musketry and the roar of cannon, all but a handful of Pickett's Virginians pass into eternity.

Ambrose Bierce

(1842–1914?)

Born in Meigs County, Ohio, Ambrose Bierce attended the Kentucky Military Institute and in 1861 enlisted as a private in the 9th Indiana Infantry Regiment. He served in the Army of Ohio under Buell and saw action at Shiloh, Chickamauga, Lookout Mountain, and Missionary Ridge. He was wounded at Kennesaw Mountain but returned to duty in time to participate in Sherman's Carolina campaign. He rose through the ranks to sergeant major, then to lieutenant in 1862, and left the army in 1868 a brevet major. In California he worked for the Hearst papers and wrote a series of articles on the Spanish-American War (1898) in which he satirized jingoistic patriotism and argued that the conflict with Spain was unnecessary and imperialistic. From 1900 to 1913 he lived in Washington, D.C., and moved in military circles. On December 26, 1913, he left for Ojinaga, Mexico, where he was probably killed in the battle he was on his way to write about.

Known as "Bitter Bierce," he entered the Civil War idealistic and emerged battle-scarred and cynical. Bierce believed that war stripped the soul naked and revealed a person's character, and at the same time he felt war was the supreme waste. In the following short story, "Chickamauga," Bierce describes the details of battle as perceived by a deaf and dumb child. Bierce believed that, like the central consciousness of the story, all men are deaf and dumb in the face of battle, and he parodies the established mythology and heroic rhetoric of war to make this point. The story begins with an indictment of martial heritage; depicts war as child's play; describes the dehumanizing effect war has on men, turning them into deformed crawling beasts; and concludes with inverted biblical imagery that debunks self-righteous justification of war. One reason this story is so effectively terrifying and wrenching is that it deliberately inverts established war rhetoric and mythology—revealing them to be cant. Bierce's postwar pessimism cancels out the optimism of the Holmes piece that follows and helps shape the thinking of later generations of Americans who were to pay more attention to the bloody means of war than to romantic and religious justifications of combat.

from Bierce's "Chickamauga"

One sunny autumn afternoon a child strayed away from its rude home
in a small field and entered a forest unobserved. It was happy in a new
sense of freedom from control—happy in the opportunity of explora-
tion and adventure; for this child's spirit, in bodies of its ancestors,
had for many thousands of years been trained to memorable feats of
discovery and conquest—victories in battles whose critical moments
were centuries, whose victors' camps were cities of hewn stone. From
the cradle of its race it had conquered its way through two continents,
and, passing a great sea, had penetrated a third, there to be born to
war and dominance as a heritage.

The child was a boy, aged about six years, the son of a poor
planter. In his younger manhood the father had been a soldier, had
fought against naked savages, and followed the flag of his country into
the capital of a civilised race to the far South. In the peaceful life of a
planter the warrior-fire survived; once kindled it is never extinguished.
The man loved military books and pictures, and the boy had understood enough to make himself a wooden sword, though even the eye
of his father would hardly have known it for what it was. This weapon
he now bore bravely, as became the son of an heroic race, and, pausing
now and again in the sunny spaces of the forest, assumed, with some
exaggeration, the postures of aggression and defence that he had been
taught by the engraver's art. Made reckless by the ease with which he
overcame invisible foes attempting to stay his advance, he committed
the common enough military error of pushing the pursuit to a dangerous extreme, until he found himself upon the margin of a wide but
shallow brook, whose rapid waters barred his direct advance against
the flying foe who had crossed with illogical ease. But the intrepid
victor was not to be baffled; the spirit of the race which had passed the
great sea burned unconquerable in that small breast and would not be
denied. Finding a place where some boulders in the bed of the stream
lay but a step or a leap apart, he made his way across and fell again
upon the rear guard of his imaginary foe, putting all to the sword.

Now that the battle had been won, prudence required that he
withdraw to his base of operations. Alas! like many a mightier con-
queror, and like one, the mightiest, he could not curb the lust for war,
nor learn that tempted Fate will leave the loftiest star.

Advancing from the bank of the creek, he suddenly found himself confronted with a new and more formidable enemy; in the path that he was following, bolt upright, with ears erect and paws suspended before it, sat a rabbit. With a startled cry the child turned and fled, he knew not in what direction, calling with inarticulate cries for his mother, weeping, stumbling, his tender skin cruelly torn by brambles, his little heart beating hard with terror—breathless, blind with tears— lost in the forest! Then, for more than an hour, he wandered with erring feet through the tangled undergrowth, till at last, overcome with fatigue, he lay down in a narrow space between two rocks, within a few yards of the stream, and, still grasping his toy sword, no longer a weapon but a companion, sobbed himself to sleep. The wood birds sang merrily above his head; the squirrels, whisking their bravery of tail, ran barking from tree to tree, unconscious of the pity of it, and somewhere far away was a strange, muffled thunder, as if the partridges were drumming in celebration of nature's victory over the son of her immemorial enslavers. And back at the little plantation, where white men and black were hastily searching the fields and hedgerows in alarm, a mother's heart was breaking for her missing child.

Hours passed, and then the little sleeper rose to his feet. The chill of the evening was in his limbs, the fear of the gloom in his heart. But he had rested, and he no longer wept. With some blind instinct which impelled to action, he struggled through the undergrowth about him and came to a more open ground—on his right the brook, to the left a gentle acclivity studded with infrequent trees; over all the gathering gloom of twilight. A thin ghostly mist rose along the water. It frightened and repelled him; instead of recrossing, in the direction whence he had come, he turned his back upon it and went forward toward the dark enclosing wood. Suddenly he saw before him a strange moving object which he took to be some large animal—a dog, a pig—he could not name it; perhaps it was a bear. He had seen pictures of bears, but knew of nothing to their discredit, and had vaguely wished to meet one. But something in form or movement of this object—something in the awkwardness of its approach—told him that it was not a bear, and curiosity was stayed by fear. He stood still, and as it came slowly on, gained courage every moment, for he saw that at least it had not the long, menacing ears of the rabbit. Possibly his impressionable mind was half conscious of something familiar in its shambling, awkward gait. Before it had approached near enough to resolve his doubts, he saw that it was followed by another and another. To right and to left were many more; the whole open space about him was alive with them—all moving forward toward the brook.

They were men. They crept upon their hands and knees. They used their hands only, dragging their legs. They used their knees only; their arms hanging useless at their sides. They strove to rise to their feet, but fell prone in the attempt. They did nothing naturally, and nothing alike, save only to advance foot by foot in the same direction. Singly, in pairs, and in little groups, they came on through the gloom, some halting now and again while others crept slowly past him, then resuming their movement. They came by the dozens and by hundreds; as far on either hand as one could see in the deepening gloom they extended, and the black wood behind them appeared to be inexhaustible. The very ground seemed in motion toward the creek. Occasionally one who had paused did not again go on, but lay motionless. He was dead. Some, pausing, made strange gestures with their hands, erected their palms upward, as men are sometimes seen to do in public prayer.

Not all of this did the child note; it is what would have been noted by an older observer; he saw little but that these were men, yet crept like babes. Being men, they were not terrible, though some of them were unfamiliarly clad. He moved among them freely, going from one to another and peering into their faces with childish curiosity. All their faces were singularly white and many were streaked and gouged with red. Something in this—something too, perhaps, in their grotesque attitudes and movements—reminded him of the painted clown whom he had seen last summer in the circus, and he laughed as he watched them. But on and ever on they crept, these maimed and bleeding men, as heedless as he of the dramatic contrast between his laughter and their own ghastly gravity. To him it was a merry spectacle. He had seen his father's negroes creep upon their hands and knees for his amusement—had ridden them so, 'making believe' they were his horses. He now approached one of the crawling figures from behind and with an agile movement mounted it astride. The man sank upon his breast, recovered, flung the small boy fiercely to the ground as an unbroken colt might have done, then turned upon him a face that lacked a lower jaw: from the upper teeth to the throat was a great red gap fringed with

hanging shreds of flesh and splinters of bone. The unnatural promi-
nence of nose, the absence of chin, the fierce eyes, gave this man the
appearance of a great bird of prey crimsoned in throat and breast by
the blood of its quarry. The man rose to his knees, the child to his feet.
The man shook his fist at the child; the child, terrified at last, ran to a
tree near by, got upon the farther side of it, and took a more serious
view of the situation. And so the uncanny multitude dragged itself
slowly and painfully along in hideous pantomime—moved forward
down the slope like a swarm of great black beetles, with never a sound
of going—in silence profound, absolute.

Instead of darkening, the haunted landscape began to brighten.
Through the belt of trees beyond the brook shone a strange red light,
the trunks and branches of the trees making a black lacework against
it. It struck the creeping figures and gave them monstrous shadows,
which caricatured their movements on the lit grass. It fell upon their
faces, touching their whiteness with a ruddy tinge, accentuating the
stains with which so many of them were freaked and maculated. It spar-
kled on buttons and bits of metal in their clothing. Instinctively the
child turned toward the growing splendour and moved down the slope
with his horrible companions; in a few moments had passed the foremost of the throng—not much of a feat, considering his advantages.
He placed himself in the lead, his wooden sword still in hand, and
solemnly directed the march, conforming his pace to theirs and occasionally turning as if to see that his forces did not straggle. Surely such
a leader never before had such a following.

Scattered about upon the ground now slowly narrowing by the
encroachment of this awful march to water, were certain articles to
which, in the leader's mind, were coupled no significant associations;
an occasional blanket, tightly rolled lengthwise, doubled, and the ends
bound together with a string; a heavy knapsack here, and there a broken musket—such things, in short, as are found in the rear of retreating troops, the 'spoor' of men flying from their hunters. Everywhere
near the creek, which here had a margin of lowland, the earth was
trodden into mud by the feet of men and horses. An observer of better
experience in the use of his eyes would have noticed that these foot-
prints pointed in both direction; the ground had been twice passed
over—in advance and in retreat. A few hours before, these desperate,
stricken men, with their more fortunate and now distant comrades,

had penetrated the forest in thousands. Their successive battalions, breaking into swarms and reforming in lines, had passed the child on every side—had almost trodden on him as he slept. The rustle and murmur of their march had not awakened him. Almost within a stone's throw of where he lay they had fought a battle; but all unheard by him were the roar of the musketry, the shock of the cannon, 'the thunder of the captains and the shouting.' He had slept through it all, grasping his little wooden sword with perhaps a tighter clutch in unconscious sympathy with his martial environment, but as heedless of the grandeur of the struggle as the dead who died to make the glory.

The fire beyond the belt of woods on the farther side of the creek, reflected to earth from the canopy of its own smoke, was now suffusing the whole landscape. It transformed the sinuous line of mist to the vapour of gold. The water gleamed with dashes of red, and red, too, were many of the stones protruding above the surface. But that was blood; the less desperately wounded had stained them in crossing. On them, too, the child now crossed with eager steps; he was going to the fire. As he stood upon the farther bank, he turned about to look at the companions of his march. The advance was arriving at the creek. The stronger had already drawn themselves to the brink and plunged their faces in the flood. Three or four who lay without motion appeared to have no heads. At this the child's eyes expanded with wonder; even his hospitable understanding could not accept a phenomenon implying such vitality as that. After slaking their thirst these men had not the strength to back away from the water, not to keep their heads above it. They were drowned. In rear of these the open spaces of the forest showed the leader as many formless figures of his grim command as at first; but not nearly so many were in motion. He waved his cap for their encouragement and smilingly pointed with his weapon in the direction of the guiding light—a pillar of fire to this strange exodus.

Confident of the fidelity of his forces, he now entered the belt of woods, passed through it easily in the red illumination, climbed a fence, ran across a field, turning now and again to coquette with his responsive shadow, and so approached the blazing ruin of a dwelling. Desolation everywhere. In all the wide glare not a living thing was visible. He cared nothing for that; the spectacle pleased, and he danced with glee in imitation of the wavering flames. He ran about collecting fuel, but every object that he found was too heavy for him to cast in from the distance to which the heat limited his approach. In despair he flung in his sword—a surrender to the superior forces of nature. His military career was at an end.

Shifting his position his eyes fell upon some outbuildings which had an oddly familiar appearance, as if he had dreamed of them. He stood considering them with wonder, when suddenly the entire plantation, with its enclosing forest, seemed to turn as if upon a pivot. His little world swung half around; the points of the compass were reversed. He recognized the blazing buildings as his own home.

For a moment he stood stupefied by the power of the revelation, then ran with stumbling feet, making a half circuit of the ruin. There, conspicuous in the light of the conflagration, lay the dead body of a woman—the white face turned upward, the hands thrown out and clutched full of grass, the clothing deranged, the long dark hair in tangles and full of clotted blood. The greater part of the forehead was torn away, and from the jagged hole the brain protruded, overflowing the temple, a frothy mass of gray, crowned with cluster of crimson bubbles—the work of a shell!

The child moved his little hands, making wild, uncertain gestures. He uttered a series of inarticulate and indescribable cries—something between the chattering of an ape and the gobbling of a turkey—a startling, soulless, unholy sound, the language of a devil. The child was a deaf mute.

Then he stood motionless, with quivering lips, looking down upon the wreck.

Oliver Wendell Holmes, Jr.

(1841–1935)

Born into the Brahmin class of Boston's cultural elite, Oliver Wendell Holmes, Jr., is best known as an independent-minded justice of the U. S. Supreme Court, but he also had a remarkable career as a soldier. Holmes was a senior at Harvard University when the Civil War started. Moved by abolitionist sympathies, he enlisted as a private, took his final exams in uniform, and entered the war. He participated in many battles, including Ball's Bluff, Antietam, the Wilderness, Spotsylvania, and Cold Harbor; was wounded three times; and left the army a brevet lieutenant colonel, a rank earned at the Battle of Chancellorsville. The war convinced him that despite the horrors, a soldier's dedication to honor was a "divine folly" that made life endurable.

The following speech delivered at Harvard on Memorial Day 1895 expresses Holmes's belief in the inevitability of war and the glory of combat. In it he calls for soldierly virtues to reform society. In many ways the culmination of traditional American war rhetoric and mythology, Holmes's speech claims that "the sword is the will of God" and that the discipline of combat ennobles the character. Although a few critics, like Ambrose Bierce, rejected this conviction, Holmes's address proves that the earliest American war myths survived well into the nineteenth century.

from Holmes's "An Address by Oliver Wendell Holmes Delivered on Memorial Day, May 30, 1895"

Any day in Washington Street, when the throng is greatest and busiest, you may see a blind man playing a flute. I suppose that someone hears him. Perhaps also my pipe may reach the heart of some passer in the crowd.

I once heard a man say, "Where Vanderbilt sits, there is the head of the table. I teach my son to be rich." He said what many think. For although the generation born about 1840, and now governing the world, has fought two at least of the greatest wars in history, and has witnessed others, war is out of fashion, and the man who commands the attention of his fellows is the man of wealth. Commerce is the great power. The aspirations of the world are those of commerce. Moralists and philosophers, following its lead, declare that war is wicked, foolish, and soon to disappear.

The society for which many philanthropists, labor reformers, and men of fashion unite in longing is one in which they may be comfortable and may shine without much trouble or any danger. The unfortunately growing hatred of the poor for the rich seems to me to rest on the belief that money is the main thing (a belief in which the poor have been encouraged by the rich), more than on any grievance. Most of my hearers would rather that their daughters or their sisters should marry a son of one of the great rich families than a regular army officer, were he as beautiful, brave, and gifted as Sir William Napier. I have heard the question asked whether our war was worth fighting, after all. There are many, poor and rich, who think that love of country is an old wife's tale, to be replaced by interest in a labor union, or, under the name of cosmopolitanism, by a rootless self-seeking search for a place where the most enjoyment may be had at the least cost.

Meantime we have learned the doctrine that evil means pain, and the revolt against pain in all its forms has grown more and more marked. From societies for the prevention of cruelty to animals up to socialism, we express in numberless ways the notion that suffering is a wrong which can be and ought to be prevented, and a whole literature of sympathy has sprung into being which points out in story and in verse how hard it is to be wounded in the battle of life, how terrible, how unjust it is that any one should fail.

Even science has had its part in the tendencies which we observe. It has shaken established religion in the minds of very many. It has pursued analysis until at last this thrilling world of colors and sounds and passions has seemed fatally to resolve itself into one vast network of vibrations endlessly weaving an aimless web, and the rainbow flush of cathedral windows, which once to enraptured eyes appeared the very smile of God, fades slowly out into the pale irony of the void.

And yet from vast orchestras still comes the music of mighty symphonies. Our painters even now are spreading along the walls of our Library glowing symbols of mysteries still real, and the hardly silenced cannon of the East proclaim once more that combat and pain still are the potion of man. For my own part, I believe that the struggle for life is the order of the world, at which it is vain to repine. I can imagine the burden changed in the way in which it is to be borne, but I cannot imagine that it ever will be lifted from men's backs. I can imagine a future in which science shall have passed from the combative to the dogmatic stage, and shall have gained such catholic acceptance that it shall take control of life, and condemn at once with instant execution what now is left for nature to destroy. But we are far from such a future, and we cannot stop to amuse or to terrify ourselves with dreams. Now, at least, and perhaps as long as man dwells upon the globe, his destiny is battle, and he has to take the chances of war. If it is our business to fight, the book for the army is a war-song, not a hospital-sketch. It is not well for soldiers to think much about wounds. Sooner or later we shall fall; but meantime it is for us to fix our eyes upon the point to be stormed and to get there if we can.

Behind every scheme to make the world over, lies the question. What kind of world do you want? The ideals of the past for men have been drawn from war, as those for women have been drawn from motherhood. For all our prophecies, I doubt if we are ready to give up our inheritance. Who is there who would not like to be thought a gentleman? Yet what has that name been built on but the soldier's choice of honor rather than life? To be a soldier or descended from soldiers, in time of peace to be ready to give one's life rather than to suffer disgrace, that is what the world has meant; and if we try to claim it at less cost than a splendid carelessness for life, we are trying to steal the good will without the responsibilities of the place. We will not dispute about tastes. The man of the future may want something different. But who of us could endure a world, although cut up into five-acre lots and having no man upon it who was not well fed and well housed, without the divine folly of honor, without the senseless passion for knowledge outreaching the flaming bounds of the possible, without ideals the essence of which is that they never can be achieved? I do not know what is true. I do not know the meaning of the universe. But in the midst of doubt, in the collapse of creeds, there is one thing I do not doubt, that no man who lives in the same world with most of us can doubt, and that is that the faith is true and adorable which leads a soldier to throw away his life in obedience to a blindly accepted duty, in a cause which he little understands, in a plan of campaign of which he had no notion, under tactics of which he does not see the use.

Most men who know battle know the cynic force with which the thoughts of common sense will assail them in times of stress; but they know that in their greatest moments faith has trampled those thoughts under foot. If you have been in line, suppose on Tremont Street Mall, ordered simply to wait and to do nothing, and have watched the enemy bring their guns to bear upon you down a gentle slope like that from Beacon Street, have seen the puff of the firing, have felt the burst of the spherical case-shot as it came toward you, have heard and seen the shrieking fragments go tearing through your company, and have known that the next or the next shot carries your fate; if you have advanced in line and have seen ahead of you the spot which you must pass where the rifle bullets are striking; if you have ridden by night at a walk toward the blue line of fire at the dead angle of Spotsylvania, where for twenty-four hours the soldiers were fighting on the two sides of an earth work, and in the morning the dead and the dying lay piled in a row six deep, and as you rode have heard the bullets splashing in the mud and earth about you; if you have been on the picketline at night in a black and unknown wood, have heard the spat of the bullets upon the trees, and as you moved have felt your foot slip upon a dead man's body; if you have had a blind fierce gallop against the enemy, with your blood up and a pace that left no time for fear—if, in short, as some, I hope many, who hear me, have known, you have known the vicissitudes of terror and of triumph in war, you know that there is such a thing as the faith I spoke of. You know your own weakness and are modest; but you know that man has in him that unspeakable something which makes him capable of miracle, able to lift himself by the might of his own soul, unaided, able to face annihilation for a blind belief.

From the beginning, to us, children of the North, life has seemed a place hung about by dark mists, out of which come the pale shine of dragon's scales, and the cry of fighting men, and the sound of swords. Beowulf, Milton, Dürer, Rembrandt, Schopenhauer, Turner, Tennyson, from the first war-song of our race to the stall-fed poetry of modern English drawing-rooms, all have had the same vision, and all have had a glimpse of a light to be followed. "The end of worldly life awaits us all. Let him who may, gain honor ere death. That is best for a warrior when he is dead." So spoke Beowulf a thousand years ago.

> Not of the sunlight, not of the moonlight
> Not of the starlight! O young Mariner,
> Down to the heaven, call your companions,
> Launch your vessel, and crowd your canvas,
> And, ere it vanishes over the margin,
> After it, follow it, follow the Gleam.

So sang Tennyson in the voice of the dying Merlin.

When I went to the war I thought that soldiers were old men. I remembered a picture of the revolutionary soldier which some of you may have seen, representing a white-haired man with his flintlock slung across his back. I remembered one or two living examples of revolutionary soldiers whom I had met, and I took no account of the lapse of time. It was not until long after, in winter quarters, as I was listening to some of the sentimental songs in vogue, such as—

> *Farewell, Mother, you may never*
> *See your darling boy again,*

that it came over me that the army was made up of what I now should call very young men. I dare say that my illusion has been shared by some of those now present, as they have looked at us upon whose heads the white shadows have begun to fall. But the truth is that war is the business of youth and early middle age. You who called this assemblage together, not we, would be the soldiers of another war, if we should have one, and we speak to you as the dying Merlin did in the verse which I just quoted. Would that the blind man's pipe might be transfigured by Merlin's magic, to make you hear the bugles as once we heard them beneath the morning stars! For to you it is that now is sung the Song of the Sword:—

> *The War-Thing, the Comrade, father of honor*
> *And giver of kingship, the fame-smith, the song master.*
>
> . . .
>
> *Priest (saith the Lord) of his marriage with victory.*
> *Clear singing, clean slicing; sweet spoken, soft finishing;*
> *Making death beautiful, life but a coin*

To be staked in the pastime whose playing is more
Than the transfer of being; arch-anarch, chief builder,
Prince and evangelist, I am the Will of God:
I am the Sword.

War, when you are at it, is horrible and dull. It is only when time has passed that you see that its message was divine. I hope it may be long before we are called again to sit at that master's feet. But some teacher of the kind we all need. In this snug, over-safe corner of the world we need it that we may realize that our comfortable routine is no eternal necessity of things, but merely a little space of calm in the midst of the tempestuous untamed streaming of the world, and in order that we may be ready for danger. We need it in this time of individualist negations, with its literature of French and American humor, revolting at discipline, loving fleshpots, and denying that anything is worthy of reverence,—in order that we may remember all that buffoons forget. We need it everywhere and at all times. For high and dangerous action teaches us to believe as right beyond dispute things for which our doubting minds are slow to find words of proof. Out of heroism grows faith in the worth of heroism. The proof comes later, and even may never come. Therefore I rejoice at every dangerous sport which I see pursued. The students at Heidelberg, with their sword-slashed faces, [dueling society wounds] inspire me with sincere respect. I gaze with delight upon our polo players. If once in a while in our rough riding a neck is broken, I regard it not as a waste, but as a price well paid for the breeding of a race fit for leadership and command.

We do not save our traditions in this country. The regiments whose battle-flags were not large enough to hold the names of battles they had fought, vanished with the surrender of Lee, although their memories inherited would have made heroes for a century. It is the more necessary to learn the lesson afresh from perils newly sought, and perhaps it is not vain for us to tell the new generation what we learned in our day, and what we still believe. That the joy of life is living, is to put out all one's powers as far as they will go; that the measure of power is obstacles overcome; to ride boldly at what is in front of you, be it fence or enemy; to pray, not for comfort, but for combat; to keep the soldier's faith against doubts of civil life more besetting and harder to overcome than all the misgivings of the battle-field, and to remember that duty is not to be obeyed unquestioning; to love glory more than the temptations of wallowing ease, but to know that one's final judge and only rival is oneself with all our failures in act and thought, these things we learned from noble enemies in Virginia or Georgia or on the Mississippi, thirty years ago; these things we believe to be true.

> *"Life is not lost,"* said she, *"for which is bought*
> *Endlesse renown."*

We learned also, and we still believe, that love of country is not yet an idle name.

> *Deare countrey! O how dearely deare*
> *Ought thy remembraunce, and perpetuall band*
> *Be to thy foster-child, that from thy hand*
> *Did commun breath and nouriture receave!*
> *How brutish is it not to understand*
> *How much to her we owe, that all us gave;*
> *That gave unto us all, whatever good we have!*

As for us, our days of combat are over. Our swords are rust. Our guns will thunder no more. The vultures that once wheeled over our heads are buried with their prey. Whatever of glory yet remains for us to win must be won in the council or the closet, never again in the field. I do not repine. We have shared the incommunicable experience of war; we have felt, we still feel, the passion of life to its top.

Three years ago died the old colonel of my regiment, the Twentieth Massachusetts. He gave our regiment its soul. No man could falter who heard his "Forward, Twentieth!" I went to his funeral. From a side door of the church a body of little choir-boys came in like a flight of careless doves. At the same time the doors opened at the front, and up the main aisle advanced his coffin, followed by the few gray heads who stood for the men of the Twentieth, the rank and file whom he had loved, and whom he led for the last time. The church was empty. No one remembered the old man who we were burying, no one save those next to him, and us. And I said to myself, "The Twentieth has shrunk to a skeleton, a ghost, a memory, a forgotten name which we other old men alone keep in our hearts." And then I thought: "It is right. It is as the colonel would have had it. This also is part of the soldier's faith: Having known great things, to be content with silence." Just then there fell into my hands a little song sung by a warlike people on the Danube, which seemed to be fit for a soldier's last word, another song of the sword, but a song of the sword in its scabbard, a song of oblivion and peace.

A soldier has been buried on the battle-field.
And when the wind in the tree-tops roared,
The soldier asked from the deep dark grave:
    "Did the banner flutter then?"
"Not so, my hero," the wind replied,
"The fight is done, but the banner won,
Thy comrades of old have borne it hence,
    Have borne it in triumph hence."
Then the soldier spake from the deep dark grave:
    "I am content."
Then he heareth the lovers laughing pass,
    And the soldier asks once more:
"Are these not the voices of them that love,
    That love—and remember me?"
"Not so, my hero," the lovers say,
"We are those that remember not;
For the spring has come and the earth has smiled,
    And the dead must be forgot."
Then the soldier spake from the deep dark grave:
    "I am content."

Conclusion

Every war is ironic because every war is worse than expected. Every war constitutes an irony of situation because its means are so melodramatically disproportionate to its presumed ends.

—Paul Fussell *The Great War and Modern Memory*

Over time, American war narratives have relied more on collective than on personal memory to organize the details of the nation's conflicts into archetypal patterns that either confirm or reject popularly held perceptions of the nation's role in history. Narratives that seek to reconcile the gruesome details of combat with culturally significant ends inevitably bog down in the irony inherent when myths attempt to justify the brutality of battle. Although historian Paul Fussell's observations on the ironic distance between war's means and rhetorical ends are directed at his study of World War I poetry, they are especially appropriate for describing the "irony of situation" inherent in America's war prose up to and including the Civil War.

Looking back on the Civil War, poet Walt Whitman wrote:

> Future years will never know the seething hell and the black infernal background of countless minor scenes and interiors, (not the official surface-courteousness of the Generals, not the few great battles) of the Secession War; and it is best they should not—the real war will never get in the books.

He believed that the restrictions placed on literature by the "mushy" tastes of his time would keep the "real war" out of popular literature. The difficulty lies beyond the subject matter, however.

Despite the eventual demise of the censorship that blocked the more distasteful details of combat from print, Whitman's prediction that "the real war will never get in the books" may still be true, because the real war must transcend "minor scenes and interiors." A book about the war narrative must try to reconcile the private suffering with the broader cultural myths, and the irony inherent in such an effort denies comfortable written resolution. If "real" war affects both individual and collective consciousness and contains

271

both bloody means and idealistic ends, then it may be too much to attempt to overcome the distance between the two.

Even a consciousness as all-embracing as Whitman's failed in just such an effort. For many years, Whitman contemplated writing a book about the Civil War. In 1863 he proposed to the publisher John Redpath "a book full enough of mosaic, but all fused into one comprehensive history." In 1875 he considered writing a history of the war, and at least flirted with producing a history of his brother George's regiment, the 51st New York. Finally, in the opening paragraph of *Specimen Days (1882–83)*, he decides he will "let the melange's lackings and want of connection take care of themselves."

His failure to find a unifying "theory" derives from the fundamental impossibility of closing the gap between the concrete reality of personal war narrative (what he knew from his experiences caring for the wounded) and the mythic ideals of America's public war rhetoric (ideals he wanted to believe and promulgate). The difficulty Whitman encounters in reconciling private memory with public myth-making further illustrates and supports Paul Fussell's conclusions about the inherent irony of war.

America's experience with war and its efforts to write about it mirror Whitman's frustration and Fussell's observations, only on a larger scale. The violent means and human suffering of combat do not lend themselves comfortably to myths of unlimited human potential and moral exceptionalism. Like Whitman, the national consciousness has to confront a "melodramatic disproportion" between means and ends.

In his poem "Elegy for a Dead Soldier," Karl Shapiro has his narrator reflect on an anonymous young soldier's "tail-gate" funeral during World War II. Shapiro's spokesman leaves the funeral service "sick with the utter silence of dispraise," and at first concludes that the soldier's death is a final deprivation, a meaningless "accident." Then he goes on to describe the dead soldier as an American everyman, his wartime "a detour that would steer / Into the Lincoln Highway of a land / Remorselessly improved, excited, new, / And that was what he wanted." The poem catalogs popular American myths that sustained the dead soldier and ends with a prayer for "peace kept by human creed." In this poem, Shapiro, a sergeant in the South Pacific, tries to reconcile the death he saw in combat with the nation's legends. He offers no easy resolution, only prayer and hope for the future.

One in search of the impact of war on the American consciousness must ask, along with Karl Shapiro's World War II narrator, "Shall we believe our eyes or legends rich with glory and rebirth beyond the void?" Shall we believe that the "real war" is the one reconstructed by memory or by imagination? Shall we believe the written record of "our eyes," or the cultural myths and "the legends rich"? Shall we look to the personal records of participants for the truth of America's experiences, or should we trust the recreation of the conflict in fiction to tell us the larger truth about Americans at war? An answer is that we must learn the lessons of American war experience from both our eyes and our myths, from those writers who write both for themselves and for a wider audience, from those who remember and report as well as from those who remember and explain, from what both private and public voices have to say about America's wars.

This anthology is obviously not a complete record of American war prose, nor is it a magic key to American culture, but its selections do record war's impact on both the individual and the national consciousness. It describes that forward edge of combat that John Ellis calls the "sharp end" of war, and it presents aesthetic strategies used to explain the cultural significance of war experience. Together, narrative accounts of war's suffering and the literary quests for its meaning provide some reconciliation of the cultural myths and the personal suffering of Americans at war. They are a revealing record of the private and the public consciousness of America at war, and perhaps the closest we can come to the "real war" in a single book.

Works Cited

Alcott, Louisa May. *Hospital Sketches.* Boston: Roberts Brothers, 1869.

Alexander, Edmund B. Special Collections, U.S. Military Academy Library. West Point, N.Y.

"An Anonymous Account of the Battle of New Orleans." *Louisiana Historical Quarterly*, 1926.

Anonymous "Reminiscences of Shiloh." In *The Civil War in Song and Story: 1860–1865,* edited by Frank Moore. New York: P. F. Collier, 1892.

Bierce, Ambrose. "Chickamauga." In *Tales of Soldiers and Civilians.* San Francisco: E.L.G. Steele, 1891.

Bradford, William. *History of Plymouth Plantation.* Boston: Wright Potter Printing Co., 1899.

Bull, Rice C. *Soldiering: The Civil War Diary of Rice C. Bull,* edited by K. Jack Bauer. San Rafael: Presidio Press, 1977.

Chesnut, Mary. *A Diary from Dixie,* edited by Isabella D. Martin and Myrta Lockett Avary. New York: D. Appleton, 1905.

Church, Benjamin. *The Entertaining History of King Philip's War.* 2d edition. Boston: Solomon Southwick, 1716.

Cooke, John Esten. *Mohun.* New York: F. J. Huntington, 1869.

Cooper, James Fenimore. *The Spy.* London: J.T. Devison, 1822.

Dana, Napoleon J.T. Special Collections, U. S. Military Academy Library. West Point, N.Y.

Doubleday, Abner. *Reminiscences of Forts Sumter and Moultrie.* New York: Harper and Brothers, 1876.

Francis, Jacob. "Petition for Pension." In *The Revolution Remembered: Eye Witness Accounts of the War of Independence,* edited by John C. Dann. Chicago: University of Chicago Press, 1977.

Franklin, Benjamin. *The Autobiography of Benjamin Franklin.* New York: Houghton Mifflin, 1889.

Grant, U. S. *Personal Memoirs.* Special Collections, U. S. Military Academy Library. West Point, N.Y.

Haley, John. *The Rebel Yell and the Yankees Hurrah: The Civil War Journal of a Maine Volunteer,* edited by Ruth L. Silliker. Camden, Me.: DownEast Books, 1985.

Holmes, Oliver Wendell, Jr. "An Address by Oliver Wendell Holmes Delivered on Memorial Day, May 30, 1895." Boston: Little, Brown, 1895.

Hutson, Charles Woodward. *Charles Woodward Hutson Papers.* Southern Historical Collection. Chapel Hill, N.C.: University of North Carolina Library.

Lee, Robert E. Special Collections, U. S. Military Academy Library. West Point, N.Y.

Martin, Joseph Plumb. *Private Yankee Doodle: Being a Narrative of Some of the Adventures, Dangers, and Sufferings of a Revolutionary War Soldier,* edited by George F. Scheer. New York: Little, Brown, 1962.

Mather, Increase. *A Brief History of the Warr with the Indians in New England.* Boston: Sign of the Dove, 1676.

Miller, James. Special Collections, U. S. Military Academy Library. West Point, N.Y.

Montgomery, Walter A. "Appomattox and the Return Home." In *Histories of the Several Regiments and Battalions from North Carolina,* edited by Walter Clark. Raleigh: North Carolina State Literary and Historical Commission, 1901.

Newsom, Nathan. *Diary of Nathan Newsom, 1812–1813.* The Ohio Historical Society, Columbus, Ohio.

Newton, James K. "Letter to Family, 12 April 1862." In *A Wisconsin Boy in Dixie,* edited by Stephen E. Ambrose. Madison: University of Wisconsin Press, 1961.

Potter, Israel. "Life and Adventures of Israel Potter." *The Magazine of History.* New York: William Abbatt, 1911.

Rathbun, Jonathan. "Narrative of Jonathan Rathbun." *The Magazine of History.* New York: William Abbatt, 1911.

Rogers, Robert. *Journals of Major Robert Rogers.* London: J. Millan, 1765.

Scribner, Benjamin Franklin. *A Campaign in Mexico or a Camp Life of a Volunteer by "One Who Has Seen the Elephant."* Philadelphia: Grigg, Elliot, 1847.

Smith, John. *Travels and Works of Captain John Smith,* edited by Edward Arber. Edinburgh: John Grant, 1910.

Stocking, Abner. "Journal of Abner Stocking as Kept by Himself, During His Long and Tedious March Through the Wilderness to Quebec." *The Magazine of History.* New York: William Abbatt, 1911.

Stubbs, Samuel. "Letter to His Brother." *The Magazine of History.* New York: William Abbatt, 1929.

Thacher, James. *The American Revolution from the Commencement to the Disbanding of the American Army.* New York: American Subscription, 1860.

Valpey, Joseph, Jr. *Journal of Joseph Valpey, Jr., of Salem.* Ann Arbor: Michigan Society of Colonial Wars, 1922.

Waldo, Albigence. "Journal of Valley Forge." *Pennsylvania Magazine of History and Biography,* Philadelphia: Historical Society of Pennsylvania, 1898.

Wheeler, Thomas. *A Thankful Remembrance of Gods Mercy to Several Persons at Quabaug or Brookfield.* Cambridge: Samuel Green, 1676.

White, Carr. "Letter to His Sister." The Ohio Historical Society, Columbus, Ohio.

Williams, John. *The Redeemed Captive Returning to Zion.* Boston: Samuel Hall, 1795.

Bibliography

Aaron, Daniel. *The Unwritten War.* New York: Alfred A. Knopf, 1973.

Ahearn, Marie L. *The Rhetoric of War: Training Day, the Militia, and the Military Sermon.* Westport, Conn.: Greenwood Press, 1989.

Aichinger, Peter. *The American Soldier in Fiction, 1880–1963: A History of Attitudes Toward Warfare and the Military Establishment.* Ames: Iowa State University Press, 1975.

Beidler, Philip D. *American Literature and the Experience of Vietnam.* Athens: University of Georgia Press, 1982.

Bercovitch, Sacvan. *The American Jeremiad.* Madison: University of Wisconsin Press, 1978.

———. "The Puritan Vision of the New World." In *Columbia Literary History of the United States.* Edited by Emory Elliot. New York: Columbia University Press, 1988. 33–44.

Brooks, Cleanth, R.W.B. Lewis, and Robert Penn Warren, eds. *American Literature: The Makers and the Making.* 2 vols. New York: St. Martin's Press, 1973.

Buck, Paul H. *The Road to Reunion.* Boston: Little, Brown, 1947.

Budhan, P.J. "War and Recovery Written with Compassion." *Army Times* 14 May 1990:78.

Burke, Kenneth. *The Philosophy of Literary Form: Studies in Symbolic Action,* 3rd edition. Berkeley: University of California Press, 1974.

Cooper, James Fenimore. *The Wept of Wish-ton-Wish.* 1820. Reprint. New York: Stringer and Townsend, 1851.

Cowley, Malcom. Letter. *The New Republic* 4 October 1933:60.

———. Reply to letter of A. MacLeish. *The New Republic.* 4 October 1933:215.

Crane, Stephen. *The Red Badge of Courage.* Boston: Riverside Press, 1960.

Crevecoeur, St. Jean de. "The Man of Sorrows." In *Sketches of Eighteenth-Century America.* Edited by Henri Bourdin, *et al.,* 1925. Reprint. New York: Penguin Books, 1981.

Davis, Rebecca Harding. "John Lamar." *Atlantic Monthly.* 51 (1862):411–23.

Davis, Richard Beale, C. Hugh Holman, and Louis D. Rubin, Jr., eds. *Southern Writing 1585–1920.* New York: Odyssey Press, 1970.

DeForest, John William. *Miss Ravenal's Conversion from Secession to Loyalty.* Edited by Gordon S. Haight. New York: Holt, Rinehart and Winston, 1962.

du Picq, Ardant. *Battle Studies. Roots of Strategy: Book 2.* Harrisburg, Pa.: Stackpole Books, 1987.

Elliot, Emory. ed. *Columbia Literary History of the United States.* New York: Columbia University Press, 1988.

Ellis, John. *The Sharp End of War: The Fighting Man in World War II.* London: David & Charles, 1980.

Fiedler, Leslie A. *Love and Death in the*

American Novel. New York: Stein and Day, 1966.

Foote, Shelby. *The Civil War: A Narrative. Red River to Appomattox.* New York: Random House, 1974.

Frohock, W.M. *The Novel of Violence in America.* Boston: Beacon Press, 1964.

Fussell, Paul. *The Great War and Modern Memory.* New York: Oxford University Press, 1975.

————. *Wartime: Understanding and Behavior in the Second World War.* New York: Oxford University Press, 1989.

Gookin, Daniel. *An Historical Account of the Doings and Sufferings of the Christian Indians in New England in the Years 1675, 1676, 1677.* 1836. Reprint. New York: Arono Press, 1972.

Grant, Jehu. "Petition for Pension." *The Revolution Remembered: Eyewitness Accounts of the War of Independence.* Ed. John C. Dann. Chicago: University of Chicago Press, 1977. 26–28.

Gray, J. Glenn. *The Warriors: Reflections on Men in Battle.* New York: Harper & Row, 1970.

Gross, Theodore L. *The Herioc Ideal in American Literature.* New York: Free Press, 1971.

Hassler, Warren W., Jr. *With Shield and Sword: American Military Affairs, Colonial Times to the Present.* Ames: Iowa State University Press, 1982.

————. *Life of Franklin Pierce.* Boston: Ticknor, Reed, and Fields, 1852.

Hemingway, Ernest, ed. *Men at War.* New York: Crown Publishers, 1942.

Higginson, Thomas Wentworth. *Army Life in a Black Regiment.* 1870. Reprint. New York: Grosset and Dunlap, 1970.

Hirst, Margaret E. *The Quakers in Peace and War.* London: Swarthmore Press, 1972.

Homberger, Eric. *The Second World War in Fiction.* London: MacMillan, 1984.

Hook, Andrew. *American Literature in Context: 1865–1900.* New York: Methuen, 1983.

Johannssen, Robert. *To the Halls of the Montezumas: The Mexican War in the American Imagination.* New York: Oxford University Press, 1985.

Jones, Katherine M. *Heroines of Dixie: Confederate Women Tell Their Story of the War.* New York: Bobbs-Merrill, 1955.

Jones, Peter. *War and the Novelist.* Columbia: University of Missouri Press, 1976.

Just, Ward. "Vietnam: Fiction and Fact." *Tri-Quarterly* 65 (1986):215–20.

Keegan, John. *The Face of Battle.* New York: Penguin Books, 1978.

Kemble, C. Robert. *The Image of the Army Officer in America: A Background for Current Discourse.* Westport, Conn.: Greenwood Press, 1973.

Lawrence, D.H. *Studies in Classic American Literature.* New York: Penguin Books, 1961.

Leonard, Thomas C. *Above the Battle: War-Making in America from Appomattox to Versailles.* New York: Oxford University Press, 1978.

Lively, Robert A. *Fiction Fights the Civil War.* Chapel Hill: University of North Carolina Press, 1957.

Lowenfels, Walter, ed. *Walt Whitman's Civil War.* New York: Da Capo Press, 1961.

Lundberg, David. "The American Literature of War: The Civil War, World War I, and World War II." *American Quarterly* 36 (1984):373–87.

McNeill, William H. "The Care and Repair of Public Myth." *Foreign Affairs* 61 (1982):1–13.

Manchester, William. *Goodbye Darkness: A Memoir of the Pacific War.* New York: Little, Brown, 1979.

Marshall, S.L.A. *Men Against Fire.* New York: William Morrow, 1951.

Melville, Herman. "Supplement." In *Battle Pieces and Aspects of War.* Gainesville, Fla.: Scholars' Facsimilies & Reprints, 1960. 259–72.

Menendez, Albert J. *Civil War Novels: An Annotated Bibliography.* New York: Garland Publishing, 1986.

Merill, James M. *Uncommon Valor: The Exciting Story of the Army.* New York: Rand McNally, 1964.

Mitchell, S. Weir. *Hugh Wynne, Free Quaker.* 1896. Reprint. New York: Century, 1915.

O'Brien, Tim. *The Things They Carried.* Boston: Houghton Mifflin, 1990.

Page, Thomas Nelson. "Marse Chan." In *In Ole Virginia*. New York: Macmillan, 1887. 1–38.

Pickering, James H., ed. *The World Turned Upside Down: Prose and Poetry of the American Revolution*. New York: Kennikat Press, 1975.

Pringle, Cyrus. *The Record of a Quaker Conscience*. New York: MacMillan, 1918.

Roberts, Kenneth. *Arundel*. 1930. Reprint. New York: Doubleday, Doran, 1941.

Rowlandson, Mary. *A Narrative of the Captivity and Restoration of Mrs. Mary Rowlandson*. New York: Garland Publishing, 1977.

Rust, Richard Dilworth. *Glory and Pathos: Responses of Nineteenth-Century American Authors to the Civil War*. Boston: Hollbrook Press, 1970.

Scheer, George F., and Hugh F. Rankin, eds. *Rebels and Redcoats: The American Revolution Through the Eyes of Those Who Fought and Lived It*. New York: Da Capo Press, 1957.

Sedgwick, Catherine Marie. *The Linwoods*. New York: Harper & Brothers, 1835.

Seelye, John. *Prophetic Waters: The River in Early American Life and Literature*. New York: Oxford University Press, 1977.

Slotkin, Richard. *Regeneration Through Violence: The Mythology of the American Frontier, 1600–1860*. Middletown, Conn.: Wesleyan University Press, 1973.

————, and James K. Folsom, eds. *So Dreadful a Judgement: Puritan Responses to King Philip's War, 1676–1677*. Middletown, Conn.: Wesleyan University Press, 1978.

Solomon, Eric. "The Novelist as Soldier: Cooke and DeForest." *American Literary Realism, 1870–1910*. 19 (1987):80–88.

Stein, Stephen J. "An Apocalyptic Rationale for the American Revolution." *Early American Literature* 9 (1975):211–25.

Thoreau, Henry David. *Walden and Other Writings*. Ed. Brooks Atkinson. New York: The Modern Library, 1950.

Tucker, Nathaniel Beverly. *The Partisan Leader*. Chapel Hill: University of North Carolina Press, 1971.

Tyler, Moses Coit. *Literary History of the American Revolution 1763–1783*. New York: Burth Franklin, 1970.

Walsh, Jeffrey. *American War Literature: 1914 to Vietnam*. New York: St. Martin's Press, 1982.

Warren, Robert Penn. *The Legacy of the Civil War: Meditations on the Centennial*. New York: Random House, 1961.

Weigley, Russell F. *History of the United States Army*. Bloomington: Indiana University Press, 1984.

Whitman, Walt. *Complete Poetry and Collected Prose*. New York: Library of America, 1982.

Index of Names